Knowing How to Know

EASA Series
Published in Association with the European Association of Social-Anthropologists (EASA)

KNOWING HOW TO KNOW

Fieldwork and the Ethnographic Present

Edited by

Narmala Halstead, Eric Hirsch and Judith Okely

Berghahn Books
New York • Oxford

First published in 2008 by

Berghahn Books

www.berghahnbooks.com

© 2008 Narmala Halstead, Eric Hirsch and Judith Okely

Library of Congress Cataloging-in-Publication Data

A C.I.P. catalog record for this book is available from
the Library of Congress

British Library Cataloguing in Publication Data

A catalogue record for this book is available from the British Library
Printed in the United States on acid-free paper

ISBN 978-1-84545-438-8 (hardback) 978-1-84545-477-7 (paperback)

Contents

Introduction

Experiencing the Ethnographic Present: Knowing through 'Crisis'[1]

Narmala Halstead

The volume focuses on anthropologists constructing knowledge through encounters which re-position the ethnographic present. The accounts bring out a notion of the ethnographic present beyond the idea of a privileged and separate time-space as one occupied by the ethnographer writing about the 'timeless' present of others (Fabian 1983). Whilst acknowledging both the use of the term as dualistic modes of the present and the critiques which argue for its necessary construction, 'an encounter outside history' as Kirsten Hastrup notes (1990: 51), this volume identifies another space in which the ethnographic present has to be located. This considers the anthropologist's engagement with doing fieldwork and writing ethnography as an ongoing and reflexive process. Thus, this is about the relationship of the anthropologist to the discipline of anthropology and the processes which constitute and demonstrate the discipline through what I term here as transformative spaces.

In these processes, the consciousness of the anthropologist is foregrounded vis-à-vis multiple influences as different moments of her/his ethnographic present. The accounts probe different aspects of the 'ethnographic present': overall, the chapters also allow for insights into the different trajectories of how the discipline is examined and reflected upon as forms of producing current anthropology. Whilst particular ethnographic moments do occur in field-sites, these moments continue at different times, in the anthropologist's study, work and social encounters to extend what Marilyn Strathern (1999) describes as the simultaneous inhabiting of ethnography's double fields – the field-site and 'back home.' Strathern (ibid.: Ch. 1) points to the notion of the 'ethnographic moment' as the 'effect of engaging the fields together' (ibid.: 6).

She notes: 'We could say that the ethnographic moment works as an example of a relation which joins the understood (what is observed at the moment of observation) to the need to understand (what is observed at the moment of analysis)' (ibid.).

The volume elaborates Strathern's 'observations': it is rather a continual process of discovery that draws on new understandings of past encounters, to result in an ethnographic present as 'multiply constituted'. In engaging with critiques of the ethnographic present, Hastrup urges that the notion should be understood beyond a construct of time between 'us' and 'them' (see also Sanjek 1991). She notes:

> The ethnographic present is a narrative construct that clearly does not represent a truth about the timelessness of the others. We know they are as historical as anybody in all possible ways. But the betweenness implied in fieldwork, and the fact of the ethnographer's sharing the time not *of* but *with* others, makes ethnography escape our ordinary historical categories. (1990: 57)

As an ongoing process, the ethnographic present in the way I am re-conceptualising it here is defined in and out of conventional field-sites[2]. It takes form through the ethnographer's reflections which may be influenced by the serendipitous encounters that occur inside and outside of these sites. In turn, anthropologists experience particular forms of their ethnographic present which contribute to changing understandings of anthropological knowledge. Thus, this construction of the ethnographic present is intertwined with the reflexive practices of ethnographers as those which constitute and re-constitute *present day* anthropology. Further, their practices are embedded in critical engagement with the history of the discipline.

Periods of reflection and scrutiny become *agents* to facilitate an idea of crisis that I argue is *the* mode of anthropological knowledge construction (cf. Kuhn 1962). This converts the idea of crisis from the conventional understanding of it being a problem, to the idea of crisis as a notion that facilitates the transformative spaces in which ethnographers do fieldwork and produce their ethnographies. Note Lila Abu-Lughod's (1991) point, for instance, where she urges that anthropologists should write against culture, a concept that has been critically interrogated in anthropology (see also Gupta and Ferguson 1992, Brightman 1995, Kuper 1999). Abu-Lughod states: 'The critiques of anthropology that have emerged recently from various quarters have encouraged us to question what we work on, how we write, and for whom we write'(1991: 157). She then points to her own work as examples to 'disturb the culture concept' (ibid.).

Matti Bunzl (2005) notes that the critiques of the 1980s vis-à-vis the 'Writing Culture' debates arose from a 'series of transformations' traceable to the 1960s. He reflects:

> ... the transformations in the recent history of anthropology need to be understood as engendered by and a reaction to the so-called 'crisis of anthropology.' This crisis

which hit the discipline in the late 1960s stood at the heart of profound reorientations in the discipline – reorientations that have, in the last forty years, shaped the anthropology of today (2005: 188).

Annette Weiner, discussing the crisis mode of the discipline[3] in terms of critical change, notes:

> Some would say that it is anthropology's propensity for crises that keeps it such an intellectually dynamic discipline. And out of these crises, anthropologists as teachers, researchers and practitioners throughout this century have made – and continue to make – profound contributions that challenge the status quo, especially Western beliefs and 'truths' about the rest of the world's populations. (1995: 14)

The idea of epistemological crisis as a framework for critical knowledge construction positions the accounts in terms of an ethnographic present that is constantly changing rather than 'unchanging.' The ethnographic present escapes 'ordinary historical categories' by emerging within and through the transformative spaces of anthropological knowledge construction. The ethnographic present, thus, co-resides and is informed by the anthropologist's engagement with the notion of crisis as the mode of knowledge construction. The chapters bring out an extended field of continual involvement: some of the accounts consider recent and ongoing research, but chapters also focus on earlier research. The authors variously engage with key debates which shift the emphasis of crisis as a problem to that of crisis as a notion that facilitates knowledge construction. Notions of the West as in Western anthropology and as in local people's inhabiting of the West acquire different nuances in the encounters and in theoretical approaches. This also brings out the situatedness of 'being local' and the processes of 'native becoming'.

Crisis and/as the Mode of Anthropological Construction

The notion of Western emerges as a term implicated in the *problem of crisis*. By engaging with positioned approaches to the term Western, the volume references the history of anthropology where this was visible through 'crisis stages.' Anthropology as *Western*, its role in colonialism, and further, its modes of constructing and representing the *other* is marked by critiques by anthropologists in the twentieth century and more recently (see, for instance, Leach 1961, Nencel and Pels 1991, Trouillot 1991, Bunzl 2005). These critiques have allowed for epistemological questioning and doubt with regard to representing the other. Anthropology's contributions to knowledge of the colonised[4] and the limitations of these contributions were explored in terms of the 'mythicising erasure' which occurred in early anthropologists accounts on the colonial presence: the accounts ignored the impact of missionaries and other evidence of the Europeans' presence (Stocking 1983, 1991, Hirsch 2001:

137). Edmund Leach (as cited in Tambiah 2002: 432–433) in an 1987 ASA lecture, discussed how 'tribal ethnographers' ignored this presence where 'in order to bring things into sharper focus palpably European elements in the ethnographer's notes were omitted from the published record or else treated as alien contamination grafted onto whatever was there before.'

Debates on anthropologists' own 'absence' from the field-site in their roles as 'objective observers' were, in turn, marked by other debates about crisis of anthropology and crisis of representation. Richard Fox (1991: 8) notes, for instance, 'how artfully Evans-Pritchard first personified himself among the Nuer and then "disappeared" himself in favor of a scientific omniscience for the remainder of his text.' Consider also Bronislaw Malinowski's diary which was produced as a separate and private journal and was never meant to be published (Malinowski 1967). This diary demonstrated his *very particular* presence in the field-site that was not reflected in his accounts (see Okely 1996: 38). The controversy with regard to the issue of its publication by his widow was, in itself, a crisis of representation within the discipline (see Geertz 1983: 55–56).

James Clifford and George Marcus' (1986) co-edited volume, *Writing Culture* brought together divergent contributions to engage explicitly with erasures and absences in the ethnographic account which also challenged the constructions of the ethnographic voice[5]. These and other expressions of dissent as a constant critical examination of anthropology and the role of anthropologists, whilst reflexive, extended the space for 'hysteria' as a space that was ostensibly self-paralysing (see Kuper 1999). Thus, Geertz (1988: 71) pointed to the 'epistemological hypochondria' which questioned how one could ever know about others with any certainty and, in effect, how one could know how to know. This emphasis, however, overshadowed the reflexive processes of knowledge construction which emerged through these forms of questioning and doubts i.e. crisis became the mode through which anthropologists came to know, as noted.

The West as Inextricably In-between

Anthropologists have had to understand how they positioned *others* from particular Western perspectives. This positioning, in turn, allowed for new perspectives of these others and for the anthropologist, in turn, to be *othered* (see, for instance, Bunzl 2004). This has been further implicated in the emergence and critiques of the so-called native anthropologist as the voice of the *other* (see Strathern 1987: 31, Narayan 1993, Weston 1997, Jacobs-Huey 2002). This voice is not singular and the 'native' anthropologist becomes located in new positions of in-betweenness that also challenges the initial construct of 'us' and 'them'. Abu-Lughod brings out the problematic of this in-between-ness where her emphasis on demonstrating the common humanity of Arabs to outsiders was viewed askance by the 'insiders' (see also Brettel 1993). She notes:

> My revelation of Bedouin individuals' attachments and vulnerabilities through their poetry, to create for Westerners a sense of recognition, not distance, has provoked several other responses in Egypt. When one woman heard someone read from a book a few of the poems she had recited years earlier, she exclaimed half-joking: 'You've scandalized us!' (1991: 159).

In general, the chapters engage in varying ways with the positioning of Western to demonstrate how the term becomes fluid as a term that is inextricably in-between. This extends the idea of the West beyond a universal category of a dominant political centre and particular ideologies. It shows its redefinition as part of a social imaginary by those who were seen traditionally outside of the West. How the West is extended and inhabited has been discussed in various ways (see Carrier 1995, Halstead 2002, Knauft 2002, Hirsch 2004). Sahlins (1993: 17) notes, commenting on the relations of Pacific islanders to western economy: '(…) The first commercial impulse of the people is not to become just like us but more like themselves. They turn foreign goods to the service of domestic ideas, to the objectification of their own reflections and notions of good life'. Clifford (1997: 4–5) discusses an account by the Indian anthropologist, Amitav Ghosh, to show the idea of the West as a site inhabited through 'travel.' Michel-Rolph Trouillot (2003: 38) discusses the notion of modernity to unveil *the* West: he notes that modernity 'was always plural, just like the West was always plural.'[6] The usage is explored beyond a select interpretation in the encounters between the anthropologist and her/his research participants which allow for different and varying understandings of the West. In this regard, *the native anthropologist, however defined, is part of the West.* The chapters bring out different ways this West is experienced. These emerge as shared experiences of variously embodied forms of knowing.

In some instances, the construction of anthropological knowledge explicitly engages with the connections between the body and person where knowing 'another' has to be experienced both through various forms of sociality and by considering the ways the body as a physical presence is placed in and becomes part of the field. This connects with critiques of the separation between the body and the thinking self. Henrietta Moore and Todd Sanders (2006: 11–12) reflecting on how anthropological knowledge is also produced through the experiences of the human body, point to the experiential contexts of the body in physical environments and to the body as a 'means of knowing the world' (see also Lambek and Strathern 1998, Okely, 2007). The ethnographer becomes a particular kind of body, occupying the interfaces between different forms of knowledge and varying periods of data collection and critical engagement.

In varying ways, all the authors engage with and question their own worldviews and particular anthropological lenses to show the shifts in their knowledge approaches over a period of time. Helena Wulff brings out her positioning of 'native' and 'ex-native' in relation to the world(s) of ballet and anthropology, where non-verbal bodily movements of the dance had to be conveyed through apprenticeship and situated practices. She carried out multi-sited fieldwork in South London and Stockholm and on tour with ballet companies in various countries. As a former dancer, she became a 'familiar other' among her research participants who, in turn, began to observe and mimic her observer pose. She was further able to appreciate and reflect on her insider and outsider positioning through 'bodily memory of dancing ballet' and personal histories. Similarly, Cristina Grasseni reflects on the acquisition of skilled vision through a landscape which incorporates her bodily movements and presence in everyday practices. Through this integrated setting, she examines her locatedness in the everyday and urges for a collapsing of world views in understanding her research participants' perspectives in Northern Italy.

Viranjini Munasinghe considers the collapsing of anthropological and local settings as a problematic which allows for new theoretical insights. Munansinghe offers a different perspective where the views of research participants may be over-privileged as a theoretical blind spot. She notes the danger of taking for granted the lay discourses among research participants in Trinidad in the collapsing of different settings. She urges for an awareness of the power of these discourses to act as substitutes for theory and argues for a necessary separation between different 'worlds'. In a related way, Crandall discusses different systems of knowledge with regard to the Himba in Southern Africa. He challenges and revises his own approach in different periods of reflection on the data. Similarly, Hirsch discusses how his understanding of a particular convention in an earlier fieldwork encounter in Papua New Guinea assumed a different meaning at a later stage to reflect his own changing historical consciousness. Both Hirsch and Crandall explicitly bring out their reflexive engagement as a theoretical repositioning which questions the assumptions of the anthropologist vis-à-vis Western knowledge conventions.

Judith Okely also re-examines the concept of Western by interrogating assumptions in her 'own' culture where she was 'forced' to do fieldwork in her 'home' settings in order to understand the Gypsy *others* in England. Her account also demonstrates the divisions between the West and its other which resurfaced on home territory as 'unanticipated fieldwork in the supposedly familiar' and where she drew on her 'own culture' to add to her understandings. Similarly, Wulff experienced a dualistic Western setting among fellow anthropologists who began to react to her in a particular way as a result of positioning her as a researcher on dance in Sweden.

Narmala Halstead, Vibha Arora and Konstantinos Retsikas engage with constructs of self and other through the ways their research participants locate them as 'Western' and or remake them into *local*. Halstead as a 'native' anthropologist discusses East Indians in Guyana. There are varied exchanges of knowledge which inscribe and suggest the presence of *persons* as a term which moves them out of bounded ethnic and cultural bodies, but which also relies on their constrasting cultural visibility as *Indians*. These are negotiations of status which define and reposition certain understandings of Western, redefine Halstead's anthropological project and her research participants' understandings of different cultural spaces. Whilst Halstead shows how her research participants position her as both insider and outsider, Arora discusses how she was always strange in the form of the 'Indian anthropologist' even though she was *not* doing fieldwork in a different country. Thus, the notion of the 'non-West' as a competing signifier for the kind of oppression usually reserved for the term 'Western' emerge in Arora's work where her visibility as the Indian anthropologist among the Sikkim in Northeast India *inevitably* attracts the hostility reserved for such outsiders. By contrast, Retsikas points out that his Western identity suggested that he had bases for familiarity with people used to dealing with the foreign (cf. Drummond 1980 and Halstead 2002). His research participants related to him on the basis of 'knowledge' about his foreign body: Retsikas points to the co-optation and refashioning of his body as definitive of the processes of knowledge construction in fieldwork encounters and as demonstrative of the ways the fieldworker's body becomes the point of access. Overall, the accounts further demonstrate an interconnected landscape of 'us' and 'them'. The accounts variously demonstrate that the anthropologist subjective immersion in the field also allows for insights into the inhabiting of *Western as both outsider and native* positions: this is further explored in the more detailed discussion of the chapters below which also demonstrates the varied ways the authors experience the ethnographic present.

The Ethnographic Present: Continual Discovery

The accounts by Crandall, Hirsch and Okely bring out the histories of their fieldwork encounters and ethnographies as complicit in *new moments of knowing* to shift the idea of anthropological knowledge as located in a select 'Western' interpretation. Specifically, these chapters illustrate the positioning of the ethnographic present as one of continual discovery over lengthy periods in terms of their reflections on fieldwork and analysis. Thus, the authors demonstrate the processes of knowing as long-term engagement across the boundaries of the academic and defined field-sites. This illustrates the ethnographic present as shaped by changing historical consciousness and embedded in processes of historicity (see Hirsch and Stewart 2005).

Hirsch points to an omission where he assumed knowledge in an early fieldwork encounter in the 1980s based on his then historical consciousness and disciplinary boundaries. His interpretation of what he was told, about a convention being abandoned, located this practice in the past. It was only later, and through a reflexive process which also demonstrates the ethnographic present as ongoing, that he was able to appreciate that this interpretation was in itself a point of access into knowing beyond particular disciplinary boundaries. He notes: 'The assumption – by Western trained anthropologists - is that matters abandoned in the past, are of the past. However, this assumption about knowledge and conduct may overlook other ways of knowing and acting that have implications for anthropological knowledge practices.'

Hirsch examines these different periods of making sense of the data by reflecting on how an anachronistic perspective meant that he implicitly overlooked the significance of his historical consciousness. He discusses the different understandings of the separation between past and present which selectively framed *knowledge* of the convention and its practice. This further allows for an appreciation of indigenous perceptions as transformed through local processes and indigenous people's conceptions of past, present and future. Hirsch's self-reflexive approach also shifts the positioning of Western practices as located in a 'Western tradition': the problems and biases of a selective Western anthropology re-emerge as transformative spaces to embody the ethnographic present.

Crandall addresses a similar point by reflecting on a different set of issues. Anthropologists have reflexively engaged with the significance of collapsing the insider-outsider boundary and understanding the position of the other in their work (see, for instance, Geertz 1983: Ch.3). What is significant in both Hirsch and Crandall's accounts is that they show how their work changed over a period of time and how this challenged earlier analysis, which also demonstrate the ethnographic present as embedded in reflexive practices and in the different periods of analysis. Their accounts illustrate reflexive stages of understanding the interfaces between fieldwork and analysis as a re-examination of access modes. Their different stages of engagement bring out a transformative space for anthropological knowledge as a construction that negotiates the positioning of both the anthropologist and his hosts.

Crandall notes that how he came to know about the Himba through an integrated system of knowledge as anthropological had to be revisited through his own appreciation of the inadequacy of this approach in relation to the Himba's forms of knowledge. His chapter on the Himba is also an engagement with the opposition which is often explicitly present in the construct of the Western. But he explores this opposition through a notion of a 'bounded system' of knowledge and by un-bounding this system. By identifying the particular systematisation of knowledge practices under which the anthropologist's account is produced, Crandall shows that this privileged an approach which missed the significance of local unsystematised ways of knowing.

His revisiting of material on the Himba brings out this key point. He considers an article published in 1996 on the Himba homestead and the symbolic dimensions of its organisation. He draws out his analysis in terms of the classificatory divide between male and female, left and right and good and evil. He notes that there were certain contradictions where their physical arrangements matched some, but not all of these categories: this emerged as a problem which then had to be resolved according to his own anthropological biases. Crandall explains that he later comes to realise that his efforts to fit the material 'in the imaginary world of (his) theoretical/analytical system' conflicted with how the Himba made sense of their world. These efforts produced, in effect, an exchange of a 'less rigid form of intellectual organisation for one of extreme rigidity'.

Crandall is concerned with showing the different 'systems' of making sense of things: he argues that the anthropologists' emphasis on system over-determines the analysis in a way that may overlook other ways people have of apprehending the world. He argues that what 'we come to recognise as a contradiction or cultural puzzle is a reflection of a mode of thinking we thrust upon the world'. This is not dissimilar to Leach's (1954) work on the Kachins where in the *Political Systems of Highland Burma*, Leach demonstrates the contradictory ideas held by individuals in relation to social structure as a distinction between the anthropologist's 'model of social reality and the inconsistencies which emerge in the data to challenge this model'(ibid.: 8).

In tracing the different periods of analysis as new ways of understanding the past and thus, re-embedding the present, Crandall, however, also addresses different kinds of consciousness by the anthropologist. Similar to the accounts by Hirsch, he reflexively examines the implications of bringing together the different periods which also alter the meaning of Western as a select anthropological bias located in 'Western practices:' this demonstrates the meaning of the term as informed through the emergence of 'others' perspectives.

In a related way, Okely's exploration of her extended field-sites synthesises self and other dichotomies: she discusses her long-term field-sites of her 'own' and 'other' culture. As in the other accounts, this emerge both as a re-examination of Western presumptions and also redefines the Western in these multiple, many-sided fieldwork encounters. By anthropologising 'her' culture she was able to extend her field-sites beyond their variously conceived boundaries and beyond the limits of a time-focused ethnographic present. This was also extended in terms of her reflection on different approaches over a period of time. Okely brings out the reflexive stages as the definitive reward for doing fieldwork: she demonstrates the extension of the field through conversations with colleagues, by exploring her own omissions and by encountering strange understandings of her research in social settings. These experiences became forms of note-taking inscribed on her own consciousness and in which she interrogated and reflected on these narratives as ways of reflexively transforming the divisive space which located the Gypsies as other. Okely's research began as a policy-oriented project and she had to convince a 'seconded civil servant' of the merits of doing ethnographic fieldwork. Both the research approach from the perspective of her employers (not just about questionnaires) and the advice about jotting down copious notes as an anthropological standard had to be re-negotiated.

Whilst Okely had to rethink the anthropological emphasis on taking notes among her research participants as an act that had its own difficulties in terms of gaining trust/knowing things, she nevertheless 'took' constant notes, outside of the notebook and in and out of the originally conceived field-sites. This became a way of knowing beyond written notes, but where constant observation brought out the 'present' of anthropologists' ethnographies as intertwined in different periods, sites and key moments of anthropological understanding. In this re-telling, she highlights both key issues affecting anthropological fieldwork when she commenced her own research and the influences and moments of knowing which shaped her ethnographic present. Okely describes the progress of the research beyond this first project where her references to various experiences in social settings illustrate the connections between the immediate research sites and the extended field within and outside academia. She points to her various encounters with those who saw the Gypsies as strange others, believed that she was complicit in their understanding of this strangeness and wanted to share their 'fractured expertise.' Her examples illustrated an unexpected 'anthropology at home.' Her field-site extended beyond the Gypsies local settings to her 'local' settings as she found it necessary increasingly to take on board the stock images which circulated in her 'own' culture and which negatively stereotyped the Gypsies.

Anthropologising the Anthropologist

The accounts further shift the notion of 'fieldwork at home' to consider how anthropologists are seen to occupy both 'Western' and 'indigenous' positions as particular and contextually-bounded categories. Helena Wulff discusses her position as a 'native dancer' to demonstrate her positioning as insider and outsider. As a former dancer, she had a particular kind of access: she was expected to understand dance. Some people knew she had been a dancer just by observing her. Yet she was also clearly visible as a separate body – the anthropologist. Wulff discusses her negotiations around these positions, her eventual awareness of being watched in similar ways to her forms of observation, of being asked not to divulge information of which she knew nothing, being assumed to be critic as part of the usual roles assigned to fieldworkers (see Freilich 1970; Abu-Lughod 1988: 146; Fowler and Hardesty 1994). She draws on these interactions to demonstrate the transformation of her role among her research participants and where this also allowed her to know the role of researcher as confidante.

Her experiences in her 'own' culture i.e. among fellow anthropologists when she announced that she was going to study dance resonate with Okely's reflections. Wulff notes that her experiences were balanced by those who saw her as someone accessible as a result of her research focus on dance. Thus, whilst the reactions of several colleagues unveiled negative understandings of dancers vis-à-vis their presumed sexual orientation and their gender, those of other colleagues contrasted with these assumptions and positioned her in a space of empathy. She notes: 'A whole new landscape opened up for me in the anthropological community. I remember how someone would stop and look at me, changing a professional expression of efficiency into a relaxed posture radiating personal warmth.'

Her bodily relationship in terms of dance is a recurring theme which allows for a narrative of various significant moments in her personal histories and in her anthropological work. How she knows and is seen to know the dance through her body further emerge through a staged performance by her research participants and reminiscent of the play staged on Kirsten Hastrup by those she studied (Hastrup 1995). Thus, her reflections on coming to know this material also rely on how she became known through the performative spaces of her field-sites. Her participant-hosts performed a sketch of her presence among them, displaying her efforts to remain in the background whilst demonstrating, however, that she was very much visible, and showing how she slowly made friends and became part of the main group.

Thus, the accounts move from a particular kind of 'anthropology at home' to anthropology in the 'extended home.' This demonstrates the dualism of the home setting, the extension of 'home' to the field through the idea of being native and the ways our participants revert anthropological focus, This allows for a more explicit focus on the anthropologist by her participant-hosts to illustrate both access into knowledge through these fieldwork encounters and the negotiation of otherness as necessary exchanges.

The anthropologising of the anthropologist emerges in Halstead's chapter through various reflections on her field-work encounters. Her chapter adds to work by so-called native anthropologists. It shows the non-West as a term which has to be challenged: it becomes contested in locals' redefinitions of the fieldworker and, in practice, in their redefining of the boundaries between West and non-West. This reverts to the theme addressed, if in different ways, by the contributors above and as a re-conceptualisation of the field in the fieldworker's varied understandings of his or her historical forms of consciousness. These forms necessarily alter and re-emerge to express the ethnographic present. She examines the idea of 'own' culture from a presumed insider perspective from which she considers her various forms of visibility as a 'native' anthropologist, woman, East Indian and Western academic. This adds to understandings of 'Western' as a term which becomes embodied through reflexivity and ethics in the fieldwork encounters: the terms of engagement redefine understandings of Western anthropology and demonstrate knowledge through shared encounters as forms of gifting.

Halstead reflects on knowing and constructing knowledge as an ongoing form of access between herself and her research participants: mutual reflections and awareness of select representative spaces allow for constructions of persons and their forms of visibility to emerge alongside the unfolding of the data. She revists one encounter where she reflects on her materialisation as insider to the culture *and* as other by exploring the implications for analysis over different periods (Halstead 2001). She teases out this process as a questioning and redefining of 'anthropology others' – those who by virtue of being the object of research are theoretically addressed in a space of distance as those who *have to be studied.* The encounters also show the shifting of her native researcher's' role: the interactions with her participant-hosts, and her different modes of representing and knowing people become a negotiation of subjectivity and academic distance. Her account shows her switching roles where she is explicitly repositioned as *participant rather than observer* by her participant-hosts.

Her contextualisation of the material is through the ways East Indians understand themselves in different cultural contexts – this emerges for instance, in the example of a food-sharer's efforts to bring attention to her 'role-switching,' after he provided her with food at a wedding, traditionally eaten in a leaf, without cutlery. Under his gaze, she changes from an observer, presumably detached, to someone being observed i.e. an East Indian woman eating with her hand and in the process *becoming* a legitimate object of anthropological interest. But, based on her experience and knowledge of other encounters, Halstead later understands that in this shift, the fieldworker identifies the display of Indian distinctiveness in a public performative space, and as one which is contextually-occupied by East Indians. In drawing attention to her role as observer/anthropologist and simultaneously to that of a woman visible through cultural practice, the food-sharer also *identifies the space for his own role to shift.* Halstead reflects on these exchanges as gifts of knowledge reliant on the mutual role-shifting of self and other.

Her participant-hosts gaze into and draw conclusions about her research agenda. Their interventions in her role and positioning, in turn, demonstrate their contextual forms of being visible in and out of a culturally-ascribed space. Halstead considers these interactions through understandings of different kinds of space. By interrogating the different gazes as an anthropologising of the anthropologist and as East Indians' interventionist approaches in their public representations, she also brings out the connections between the anthropological project of understanding difference and the ways East Indians construct and erode difference.

Konstantinos Retsikas'chapter on the East Javanese allows for a different perspective to show how he becomes embodied as the other from a positioning where he is explicitly visible as Western and where, for instance, there are efforts by his participant-hosts to challenge his difference or explore the possibility of mutual origins. The contrast of this re-making of his body with classic anthropological ideas of 'going native' is indicative of the changing nature of anthropological knowledge construction and how this emerges through reflexive accounts of fieldwork and ethnography. Further, it again brings out the mutually-interventionist roles of fieldworker and research-participants in the debates on knowledge and reflexivity.

He demonstrates forms of the anthropologist being anthropologised in his reflections on how his body is produced and probed as foreign by people accustomed to dealing with foreigners through their own 'foreign past'. Retsikas explores these fieldwork encounters through the ways he is transformed and where this 'new kind of body' informs his understandings which are always in process – 'incomplete and partial'

In foregrounding his ethnographic present in this incompleteness, he comes to understand how his 'otherness' is refashioned by people who themselves have gone through the process of being from elsewhere in a locality marked by centuries of migration and 'mixed-ness' as part of 'intermingled living'. He notes that the explicit nature of his research assumes new forms in the efforts of the East Javanese to transform his body as 'a moral Muslim human subject': their efforts to refashion his body, in turn, *become* his moments of knowing.

Retsikas discusses the contemporary setting of public violence as one which addresses his visibility as a researcher from the West. His presence added to this violence through the ways his person as an outsider also signified danger. His anxiety about being safe from violence had to be balanced by his need to become part of the setting – to some extent, this localisation required a re-materialisation of himself as a 'safe person'. The chapter brings out this idea of being seen to be safe as a process of becoming *local* through the ways he is scrutinised as Westerner and outsider.

These processes of *becoming* enter into his understandings of the ways locals are visible through 'mixed personhood,' the ways mixedness speaks to an interrogation and claiming of people around their ideas of difference and as those who belong through the visibility of their partial selves. First discussing mixedness as a space for 'intimate others', Retsikas offers detailed accounts of how his body was 'localised' to become 'a living, physical, sensing and experiencing agent enmeshed in practical and intimate encounters,' and how these bodily transformations informed his anthropological understandings.

Mixedness and the localising of the anthropologist emerge in a different way in Arora's work. Although Arora was not in a different country, the area had restricted access and she had to obtain a fieldwork permit which had to be renewed every ninety days. Arora notes: 'I was neither exploring another land nor did I ever feel that I was conducting fieldwork in my own society and culture.' This ambiguous setting allowed for particular political contours where Arora had to constantly assess the political inscribing of her research sites and the ways she entered into an 'ethnically fissured' landscape. Her access of these sites is intertwined with the efforts of her research-participants to 'rescue' themselves from the partiality of mixedness in their attempts to present ethnic and culturally bound identities. At the same time, Arora achieves various partial selves through her hosts' attempts to find meaning for her presence vis-à-vis their own concerns.

Thus, although Arora explores her various roles in a different way to the account of Retsikas who explicitly focuses on the body, she is nevertheless moulded into a particular kind of localness through moving from 'idiot' to 'aunt' to knowledgeable person who knew doctors. Arora points to serendipity and complicity to argue against expectations of scientific designs in conducting research. In discussing her approach she has to consider her positioned role as 'witness' and her self-reflexive understanding of her presence: she considers ethical issues and her 'privileged access'. Her awareness of occupying a public representative space where she was expected to document the Lepcha and Bhutia groups' ceremonial assertions of their rights frames her efforts to know beyond prescribed spaces. Further, this allows for an exploitation of unexpected events. Yet, this self-awareness has to be balanced in terms of the sacredness invested in the landscape: Arora's focus is also about validating the sacredness of Mt Tendong to others. The emphasis allows her to make use of both ethnographic and archival research and for her to probe her role as circumstantial activist. In coming to understand this landscape in a particular mode, Arora demonstrates choices made by the fieldworker vis-à-vis the aims of the research and how the interventions of research participants relate to these choices. Thus, the Lepcha and Bhutia who focused on her ethnic and researcher's presence to discuss ethnicity and unpack earlier representations of themselves in ethnographic accounts retain distinctive politicised identities in the analysis: this is particularly around the discussion of the Bhutanisation of the Lepcha.

Practising Theory: Seeing through Epistemological Crisis

Grasseni's chapter shifts the discussion on the mixedness of persons and groups to argue for a 'mixedness' in world views. This brings out themes in the volume around the coalescing of knowledge practices by the researcher and researched. In her focus, Grasseni argues for the synthesis of different knowledge settings by attending to other kinds of vision beyond that of the physical eye. In recognising the distinctions between her worldview and that of her participants, she argues for a collapsing of these distinctions through practices which have to incorporate the 'leisurely manner of her research participants' apprehension of their settings. Her initial understanding of this difference and her various attempts to gain an access beyond her worldview draws attention to an 'epistemological crisis.'

Her access to knowledge through crisis teases out the varying 'everyday' modes her research participants have of knowing the world around them as an 'enskillment of the senses,' and the ways she as the 'ethnographic other' has to learn to combine her ways of seeing with these modes. Thus, she emerges as apprentice by going through the processes of acquiring enskilled vision which, in turn, allows her to appreciate the ways her research-participants 'see' through being embedded in their everyday practices. Her accounts focus on residents in the valleys of North of Bergamo in northern Italy among dairy farmers. She explores her 'ethnographic apprenticeship' through her observations of cattle and her attempts to inhabit shared spaces through 'local ecologies of vision'. Grasseni argues for these forms of enskilled visions as background settings and draws on visual media to develop her accounts of an 'anthropology of the senses.' Grasseni discusses her making of an ethnographic film as an effort to access her research participants' worldview through their practices and demonstrates how film became a 'trace of (her) own outlook on fieldwork' which then allowed her to trace different moments of engagement with varied settings and practices.

She offers an overview of visual anthropological methods outside of traditional ethnographic approaches and brings out the emphasis on human cognition as social. Grasseni discusses the varied development of scholarly dissemination of the visual to demonstrate the way the ethnographer has to go beyond 'simple application of analytical grids' as a way of learning to see through local practices. She points to this becoming of the ethnographer as a space of 'learning how to learn.' Grasseni sees these modes of learning as shared spaces and develops the ethnographer's participation in them by bringing out philosophical connections to the anthropological inhabiting of other worldviews. Her argument draws on Ludwig Wittgenstein and Ian Hacking to bring out different kinds of knowledge practices in *becoming an ethnographer*. The sharing of worldviews is facilitated through her bodily experiences of other people's practices.

Munasinghe's chapter concludes the volume by arguing that we should turn our attention to the need to treat moments of epistemological collapse – the coalescing of theory and data – as ethnographic evidence which then has to be theorised to avoid 'blind spots.' In this regard, she provides a different approach to the collapsing of different settings of academic and lay discourses by arguing that the distinctions need to be carefully re-imposed. She discusses the field as one where the academic setting has to be re-examined in terms of its easy complicity with the research setting and in order to avoid certain discourses to re-merge as givens in the analysis. Munasinghe engages with the idea of the nation to consider the unexamined entanglement of theory and data as problematic for anthropological analysis through the concept of epistemological collapse. Here she discusses the work of Benedict Anderson and Alfred Cobban to bring out the 'schizophrenic nature of this concept' and to draw an analogy with how theory is appropriated through lay discourses. She notes that the recognition that 'our informants are speaking our language' blurs the distinction between researcher and research participant and between theory and data. She argues for the need to reclaim theory by interrogating how theory is confused or substituted with 'layers of historicity.'

Munasinghe draws on her fieldwork in Trinidad to demonstrate this entanglement. She interrogates the concept of Creole to show that while it is inextricably intertwined with the idea of the nation in the Caribbean in both lay and academic discourses, it also represents a specific exclusion from the nation. This is where the East Indian is seen as 'culture- carrier' rather than someone who is Creole or a 'creator of culture' and in contrast to the Afro-Trinidadian. The symbolic equation of the Afro-Trinidadian with the concept of Creole also became a theoretical failure of addressing how this historical understanding erased the presence of East Indians within this notion. In arguing for theory to be rescued outside the spaces of lay political discourses, Munasinghe also argues for an accounting of the historical perspective as one to be included in the ethnographic material. This entanglement shows how the collapsing of 'world-views' have to be critically re-examined in instances where lay discourses on certain issues appropriate the spaces for theory. Thus, it remains the task of ethnographers to reclaim space for theorising where objects of anthropological analysis are also represented through local discourses. This suggests that while boundaries have to be re-examined in privileging the perspectives of other world views, some caution is necessary in order to retain analytical efficacy.

Conclusion: Knowledge Interfaces between Self and Other

In the chapters, there is a recurring theme of the positioning and re-positioning of self and other which allows for different perspectives, insights and discussion of fieldwork material and theoretical approaches. This is necessarily a discussion of the distinctions which challenge and produce *Western* anthropology: the interfaces between fieldworker, research participants and the extended field are ways of understanding how we come to know by *becoming or re-positioning the other*. The chapters, in dealing with or highlighting particular crises of knowledge construction, offer specific accounts as an integrated landscape of different ways of questioning the boundaries and unveiling the negotiated spaces between the anthropologist, her/his field participants and particular paradigms and debates.

The focus on historical consciousness which allows for the anthropologist to question assumptions and extend disciplinary boundaries in one example is returned to in another as an explicit discussion of the anthropologist's reliance on a particular system of knowledge construction and the need to question this system. These distinctions and their subsequent collapsing in different worldviews are further brought out where the field-site as the anthropologist's home territory allows for both an interrogation of the narratives within one's 'own culture' as the problem and the need to re-position a maligned other through explicit distancing from this own culture. Subsequent accounts bring out the embodiment of the anthropologist in the encounters between observer and observed: the shifting of this role and particular kinds of visibility for the anthropologist facilitate interventionist spaces. Observer as participant and observed as actor/participant reflect on and *know* each other through 'Western' and 'local' identities which in themselves become the medium of questioning that which is known and thus both facilitates and dislodges otherness.

It is by being *othered* that the anthropologist comes to see: this is in the sense of occupying distance through the perspectives of those being studied, occupying distance from the perspectives anthropologists bring to the study and or finding a space of distance within the study. This othering becomes a process where the anthropologist moves between self and other as a constant positioning and re-positioning of immersion and distance. In the interfaces, there is an interrogating of the distinctions between different worldviews and the ways these distinctions can collapse. How we come to know is also about how we experience and question what is given: the ethnographic present emerges in this process and is produced as continual.

Notes

1. I thank Eric Hirsch and Judith Okely for looking at several versions of this chapter. I am also grateful to Jaro Stacul and Darshan Ramdhani for their comments.
2. The 'known' field-site, in itself, has shifted from remote places to anthropology at home, in organisations and in 'sites' of people in the study of transnational families (see Jackson 1987; Okely 1992; Olwig and Hastrup 1997; Eriksen and Nielsen 2001: 49; Gellner and Hirsch 2001). The field also extends through the changes and gains since the legitimising of the self-reflexive anthropologist and her/his subjective immersion, and in debates about 'the field' and the 'other.' This is where these debates are, in turn, shaped or transformed by the gaze from anthropology's object (see Clifford 1997: 22; Gupta and Ferguson 1997; Bunzl 2004).
3. See also Joan Vincent's (1991: 50) discussion of crisis as a 'call for engagement' in relation to departmental and inter-disciplinary imperatives. She further noted: 'Anthropology required in the 1980s, I would argue, not an experimental moment but a sense of crisis: an educated knowledge of unending crisis, or contention' (ibid.: 49).
4. Asad (1991: 314–16) describes the narratives of anthropology and colonialism, in which the initial encounters between Europeans and their non-European subjects are dealt with by the latter in terms of resistance, assimilation and attempts 'to reinvent their disrupted lives' (ibid.: 314). While Asad argues for the role of anthropology in colonialism to be 'relatively unimportant', he notes the centrality of the 'process of European global power' to the anthropological task of understanding colonial populations (1991: 315).
5. See Fox (1991), for instance, for a historicising of the writing culture debate.
6. Bruce Knauft's (2002) volume as a focus on plural modernity and the 'alter-natively' modern also demonstrates different understandings of the term Western.

References

Abu-Lughod, Lila. 1988. 'A Dutiful Daughter', in Soraya Altorki and Camilla Fawzi El-Solh (eds), *Arab Women in the Field: Studying Your Own Society*. Syracuse, NY: Syracuse University Press, pp. 139–61.
––––––. 1991. 'Writing against Culture', in Richard G. Fox (ed.), *Recapturing Anthropology: Working in the Present*. New Mexico: School of American Research Press, pp. 137–62.

Asad, Talal. 1991. 'Afterword: From the History of Colonial Anthropology to the Anthropology of Western Hegemony', in George W. Stocking Jr (ed.), *Colonial Situations: Essays on the Contextualization of Ethnographic Knowledge*. London: University of Wisconsin Press, pp. 314–24.

Brettell, Caroline B. (ed.). 1993. *When They Read What We Write: The Politics of Ethnography*. London: Bergin and Garvey.

Brightman, Robert. 1995. 'Forget Culture: Replacement, Transcendence, Relexification'. *Cultural Anthropology* 10(4): 509–546.

Bunzl, Matti. 2004. 'Boas, Foucault, and the "Native Anthropologist": Notes toward a Neo-Boasian Anthropology', *American Anthropologist* 106(3): 435–42.

———. 2005. 'Anthropology Beyond Crisis', *Anthropology and Humanism* 30(2): 187–95.

Carrier, James. (ed.). 1995. *Occidentalism: Images of the West*. Oxford: Clarendon Press.

Clifford, James. 1997. *Routes: Travel and Translation in the Late Twentieth Century*. London: Harvard University Press.

Clifford, James and George Marcus (eds). 1986. *Writing Culture: The Poetics and Politics of Ethnography*. Berkeley: University of California Press.

Drummond, Lee. 1980. 'A Cultural Continuum: A Theory of Intersystems', *Man* 15(2): 352–74.

Eriksen, Thomas Hylland and Finn Sivert Nielsen. 2001. *A History of Anthropology*. London: Pluto Press.

Fabian, Johannes. 2002 [1983]. *Time and the Other: How Anthropology Makes its Object*. New York: Columbia University Press.

Fowler, Don D. and Donald L. Hardesty. 1994. 'Introduction', in D.D. Fowler and D.L. Hardesty (eds), *Others Knowing Others: Perspectives on Ethnographic Careers*. London: Smithsonian Institution Press, pp. 1–14.

Fox, Richard G. 1991. 'Introduction', in Richard G. Fox (ed.) *Recapturing Anthropology: Working in the Present*. New Mexico: School of American Research Press, pp. 1–44.

Freilich, Morris. 1970. 'Field Work: An Introduction', in *Marginal Natives: Anthropologists at Work*. London: Harper and Row, pp. 1–37.

Geertz, Clifford. 1988. *Works and Lives: The Anthropologist as Author*. Cambridge: Polity Press.

———. 1993 [1983]. *Local Knowledge*. New York: Basic Books.

Gellner, David N. and Eric Hirsch. 2001. *Inside Organizations: Anthropologists at Work*. Oxford: Berg.

Gupta, Akhil and James Ferguson. 1992. 'Beyond "Culture": Space, Identity, and the Politics of Difference', *Cultural Anthropology* 7(1): 6–23.

———. 1997. 'Discipline and Practice': "The Field" as Site, Method and Location in Anthropology', in Akhil Gupta and James Ferguson (eds), *Anthropological Locations: Boundaries and Grounds of a Field Science*. London: University of California Press, pp. 1–46.

Halstead, Narmala. 2001. 'Ethnographic Encounters: Positionings within and Outside the Insider Frame', *Social Anthropology* 9(3): 307–21.

———. 2002. 'Branding "perfection": Foreign as Self – Self as Foreign-foreign', *Journal of Material Culture* 7(3): 273–93.

Hastrup, Kirsten. 1990. 'The Ethnographic Present: A Re-invention', *Cultural Anthropology* 5(1): 45–61.

_____. 1995. *A Passage to Anthropology: Between Experience and Theory*. London: Routledge.

Hirsch, Eric. 2001. 'When was Modernity in Melanesia?', *Social Anthropology* 9(2): 131–46.

_____. 2004. 'Techniques of Vision: Photography, Disco and Renderings of Present Perceptions in Highland Papua', *Journal of the Royal Anthropological Institute* 10(1): 19–39.

Hirsch, Eric and Charles Stewart. 2005. 'Introduction: Ethnographies of Historicity', *History and Anthropology* 16(3): 261–74.

Jackson, Anthony. (ed.). 1987. *Anthropology at Home*. London: Tavistock Publications.

Jacobs-Huey, Lanita. 2002. 'The Natives are Gazing and Talking Back: Reviewing the Problematics of Positionality, Voice and Accountability among "Native" Anthropologists', *American Anthropologist* 104(3): 791–804.

Knauft, Bruce (ed.), 2002. *Critically Modern: Alternatives, Alterities, Anthropologies*. Bloomington: Indiana University Press

Kuhn, T. 1962. *The Structure of Scientific Revolutions*. USA: University of Chicago Press.

Kuper, Adam. 1999. *Culture: The Anthropologists' Account*. London: Harvard University Press.

Lambek. Michael and Andrew Strathern (eds). *1998. Bodies and persons. Comparative perspectives from Africa and Melanesia. Cambridge: Cambridge University Press.*

Leach, E.R. 1961. *Rethinking Anthropology*. London: Athlone Press.

_____. 1954 (2002). *Political Systems of Highland Burma: A Study of the Kachin Social Structure*. Oxford: Berg.

Malinowski, Bronislaw. 1967. *A Diary in the Strict Sense of the Word*. London: Routledge and Kegan Paul.

Moore, Henrietta L. and Todd Sanders. 2006. General Introduction, in H.L. Moore and T. Sanders (eds), *Anthropology in Theory. Issues in Epistemology*. Oxford: Blackwell Publishing, pp. 1–21.

Narayan, Kirin. 1993. 'How Native Is a "Native" Anthropologist?' *American Anthropologist* 95(3): 671–86.

Nencel, Lorraine and Peter Pels (eds). 1991. *Constructing Knowledge: Authority and Critique in Social Science*. London: Sage Publications.

Okely, Judith. 1996. *Own or Other Culture*. London: Routledge.

_____. 1992. 'Anthropology and Autobiography: Participatory Experience and Embodied Knowledge', in Judith Okely and Helen Callaway (eds), *Anthropology and Autobiography*. London: Routledge, pp. 1–28.

_____. 2007. Fieldwork Embodied in Shilling (ed.). *Embodying Sociology: Retrospect, Progress and Prospects*. Oxford: Blackwell Publishing Ltd.

Olwig, Karen Fog and Kirsten Hastrup (eds). 1997. *Siting Culture: The Shifting Anthropological Object*. London: Routledge.

Sahlins, Marshall. 1993. 'Goodbye to *Triste Tropes*: Ethnography in the Context of Modern World History'. *Journal of Modern History* 65(1): 1–25.

Sanjek, Roger. 1991. 'The Ethnographic Present'. *Man* (New Series) 26(4): 609–28.

Stocking, George W. Jr. 1985 [1983]. 'History of Anthropology: Whence/Whither', in George W. Stocking (ed.), *Observers Observed: Essays on Ethnographic Fieldwork*. London: University of Wisconsin Press, pp. 3–12.

———. 1991. 'Maclay, Kubary, Malinowski: Archetypes from the Dreamtime of Anthropology', in George W. Stocking Jr (ed.), *Colonial Situations: Essays on the Contextualization of Ethnographic Knowledge*. London: University of Wisconsin Press, pp. 9–74.

Strathern, Marilyn. 1987. 'The Limits of Auto-anthropology', in Anthony Jackson (ed.), *Anthropology at Home*. London: Tavistock Publications, pp. pp 16–37.

———. 1999. *Property, Substance and Effect: Anthropological Essays on Persons and Things*. London: Athlone Press.

Tambiah, Stanley J. 2002. *Edmund Leach: An Anthropological Life*. Cambridge: Cambridge University Press.

Trouillot, Michel-Rolph. 1991. 'Anthropology and the Savage Slot: The Poetics and Politics of Otherness', in Richard G. Fox (ed.), *Recapturing Anthropology: Working in the Present*. New Mexico: School of American Research Press, pp. 18–44.

———. 2003. *Global Transformations: Anthropology and the Modern World*. Hampshire: Palgrave Macmillan.

Vincent, Joan. 1991. *Engaging Historicism in Recapturing Anthropology: Working in the Present*, ed. Richard G. Fox. Sante Fe, New Mexico: School of American Research Press.

Weiner, Annette. B. 1995. 'Culture and Our Discontents'. *American Anthropologist*, New Series, 97(1): 14–21.

Weston, Kath. 1997. 'The Virtual Anthropologist', in Akhil Gupta and James Ferguson (eds), *Anthropological Locations: Boundaries and Grounds of a Field Science*. London: University of California Press, pp. 163–84.

Chapter 1

Knowing, Not Knowing, Knowing Anew[1]

Eric Hirsch

Introduction: On Not Knowing

In 1999 I returned to the Upper Udabe Valley to revisit the people I had first lived and worked among as an anthropologist. I initially went to live there during the mid-1980s. Among the many things I learned or re-learned during my return one stands out in particular. It concerns a convention that I had thought was no longer performed, but was actually currently engaged in. More significantly, and more surprising for me, the convention was current practice during my initial fieldwork, although I thought its abandonment in the past *had consigned it to the past*.

The convention I am referring to is the ceremonial splitting of *teb* (sugarcane) at principal moments of the ritual known locally as *gab* (see below and Figure 1). I first saw this performed during my stay in 1999. It was during my stay at Yuvenise with my friend and host Alphonse Hega and his relations that I was told the circumstances in which this convention had been re-established. This re-establishment predated my first fieldwork. In principle, then, I should have known about it, but I did not.

The chapter takes up this problem of knowing in the fieldwork context. It considers how my expectations about knowledge and about the past created the conditions for me to assume that the abandoned convention of ceremoniously splitting *teb* would always remain so – always remained abandoned and of the past. But as I now see more clearly I was operating with a *historical* perspective and specifically a view about anachronism that was

Figure 1. The ritual splitting of sugar cane (reb) at Hausline, August 1999. (photo: E. Hirsch)

inappropriate. Anachronism, according to the OED, is 'anything done or existing out of date; hence, anything which was proper to a former age, but is, or, if it existed, would be, out of harmony with the present'. I now understand that my view accorded with this definition. When I learned that the ceremonial splitting of *teb* was a practice abandoned in the past – I will clarify the circumstances for its abandonment below – the way I interpreted such a detail suggested that it was of the past, and remained as such.

In this light, the chapter critically engages with the 'historical turn' in anthropology and certain assumptions that are associated with the value attributed to an 'anthropology of history' (or 'historical anthropology'). According to the historical turn, history is seen as a necessary corrective to the conventional a-temporal ('out of time') perspective of anthropology. By aligning anthropology and history more closely, the limitations of each, it would seem, can be diminished. This is a view I subscribed to as well but more recently have come to question some of its suppositions. I can illustrate my hesitation by reference to an interesting observation made by Thomas (1989: 6, emphasis added) about ethnographies written with a historical anthropological outlook:

> Some works add much to our knowledge of indigenous perceptions of history or tradition, but do not *historicize* the indigenous perceptions themselves: the overarching context, and reference point for interpretation, remains an intransigently atemporal culture, rather than a *historical process*.

The idea that indigenous perceptions need to be historicised and that the context of anthropological investigation is a historical process is persuasive and seemingly self-evident. At the same time, the emphasis on 'historicising' is a profoundly Western[2] view (see Burke 2002). The view opens up certain possibilities, and forecloses others. The material presented in this chapter is a case in point: the changes I document are an outcome of (historical) colonial entanglements, but the enduring significance of these changes is not necessarily elucidated by the historical context, or the historicising of indigenous perceptions. Rather, the enduring significance of the changes is disclosed by attention to the possibilities inherent in indigenous perceptions about the relations and potential conversions[3] between past, present and future. I suggest that the emphasis on historical contextualisation is associated with Euro-American knowledge conventions – a convention of historical perspective is that anachronism must be avoided. It was precisely my implicit attitude towards anachronism and my implicit historical attitude that was the problem. Contrary to authors such as Thomas, the ethnographic present should not be displaced because it fosters an a-historical (or even anti-historical) outlook. Rather, attention needs to be focused on the potential for conversions in local perceptions: of transformations of the past in the present and transformations of versions of the future in the present.

The people who reside in the upper Udabe Valley, who are the focus of this chapter, are part of a language and culture known since colonial times as Fuyuge. The approximately 14,000 Fuyuge live in the Wharton Ranges, 100 km north-west of Port Moresby, the national capital. The Udabe Valley is one of five Fuyuge river valleys and has the largest population, of about 6,000. Fuyuge speakers reside in named territorial and dialect areas, known as *em* (home), within these valleys. There is no vehicular road to this mountainous region and during the mid-1980s I first arrived by light aircraft at the recently constructed mission airstrip at Ononge. Not long after my arrival I befriended Alphonse and his relations. They live at Yuvenise, a village nearby the Ononge mission station.[4] It was through these initial discussions with Alphonse's father, Hega, that I was able to move further down the valley to Visi and live with Hega's brother, Kol. At this time Kol was living at Fuda, the place of a *gab* ritual and it was here that I also came to reside.

During my initial fieldwork with the people of Visi I became interested in the organisation and structure of their *gab* ritual. *Gab* is the name that Fuyuge-speakers give to both the village in which the events of the ritual are performed and unfold, and to the whole performance of events: dances, pig-killings and ceremonial exchanges, all accomplished in the name of the young, old and dead. A *gab* is performed to 'wash away' the shame of life-crisis transitions. My interest was incited by Visi peoples' own keen interest in their ritual and the amount of effort they devote to its preparation and performance. One of the central elements of current *gab* arrangements is the concentration, display, ceremonial splitting and distribution of vast quantities of *inae* betel nut and in conjunction with this (although its bunches are not split) *solon* betel nut. *Inae* is a mountain variety of betel nut with a small nut that is not greatly valued as a chew. *Solon*, by contrast, is a coastal variety of betel nut with a large nut that is greatly valued as a chew and is lucratively marketed (see Hirsch 1990).

However, the contemporary value accorded to betel nut was not evident in the past. The concentration of betel nut in this manner, for instance, is not present in Williamson's (1912) early colonial-period monograph on the Mafulu (Mabula) Fuyuge-speakers. Several decades later a form of it is present in the accounts written by the missionary Dupeyrat. In his book, *Festive Papua* (see Dupeyrat 1955: 54) he describes peoples resident in the same Fuyuge river valley as that of the Mafulu (the Auga Valley) but further to the north-east and living at a higher altitude. I was interested in the expansion of this convention with betel nut and during my initial fieldwork asked my hosts about it. How was it possible for this practice to have emerged in the Upper Udabe Valley? How was it possible for these Fuyuge-speakers to imagine themselves in this different way (cf. Hacking 2002).

At this time Kol Usi told me that men from Pata (the Udabe Valley name for people living in the Auga Valley) had introduced the convention of splitting *inae* in the past to those in Visi. He said this was at the time he first wore the loincloth (*haning*), one of the rites that is performed in *gab*. From my estimations this would have been sometime around the early 1930s. I asked Kol what convention that of *inae* splitting had replaced. He told me that previously they had split *teb* but, as he put it, Visi became 'scared' (*hogaiya*) of it.[5] This was after the colonial reprisals for Fuyuge warfare and revenge killings with neighbouring collectivities, and the association of *teb* splitting with this legacy. My understanding was that *teb* splitting had been abandoned and although I asked how it was conducted in the past, I did not ask about its relevance in the present. When I heard it had been abandoned I summoned an image of it being in the past. It was 'history' and the domain of historical inquiry.

Upon reflection, I was, implicitly, conflating the past with history (see White 2002: 111–12). I was separating past from present in the way that is conventional for historical understanding. What I was not doing was considering this narrative about the past as a *present concern*, as a concern relevant to the present. What I was ignoring or failing to see was the potential of conversion: the manner in which one can appear and be effective by performing conversions upon (past) forms (see Strathern 1985). Because I did not inquire further, Kol assumed, I now imagine, that I knew all I needed to. Perhaps he believed that I knew, as he knew, that *teb* splitting had been brought back into use in the not too distant past. This is not simply an issue of me forgetting or overlooking to pursue a particular line of questioning – although it is clearly this to some extent, as well.

Rather, it was my understanding that a convention abandoned in the past was of the past, especially when I saw no evidence of it in the present. My supposition was that the present was separate from the past. This is not to suggest that past Fuyuge conventions are not evident in the present – *gab* is a case in point. The problem, as I now see it, was my unstated adoption of an attitude towards anachronism – an outgrowth of my profoundly *historical consciousness*. It is this consciousness, I suggest, that is not necessarily relevant to the consciousness of my Fuyuge interlocutors. Recognition of my unstated historical consciousness might not have made a difference to whether I came to know about *teb* splitting in the way I subsequently did. What it would have done was to prevent me from implicitly seeing the past as radically different and separate from the present.

Historical Consciousness

The title of Lowenthal's (1985) tome is instructive: *The past is a foreign country*. This is a view of the past as distant and dissimilar. 'The past is a foreign country' is a trope that resonates with a consciousness of the past that emerged over several centuries in Western Europe. What Whitehead (1967) refers to as the 'historical revolt' was the decisive moment in this process of transformation. A historical consciousness that we now understand and take for granted is the outcome of a humanist movement during the sixteenth century. This violent affair sought to rest political and temporal control away from the Papacy and Holy Roman Emperor. Thus, subsequently, the fundamental connections between sovereign subjects and historical time were forged. It is the 'subjectivity' that westerners (and Western trained anthropologists) imbibe as part of their modern education and socialisation.

Here I draw on Fasolt's (2004) provocative account where he suggests three principles that inform Western attitudes towards the past (and by implication that of historical consciousness): '1. the past is gone forever; 2. to understand the meaning of a text, you must first put it in the context of its time and place; 3. you cannot tell where you are going unless you know where you are coming from' (Fasolt 2004: ix). To know the past in this way, then, requires a certain kind of awareness. It is an awareness of the present as alive and the past as dead and gone. But without an awareness of this past it is not possible to know where one is going. Thus, attention to the past is both fundamental and fundamentally proliferating because there is not just one 'past' to know, but a seemingly infinite number, that keep growing. It is through the study of history of various kinds that these pasts are understood (see Samuel 1994). The knowledge thus accumulated is contextual, sensitive to the settings in which it derives. As such, anachronism must be avoided as this contaminates the history constructed. At the same time, this is not really possible, as all history is constructed from the perspective of the present (Collingwood 1961) and 'creative anachronism' flourishes (Lowenthal 1985: 363–412). But the ideal endures even as it is continually subverted (see Burke 2002: 19–20). As Burke (2002: 17–19) has suggested:

> The most important, or at least the most obvious characteristic of Western historical thought is its stress on development or progress, in other words its 'linear' view of the past. The term 'progress' is used here in a broad sense, to refer to the idea that change is cumulative (one generation standing on the shoulders of another), or that it is irreversible (summed up in the popular phrase, 'you can't put back the clock') ... Linked to the idea of progress but distinct from it is the Western concern with historical perspective. By 'concern with historical perspective' or the 'sense of anachronism', I mean the idea that the past is not uniform, more and more of the same thing, but on the contrary extremely variable, each historical period having its own cultural style, its own personality. One might describe this idea as a sense of 'cultural distance', a view of the past as 'a foreign country'.

These reflections on historical consciousness are as much about its conventional form as its limits and limits that anthropology, I suggest, needs to attend to. It is only recently that I have come to understand better these limits as well as the powerful hold such a consciousness has on Western perceptions as much as Western views of others (cf. Lévi-Strauss 1966: 245–70).[6] In short, historical consciousness and history are particular kinds of knowledge, associated with particular kinds of societies. Such perceptions have profound implications for the way the world is understood, and the principles mentioned above often shape that understanding, even when these principles are not explicitly evoked or acknowledged. This, I suggest, was the case with my initial attention to the 'abandoned' convention of *teb* splitting.

An inherent feature of historical understanding is periodisation. Leff (1969: 130) states categorically: '[P]eriodization is indispensable to historical understanding of any kind'. He goes on to highlight the importance of context. 'But a context must itself be defined in terms which are appropriate to the events which come within it. This entails marking it off from other contexts which, since they apply to events in time, must constitute a temporal division' (Leff 1969: 130). The crucial issue with periodisation is not whether history should be so divided, but the criteria by which one period is distinguished from another (Leff 1969: 130). It is these unstated assumptions about periodisation and history that informed the way I placed *teb* splitting into one period and that of *inae* splitting into another. I do not recall consciously making this separation. It is only in retrospect that I can see how it might have operated in the way I created anthropological knowledge for myself about Visi conventions. To put it bluntly, I saw the past as dead and gone forever and the present as alive. *Teb* splitting was of the past, was of another 'period', compared to that of *inae* splitting, which was of the present. This was not how my Visi hosts saw matters. Although they did say that *teb* splitting was of the *aked inoge* (lit. great men; the men from before), this was not in terms of explicit temporal periods.

Teb Splitting in the Present

So how did *teb* splitting come to be current convention again and why did I not see it performed during my initial time in Visi? As Kol Usi explained to me during 1999, *teb* was taken up again after Father Charles, one of the Ononge French Catholic missionaries, asked about this practice from the past, which he had heard about from the Visi people. This was during one of his pastoral visits to Visi. I was not able to ascertain the specific time this happened, but it was probably during the mid to late 1970s. Kol told me that Yavu Inoge (his elder brother and Visi *amede*[7] along with Kol) demonstrated the act of *teb* splitting to Father Charles in the Visi chapel on one occasion. He described how Yavu stood at the front of the chapel, near the missionary, and suddenly and loudly called everyone present to be silent and motionless. This is what happens before *inae* is split and would have occurred with *teb*. Yavu's forceful call surprised the missionary, which Kol particularly emphasised in his account. Kol then said that the Visi *aked* (the efficacious men of Visi) decided to make *teb* splitting current convention again. Yavu and Kol then agreed that Yavu would continue to 'look after' *inae* and Kol would 'look after' *teb*, each splitting these respectively in *gab*.

Although *teb* splitting had been abandoned in the past, as I was told, this was not a past that was radically separate from the present. The Fuyuge notion of *ilofe* (before) is how this is understood: persons and events that are recalled and that continue to exert an influence on the social relations constituted in the present (cf. Bird-David 2004). A case in point was Kol's continual reference, during 1999 when I spoke with him, to killings in the past between Visi and their neighbour Kase. These actions, he said, informed their current coercive relations enacted in *gab* (see Hirsch 2001). Those in Visi who knew about *teb* splitting, knew why it had been abandoned, but also knew why its abandonment was still significant. Its significance is associated with what people in Visi and other Fuyuge places say they came to take up after having been 'scared' of *teb* (see above). They say they came to know the 'law', that it was 'put into their heads', as this was stated to me. This is 'law' deriving from colonial agents and from the missionaries (the law of the government and that of God). It meant that Visi people now knew how to live 'properly', 'well' (*ife*), where fear of explicit killing and warfare was no longer viewed as conventional. It is this alteration of conventions that enabled, I suggest, the innovative take-up of *teb* splitting, after Father Charles's interest in this practice. Visi people no longer had to be 'scared' of *teb* in the way they had because now they knew the 'law'; they knew how to conduct themselves in a way the *aked inoge* did not. The convention of 'law' could now be potentially 'knocked off balance' (Wagner 1975) by the innovative take-up of *teb* splitting.

This is, of course, my post-hoc interpretation of what I perhaps should have known at the time but did not. Why was this the case? Why, in particular, did I not see this practiced during my time in Visi when it was 'current'? Here the answers are more straightforward. During the mid-1980s when I first lived in Visi there were two *gab* performed. One was at Fuda and the second was at Uyams. Fuda is in the part of Visi known as Yago. As noted above, I followed a path (*enamb*) to Fuda from Yuvenise via the relations between Kol and Hega, Alphonse's father. The *gab* at Fuda was organised for among others, Kol himself. Given these circumstances, he would not have split *teb* in the *gab* plaza centre. As a *mal* – a person of 'white hairs' – for whom others killed pigs, Kol would not be able to enter the village plaza. To do so would bring him illness and possibly his early demise.

The second *gab* at Uyams was one where new *amede* were to be given the power to split *inae*. This *gab* was in a part of Visi known as Ambabu. The name Ambabu derives from across the Udabe Valley, from the *em* (home) known as Kambisi. As such, Ambabu are 'guests' (*vas*) in Visi. There are men with 'skin' (*hode*) from Visi Yago, the 'true' Visi, that reside in Ambabu and have the capacities to be *amede*. The father of one of these men recently died before he was able to hand over his power. His son and two other men were perceived by the Visi *aked* as able to handle and talk over *inae*. Yavu Inoge and Kol were both at Uyams to give these new men this power. As such, *teb* would not be split at Ambabu because it was only *inae* that was to be passed on.

Given the above conditions, it is clear why I did not witness the practice of *teb* splitting during my initial fieldwork. However, the fact that I did not consider the *enduring significance* of this convention in the present, this was an outcome of my historical consciousness and distinct attitude about anachronism. It was my taken for granted outlook about the past as separate from the present that prevented me from pursuing my inquiries in a way that *might* have enabled me to know what I should have known.[8]

So why was it revived? I suggest that it was an outcome of the way the Fuyuge recurrently attempt to innovate their performance of *gab*, within the constraints of ancestrally derived conventions. That is, to 'knock the conventional off balance' in order to appear powerful (see Wagner 1975). The initial abandonment of *teb* in the past, and the innovation of *inae* adoption is a case in point. Under the current conventions of 'law', the revival of *teb* splitting is an analogous kind of innovation of its time.

When I returned to the Udabe Valley during the summer of 1999 I was told that Sol, one of the younger brothers of Alphonse, would be splitting *teb* at the *gab* at Hausline. This village is located in Evese, a home to the north of Visi, nearby the central mission station at Ononge. Why, though, was Sol now splitting *teb* instead of Kol and why was it not given to a man in Visi? Kol explained to me that he wanted to pass his power on – as he was getting old – but there was no one in Visi seen as capable of doing this. Sol is the son of Kol's brother, Hega. Kol and Hega both have the same father but different mothers and Hega was adopted by an Evese *amede* who had no sons. Although the *teb* had passed to Evese, a different home from that of Visi, its path (*enamb*) to this place was from Visi and this base or origin (*apude*) would be evident in the ancestral name of the *teb* and the words spoken when splitting it. A similar problem affected the passing on of *inae* in Visi, a problem that was also discussed during the mid-1980s. At this time, a young Visi man named Yavu Kasin was seen by the *aked* to have the requisite qualities to be able to handle and to speak over *inae*. He was said to have good qualities (i.e. not stealing, fighting and knowing how to look after people, things and the land). However, between the time of this talk in the mid-1980s and 1999 – when I returned – Yavu Kasin died. Other men of a similar generation and of similar *amede* origins were either seen as unsuitable to take the power of *inae*, or were scared: scared to speak publicly or scared they may be attacked with sorcery or poison by jealous others. One needed to be strong to speak in the *gab* plaza in front of hundreds of others and to hold and split these entities. It is for similar reasons that Kol decided to pass his power onto Sol who had the requisite qualities.

Too Little History?

It would be wrong to assume that my ignorance of the re-enactment of *teb* splitting was due to an a-historical perspective. Although my initial study was not historically orientated, an implicit historical perspective was at work in my fieldwork techniques, as I have indicated. A greater attention to history, I think, would not have been an advantage. Rather, what was required was a greater awareness of the profound connections of past, present and future, which is not the same thing as history. Thomas (1989: 120) argues that one of the limitations of the modern ethnographic method is its tendency to situate the object of study 'out of time'. He advocates a greater attention to history in order to overcome this 'static' emphasis on the present. And yet, it was my unspoken historical consciousness, I suggest, that was the problem. I was attempting to place *teb* splitting in a different historical epoch from that of *inae* (see Leff 1969, cited above). I was attributing to Fuyuge perceptions a way of reckoning events that was not appropriate to their perception and evaluation of events (see Strathern 1990). It was because I did not appreciate that pasts are always future orientated, that I did not understand that the abandonment of *teb* splitting could be implicated in futures present (see Chakrabarty 2000: 249–53).

Consider the event of Father Charles's question about *teb* and its later enactment in the Visi mission chapel as told to me by Kol. Father Charles was asking a question about the Fuyuge past ('history') and the response he received was in the form of a performance of the 'abandoned' convention. His question prompted the conversion of this knowledge about the past into an enactment in the present. Men such as Kol had this knowledge. It was a form that could be converted into another form (its ritual enactment). This is how Fuyuge and other Melanesians act and appear effective, by converting forms (see Strathern 1985). This is what I had not appreciated about the knowledge I had been told, that it was potentially transformable ('alive' and not 'dead'). However, this could only occur when the moment was appropriate. Unlike the time of its 'abandonment' – when people became scared of this practice – 'law' had become conventional by the time of Father Charles's question. It was not that the Fuyuge were 're-inventing tradition' but performing their knowledge in appropriate circumstances of the present.

Father Charles's question from the Fuyuge perspective needs to be understood not as an event in need of historical contextualisation but as a performance, evoking past and future simultaneously. *Teb* splitting of the past and its future re-enactment were disclosed in the present, a present now informed by law. Now was the time of law, a time vividly disclosed to me in a narrative I was told not long after my initial arrival in the Upper Udabe Valley (see below). Father Charles's question and the initial re-enactment of *teb* splitting disclosed a 'presence of time'.

When I speak of 'now' or the presence of time I am drawing on notions elaborated by Wagner (1986) in his discussion of epoch. Epoch is time that stands for itself in contrast to the measurement of time that clocks, calendars and history itself discloses. As Wagner (1986: 81) notes, it is an organic time, 'for the events occurring within it have a definitive and nonarbitrary – in fact, an organic or constitutive – relationship to the sequence as a whole, as in the plot of a myth … its events are in themselves relations, each one subsuming and radically transforming what has gone before'. This is how we understand historical epochs and it is this understanding of epoch with which, as Western trained analysts, we are most familiar. As the quote from Leff above indicates, we take epoch in this manner as a given. And it is because historical epoch so much informs our perceptions that we find it difficult to appreciate the relevance of epoch in a non-historical way.

With regard to the upper Udabe Fuyuge, epoch is poignantly disclosed in the ritual of *gab*, among other forms, including what Fuyuge refer to as *tidibe*. The notion of *tidibe* refers to two connected forms: to a singular creator force or power from which everything derives and a multiplicity of human-like characters whose movements and actions are narrated in specific stories – both the characters and narratives are known as *tidibe*. The *tidibe* narratives account for how current conventions came to appear – their present obviousness. The *emergence* of *tidibe*, then, reveals a new presence of time, a new kind of epoch, as I came to find out through my archival (historical) research.

During the mid-1960s, in the run-up to self-government (1972)[9] a *tidibe* is explicitly recorded in a patrol report of a visiting patrol officer to the Upper Udabe Valley. I consulted this report, among dozens of others that were written during the period of colonial control from the late nineteenth century until the mid-1970s. Nearly twenty years after this report was written I was told a version of this *tidibe*. The narrative I was told ends by disclosing how the Visi and other Fuyuge 'got the law into their heads' (see Hirsch 2001). This aspect is not apparent in the 1960s version. Rather, in that story (as in the one I was told) the emphasis is on how the government (and by implication missionaries) were pulled into their lands. The acquisition of law caps the version I was told. It was this perception, I want to suggest, that was of significance when Father Charles asked about the convention of *teb* splitting. The performance of the rite could now be undertaken in the time of law; Visi people no longer needed to be 'scared' about the practice of splitting *teb*.

Although I knew these ethnographic 'facts' at the time of my initial fieldwork – the *tidibe* where law is 'put into Fuyuge heads' and the past abandonment of *teb* splitting, I did not then connect them. I did not consider the possibility that *teb* splitting might be thought of in a different way given what the *tidibe* disclosed about the present. Father Charles's question could be understood from the perspective of (anthropological) history as a contingency, a chancy event in relation to the cultural structure or system (Sahlins 2004). According to this historical view, his question would then be 'domesticated' through (local) cultural interpretation (Sahlins 1985: 153). In other words, the event of his question was locally contextualised in an analogous way to the historian placing events in relation to one another in a kind of progression.

The alternative local perspective I am suggesting would understand the event in a different way. If we understand the event of Father Charles's question instead as a kind of performance, then it would be known by its effects – like an image that conceals or reveals, through the way it is registered by those who witness it (Strathern 1990: 28–29). In this way, his question is analogous to the *tidibe*: that is, each *tidibe* is a succession of images, where each image is a substitution for what has gone previously, containing the images that have preceded it, and containing the effects it has on those the *tidibe* engages. The event of Father Charles's question is not so much 'contingency' – an event in need of structural domestication – as an evocation of past and future simultaneously. That is, a past of being scared of *teb* splitting and a future where this convention is now possible because people know the law – a new presence of time.

In fact, I met Father Charles during my first fieldwork, but the topic of his question to Visi never arose in our brief conversations. He told me other interesting observations, such as when he first saw money transacted in *gab* ritual exchanges (ca. 1950s). It never occurred to me to ask him about this 'past' practice, as I assumed he would not have observed it, and was not interested in it. My view was formed by the way the missionaries talked about *gab*. In general, they were very negative about what they saw as its constant performance and the proliferation of 'parties', as they called them.

In retrospect, I see now that my attitude towards the missionaries was too limited, and a view correctly criticised by Thomas (1989: 14–15). Their negative views towards *gab* were matched by a long-standing familiarity with the people and an intimate knowledge of local conventions. At the time of my initial fieldwork, though, I tended to assess the missionaries as a 'foreign' intrusion, a sort of 'hindrance' to my understanding of Visi and other Fuyuge. This was an outcome of the 'mythicising erasure' I imbibed as part of the Malinowskian legacy of the lone, 'heroic' fieldworker. As I later came to appreciate, I should have seen the missionaries as an intrinsic feature of this 'ethnographic present'. But this is not just a matter of attending to historical time and the significance of historical processes in local relations (see Thomas 1989: 5). Attention to historical documentation is important ethnographically in relation to what is revealed through the encounters of fieldwork and the 'ethnographic present' and how this is formed through the process of interpretation and writing.

Thomas's (1989: 5) concern with the absence of historical time in many anthropological accounts appears straightforward and almost self-evident – in particular 'with the explicit or implicit negation of the notion that history [read mission and colonial relations] has any constitutive effect in the social situation under consideration'. The issue, as I understand it, is how mission and colonial influences are implicated in current social situations – 'the ethnographic present'. This is not a problem of history (or its lack) per se, but the relevance of these agents and organisations *in the present*. To understand this present may require a turn to historical materials (mission and colonial archives) and one may write an historical account of how local people came to be implicated with missionaries and colonialists (cf. Hirsch 2003). However, this history can only be used to enlarge what is understood as the ethnographic present; what is examined through fieldwork in a system of relations with a past, present and future (including relations of the anthropologist with anthropology, as much as the local people).

Does history tell us how change occurs? Or does the *tidibe* render this obvious. Which is more accurate and appropriate? This is not recourse to relativism but to the 'limits of history' (Fasolt 2004) and the often unquestioned status history has in the self-understandings of Western peoples. As I indicated above, history is written with respect to epochs, periods as an unquestioned aspect of modern historical practice. The historical understanding produced by writing with respect to epochs is what renders the past apparent in particular ways. In this way, historical epochs are analogous to *tidibe* or the performance of *gab* as each manifests organic time in which past, present and future are mutually implicated.

Conclusion: Blind Spot

There was something I should have known in the present, about something that had altered in the past. My lack of knowledge of both I have suggested was conceivably an outcome of my implicit historical consciousness and my unspoken attitude to anachronism. There was a 'gap' in my knowledge that I subsequently came to recognise. But there are always such gaps; anthropological knowledge can only ever be partial. At the same time, though, anthropologists attempt to overcome present gaps while inevitably revealing new ones: 'We become aware of creating more and more gaps' (Strathern 1991: 119). The 'historical turn' in anthropology was meant to overcome limits in understanding, as exemplified in texts such as the one produced by Thomas (1989). The assessment that colonialism and missionisation had profound influences on the societies conventionally studied by anthropology was a spur to a certain kind of ethnographic research. But even here the idea that 'the present' studied by anthropologists was the outcome of this history was by no means certain or uncontested. And the reason for this is that history is based on the study of a certain kind of evidence (archives, etc.) and a translation of such past evidence in the present. The influence of colonialism and missionisation may have been profound, but it is not enough to say that what is observed and understood during fieldwork is the outcome of that 'history'.

Ironically, I have undertaken historical research in the colonial (post-colonial) and mission archives that pertain to the Fuyuge, and never come across reference to *teb* splitting in these archives. So, greater attention to history would not have been the answer. In a sense, I already possessed the 'answer' but was not in a position to ask the appropriate question about what I knew.

My lack of knowledge of *teb* splitting during my initial fieldwork and my subsequent knowledge about this convention during my return visit is what has guided the discussion here. I have suggested that this gap in my knowledge may have been the unintended consequences of my significant, but implicit historical attitude. What I have learned, and what I should have already known is that past, present and future are not radically separated (as presupposed by history and historians) but are deeply connected in ethnographically unique ways.

The abandonment of *teb* splitting was, as the Fuyuge told me, the outcome of encounters in the colonial past. In this sense, then, we could say that its abandonment was the product of colonial history. However, the enduring significance of this convention was not revealed by that history. Rather, matters revealed it in the present that, for reasons I have tried to address here, remained obscured to me. The research and writing of ethnography is, in this manner, a constant process of 'discovery' or disclosure involving the people one lives among, others they have encountered (directly or indirectly), as much as oneself. Knowing, not knowing and knowing anew might be how best to describe this kind of anthropological inevitability.

Notes

1. A version of this chapter was presented in a seminar at Brunel University. For their very helpful comments and criticisms at the time and subsequently, I thank Nicolas Argenti, Adam Kuper, Alexandra Ouroussoff and Christina Toren. For all errors in either fact or form that remain, I only have myself to thank. The chapter draws on different periods of fieldwork (from the mid-1980s), most recently supported by the Cambridge and Brunel Universities joint research project, 'Property, Transactions and Creations: New Economic Relations in the Pacific', funded by the UK Economic and Social Research Council (grant no. ROOO237838). I am most grateful to Alphonse Hega, Kol Usi and my other recent hosts in Yuvenise.

2. The use of Western or European in this chapter refers both to people associated with areas conventionally understood as distinctly 'Western' or 'European', that is, North America, Western Europe, Australia, among other historically connected areas. Western or European also refers to knowledge conventions that were historically formed in these places but whose use is not restricted to these contexts.

3. The way I am using conversion in this chapter derives from Strathern (1985: 124). She deploys the notion to counter the idea that dispute settlements in the New Guinea highlands, for example, are motivated by a form of local reparation, where something 'broken' is then made 'whole' again. She suggests that this is a distinctly Western evaluation, based on the sense of persons or societies as 'whole', which is subject to shattering. By contrast, she argues, Melanesian persons – as 'partible' – continually circulate objects between themselves: 'what counts less than the repair of a broken connection (our own metaphor) is the *conversion* of one type of flow (e.g. blood) into another type (e.g. pigs). Power is shown in the ability to effect conversions (Strathern 1985: 124, emphasis added). Here I augment the use of the notion of conversion to understand the way relations between past, present and future are reformed.

4. At the time, I wanted to situate myself further away from the mission station. I thought that I needed to separate physically myself from such influences as much as possible. These influences, as I conceived them then, were not the proper focus of my anthropological research (cf. Barker 1990). As I came to realise subsequently, this was an incorrect view and one informed by the idea of anthropology I had imbibed before going to do fieldwork.

5. The fact that both *inae* and *teb* are split is significant. There is a category of men among the Fuyuge known as *amede*. The closest English equivalent used in the Melanesian literature to describe such men is that of 'chief' (cf. Hallpike 1977: 138–61). *Amede* take the place of their

fathers and are perceived to have excellent qualities. Today *amede* make speeches over and split bunches of *inae* at key moments of the *gab* ritual (in the past, a similar process would have occurred with *teb*). When they do so they articulate the archetypal name of *inae*, such as *yabdu kes*, where *yabdu* is a hand without fingers, i.e. a hand that does not steal. The name exemplifies the excellent qualities meant to be disclosed by splitting the bunch and of the *amede* performing the action. Without the performance of these actions the life cycle transitions enacted in *gab* could not be accomplished. In a connected way, there is a Fuyuge myth – such narratives are known as *tidibe* (see below) – called Hufife and Aling. They are a primordial husband and wife, respectively. A central image in this myth is where Hufife tricks Aling into having herself split between the legs, so that a vagina can be formed. In this way all women have vaginas and children can be born. In their unique, but connected ways, both *amede* and woman sustain existence through the 'splitting' each embodies.

6. Modern (i.e. post-Malinowskian) social anthropology defined itself with a particular relation to the historical situation of fieldwork and ethnography. The anthropologist sought to capture the 'ethnographic present' by deleting the effects of historical contacts and influences, what Stocking (1991: 10) refers to as a 'mythicising erasure'. With the 'historical turn' in anthropology during the 1980s and since, the fiction of the 'ethnographic present' has come to be seen more as an obstacle to anthropological understanding (cf. Comaroff and Comaroff 1992). The influences of colonialism, missionisation and capitalism are more explicitly brought into the analysis. In short, the present cannot be adequately understood, it is argued, unless history is integrated into the account (see Carrier 1992; Thomas 1989). In either case, then, an attitude to history and historical consciousness prevails: to create 'mythically' a moment outside its influences or one inside. What is understood as the ethnographic present is related, then, in often contradictory ways, to Western history and historical consciousness.

7. See note 4.

8. My anthropological training at the LSE during the early 1980s was highly influenced by the legacy of Malinowski. Not so much theoretically ('functionalism') as the influence of Lévi-Strauss was very prominent: my supervisor's monograph (Gell 1975) that was much debated at the time was heavily influenced by structuralism. But the legacy was there in the kind of 'mythicising erasure' discussed by Stocking (1991: 10). Issues to do with colonialism, history and missionisation were not really addressed in this environment. Although Bloch's (1986) monograph appeared shortly after my return from fieldwork, this was a very particular kind of historical anthropology, a use of history to disclose the a-historical structure of ritual. At this same time the work of Comaroff (1985), Sahlins (1981, 1985) and others began to appear and I began to become interested in the historical matters they raised and to see the limits of my previous work. This led to sustained research with colonial government and missionary archival materials and to a number of publications that began to analyse these historical influences on Fuyuge persons, personhood and changes in their spatial and temporal horizons (e.g. see Hirsch 1999). As an outcome of this research I began to re-analyse a number of Fuyuge *tidibe* that emerged and/or transformed in the context of these historical situations. As I discuss in the next section below, *tidibe* are known and told to account for how present arrangements and conventions came to be formed. These narratives are different from the historical accounts that the missionaries (e.g. Delbos 1985) or I have fashioned. Both are epochal, in the sense described by Wagner (1986): that is, both disclose the presence of time in distinctive ways (again, as I elaborate in the next section below). It is this work, in particular, that led me to the issues discussed in this chapter.

9. And later national independence from Australia in 1975.

References

Barker, J. (ed.). 1999. *Christianity in Oceania: Ethnographic Perspectives*. Lanham, MD: University Press of America.

Bird-Davis, N. 2004. 'No Past, No Present: A Critical-Nayaka Perspective on Cultural Remembering', *American Ethnologist* 31: 406–21.

Bloch, M. 1986. *From Blessing to Violence: History and Ideology in the Circumcision Ritual of the Merina*. Cambridge: Cambridge University Press.

Burke, P. 2002. 'Western Historical Thinking in Global Perspective – 10 theses', in J. Rusen (ed.), *Western Historical Thinking: An Intercultural Debate*. Oxford: Berghahn, pp. 15–32.

Carrier, J. (ed.). 1992. *History and Tradition in Melanesian Anthropology*. Berkeley: University of California Press.

Chakrabarty, D. 2000. *Provincializing Europe: Postcolonial Thought and Historical Difference*. Princeton: Princeton University Press.

Collingwood, R. 1961. *The Idea of History*. Oxford: Oxford University Press.

Comaroff, J. 1985. *Body of Power, Spirit of Resistance: The Culture and History of a South African People*. Chicago: University of Chicago Press.

Comaroff, J. and J. Comaroff. 1992. *Ethnography and the Historical Imagination*. Boulder, CO: Westview.

Delbos, G. 1985. *The Mustard Seed: From a French Mission to a Papuan Church*. Port Moresby: Institute of Papua New Guinea Studies.

Dupeyrat, A. 1955. *Festive Papua*, trans. E. de Mauny. London: Staples Press.

Fasolt, C. 2004. *The Limits of History*. Chicago: University of Chicago Press.

Gell, A. 1975. *Metamorphosis of the Casowaries: Umeda Society, Language and Ritual*. London: Athlone.

Hacking, I. 2002. *Historical Ontology*. Cambridge, MA: MIT Press.

Hallpike, C. 1977. *Bloodshed and Vengeance in the Papuan Mountains: The Generation of Conflict in Tauade Society*. Oxford: Clarendon Press.

Hirsch, E. 1990. 'From Bones to Betelnuts: Processes of Ritual Transformation and the Development of "National Culture" in Papua New Guinea', *Man* 25(1): 18–34.

———. 1994. 'Between Mission and Market: Events and Images in a Melanesian Society', *Man* 29(3): 689–711.

———. 1999. 'Colonial Units and Ritual Units: Historical Transformations of Persons and Horizons in Highland Papua', *Comparative Studies in Society and History* 41(4): 805–28.

———. 2001. 'Making up People in Papua', *Journal of the Royal Anthropological Institute* 7(2): 241–56.

———. 2003. 'A Landscape of Powers in Highland Papua, c. 1899–1918', *History and Anthropology* 14(3): 3–22.

Leff, G. 1969. *History and Social Theory*. London: Merlin.

Lévi-Strauss, C. 1966. *The Savage Mind*. Chicago: University of Chicago Press.

Lowenthal, D. 1985. *The Past Is a Foreign Country*. Cambridge: Cambridge University Press.

Sahlins, M. 1981. *Historical Metaphors and Mythical Realities*. Ann Arbor: University of Michigan Press.

———. 1985. *Islands of History*. Chicago: University of Chicago Press.

_____. 2004. *Apologies to Thucydides: Understanding History as Culture and Vice Versa*. Chicago: University of Chicago Press.

Samuel, R. 1994. *Theatres of Memory*. London: Verso.

Stocking, G. 1991. 'Maclay, Kubary, Malinowski, Archetypes from the Dreamtime of Anthropology', in G. Stocking (ed.), *Colonial Situations: Essays on the Contextualization of Anthropological Knowledge*. Madison: University of Wisconsin Press, pp. 9–74.

Strathern, M. 1985. 'Discovering "Social Control"', *Journal of Law and Society* 12(2): 111–34.

_____. 1990. 'Artefacts of History: Events and the Interpretation of Images', in J. Siikala (ed.), *Culture and History in the Pacific*. Helsinki: Suomen Antropologien Seura, The Finnish Anthropological Society, Transactions No. 27, pp. 25–44.

_____. 1991. *Partial Connections*. Savage, MD: Rowman and Littlefield.

Thomas, N. 1989. *Out of Time: History and Evolution in Anthropological Discourse*. Cambridge: Cambridge University Press.

Wagner, R. 1975. *The Invention of Culture*. Chicago: University of Chicago Press.

_____. 1986. *Symbols that Stand for Themselves*. Chicago: University of Chicago Press.

White, H. 2002. 'The Westernization of World History', in J. Rusen (ed.), *Western Historical Thinking: An Intercultural Debate*. Oxford: Berghahn, pp. 111–118.

Whitehead, A. 1927. *Science and the Modern World*. Cambridge: Cambridge University Press.

Williamson, R. 1912. *The Mafulu Mountain People of British New Guinea*. London: Macmillan.

Chapter 2

The Transformation of Indigenous Knowledge into Anthropological Knowledge: Whose Knowledge Is It?

David P. Crandall

Introduction

The creation of anthropological knowledge is a complex, interpretive, analytical and transformative process of taking what is foreign and 'other' and domesticating it – making it our own. By congealing the individualised knowledge of many persons into a single intellectual object and setting that object within a form of interpretive discourse of the anthropologist's own choosing, the transformation is complete and anthropological knowledge is born. Though this process may seem ominous, I think it is not much different from what happens in ordinary conversation and is simply the way human beings engage the thought of others. This does not mean that all schools of interpretation are equal. In this paper I argue, based on reflections of my own fieldwork, that some of the interpretive and analytical tools we bring to this process offer greater fidelity to our ethnographic experience than others; and that though we cannot alter the basic innate mechanisms of engaging the thought of others, we can choose analytical tools that are less distorting than others. In particular, I argue that the concept of the integrated system, as the assumed basis of order for human thought, gravely distorts and warps our ethnographic analyses, leading us astray in our characterisations of the thinking and actions of other peoples. Finally, I suggest several other analytical/interpretive approaches for understanding the organisation of human thought which offer a far more accurate depiction of the ordering of human thought and, hence, may lead to an anthropological knowledge that has a greater fidelity to the ethnographic experience.

In Henri Junod's introduction to his well-known, two volume work, *The Life of a South African Tribe*, he remarks upon the 1895 visit of Lord Bryce to his missionary outpost in Mozambique. Bryce, who had spent considerable time journeying through South Africa and visiting native peoples, lamented the dearth of knowledge European settlers possessed of them. 'How thankful we should be', Bryce mused, 'we men of the XIXth century, if a Roman had taken the trouble fully to investigate the habits of our Celtic forefathers! This work has not been done, and we shall always remain ignorant of things which would have interested us so much!' (1966: 1). After pondering this statement, Junod (the Roman) took its challenge to heart and began recording the observations that resulted in his large and useful catalogue of organised ethnographic bits and pieces – interspersed with well-considered commentaries and explanations – about the life of the Thonga. That this is a significant piece of ethnographic knowledge is not in doubt. However, can Junod's essentially fact-finding activity be properly considered anthropological knowledge?

If one follows Evans-Pritchard's observation on the matter, the answer is firmly, no. For the production of anthropological knowledge is much more than mere fact gathering and compilation. 'Anyone who is not a complete idiot can do fieldwork, and if the people he is working among have not been studied before he cannot help making an original contribution to knowledge. But will it be to theoretical, or just to factual, knowledge? Anyone can produce a new fact; the thing is to produce a new idea ... Can it be too often said that in science ... [if] empirical observation [is] to be of value [it] must be guided and inspired by some general view of the nature of the phenomena being studied? The theoretical conclusions will then be found to be implicit in an exact and detailed description' (1976: 243).

Though much has changed in the world of academic anthropology in the five or six decades since Evans-Pritchard first made these comments, his view that anthropological knowledge is not simply an accumulation of ethnographic facts, but ethnographic facts set within an explanatory framework that gives those facts additional depth, weight, meaning and coherence, and connects them to a far wider academic discourse on the subject, is still essentially correct.

The creation of anthropological knowledge involves taking what is 'foreign' and 'other', and domesticating it – that is, making it our own, couching things in terms familiar to us, sorting through the ethnographic facts *we* determine to be important and placing them in an intellectual context that is not only the invention of our own minds, but one we have selected from a range of competing constructs because we, for some inexplicable reason, have found it more intellectually agreeable than its competitors. 'Cultural translation' is inherently an idiosyncratic process, and in the current intellectual climate, confidence in being able to produce a straightforward, accurate and perhaps even objective ethnographic result – confidence of the sort ostensibly possessed by anthropology's 'golden-age' ethnographers – has simply fallen to the wayside. Still, the widely acknowledged problematic nature of anthropological knowledge has hardly resulted in less ink on fewer pages. Indeed, the ever-increasing production of ethnographic monographs, as well as the proliferation of new anthropological journals, suggests that despite Fabian's (1991: 191–206) inescapable conclusion that we ultimately create the object of our studies, we still feel confident we have something to report.

At least partially couched in the ideas of Foucault and Derrida, recognition that the foundations of anthropological knowledge are complex, even tenuous, provoked the soul-searching critiques of ethnography in the 1980s and 1990s (e.g. Clifford 1986; Marcus 1986) that focused on often hidden issues such as power relations, the authoritative voice, the all-seeing ethnographic eye, the many missing voices, the inability to fully understand another person, complicity in colonialism (even if unaware) and a number of other analytical blinders (ranging from Christianity to capitalism, and from homophobia to sexism) reputed to be deeply embedded in anthropological texts. Even if subsequent works have proven to be no less biased, at least the ethnographer has the pleasure of unburdening his or her inherited guilt by full or partial disclosure of the postmodern facts of life. Yet none of the effects of ethnographic catharsis mitigates the fact that anthropological knowledge is anything other than what Fabian concludes it to be – the inescapable remains inescapable. While it is useful to remain circumspect in our attempts at producing anthropological knowledge, these issues are hardly unique to anthropology, or to the academic world as a whole. Indeed, they seem to be part and parcel of the way human beings construct knowledge in virtually every avenue of life. If, for instance, one sits down to chat with a group of acquaintances, or even strangers, is it not typical – perhaps fundamentally necessary – to refer all the information conveyed in conversation back to one's own private intellectual world (one's most deeply held ideas concerning what is really real, what is good and correct, and what is morally untenable) to be processed, to be made sense of, in order that it might become known, connected and useful information? In this process, does one not take another person's knowledge and make it meaningful and useful by altering it – however slightly – as one connects that information to ideas one already accepts as important? By so doing, one may well give this 'new' information an elucidative power to be employed in stitching together explanations in ways fully unintended by the person who conveyed that information in the first place. I contend that the creation of anthropological knowledge follows this same basic course.

I am not arguing this as a means of legitimising what might well be an illegitimate way of doing things (unless the apparent lack of an alternative confers legitimacy); I am simply arguing that it is the inescapable manner in which it is done. The only alterable aspect of this seems to be the ideas – the intellectual tools – one holds as correct about the nature of the world; these can, and occasionally do, change. As these change, so changes the state of human knowledge – a fact to which any intellectual history of a subject attests (see Kuper 1989; Kuhn 1996; Grene 2004). But this is hardly to be equated with the sweeping away of prejudices; indeed, it is merely the switching of one bundle of preconceived ideas for another.

In this essay, I wish to explore this issue a bit more fully, focusing on the result of ethnographers engaging the knowledge of a particular people and transforming the individualised knowledge of many 'informants' into anthropological knowledge by strategically fitting that information into the strait jacket of an analytical framework. In particular, I am interested in the issue of systemisation and how the mostly unthinking employment of traditional conceptions of 'system' – an element so fundamental to anthropological analysis, yet so fundamentally ill-suited to it – not only distorts ethnographic reality, but calls into question the foundations of anthropological knowledge.

To this end, I wish to revisit an article I published in 1996 on the symbolic dimensions of the organisation of a Himba homestead (Crandall 1996). In this piece I argued that the physical arrangement of the homestead posed a curious problem for the near universal organisational feature, and its distinctive correlates, of the left/right, female/male, evil/good, classificatory divide. The basic arrangement of a Himba homestead contradicted the typical associations of the left/right divide – notwithstanding the fact that common left/right, female/male, weakness/strength, evil/good associations were widely used and acknowledged organisational features of Himba physical and intellectual life. As I saw it then, this was a puzzle wanting resolution, and I happily complied.

With hindsight, however, I have come to understand that I embarked on my brief study because I saw a problem that existed not in the Himba world, but in the imaginary world of my theoretical/analytical system. To resolve the problem, I transposed a non-parallel way (i.e. Himba) of ordering the world into the world of formal analysis. These two worlds did not, and do not, correspond. But I pursued the analysis and reached a conclusion that has, I believe, some affinity with the truth, a kind of rough-hewn resemblance, but my analysis inevitably distorted some things in the process. This is why I have come to view the assumed utility of traditional conceptions of system and systemisation as greatly exaggerated; and I shall argue that far softer approaches such as shreds and patches, bricolage, family resemblance, and fuzzy sets are far more useful and accurate ways of understanding supposed systems – be they systems of thought or social systems.

Himba, Himba Space and a Puzzle Solved

The Himba are a Herero-speaking people who live in the north-west corner of Namibia (southern Africa) and in the adjoining provinces of Angola. About 15,000 Himba live widely dispersed in the northern section of the Kunene Province of Namibia, commonly known as Kaokoland, with perhaps half that number settled across the Kunene River in Angola. Kaokoland, where my fieldwork takes place, is a vast and rugged territory of approximately 20,000 square kilometres occupied mainly, though not exclusively, by Himba. The landscape is broken with hills and mountains creating latitudinal chains of valleys perhaps 20–25 km in length, and about half that distance in width. In central Kaokoland, mountain peaks reach an elevation of over 1,500 metres. The valley floors are arid savanna and savanna woodland, and rainfall throughout the whole of Kaokoland is sporadic, ranging from 100 mm to 300 mm per annum.

The Himba economy is still largely pastoral with comparatively few opportunities to participate in the larger cash economy of Namibia. Himba herd great numbers of sheep and goats, yet Himba men predominantly think of themselves as cattle-herders – traditionally the only economic activity worthy of masculine attention. Unlike sheep and goats, which are non-distinct animals, within the community of cattle there are rigid distinctions between sacred (patrilineal) and secular (matrilineal) beasts. Horticulture is practiced during the rainy season, when maize, pumpkins and calabashes are cultivated on flood plains; wild foods are also gathered during this season of the year (see Crandall 1992).

Perhaps the most remarkable organisational feature of Himba society is its system of dual descent, with the combination of matri- and patrilineal descent used to establish social, economic and moral/ritual identity. Matrilineal descent confers rights to matrilineal inheritance which, in the case of the Himba, constitutes the majority of wealth in livestock, as well as all non-sacred, non-consecrated wealth. Matrilineal relations also provide for the extension of long-ranging kinship ties within the whole of Himba society, even branching out to neighbouring peoples with whom the Himba share common matriclans. Patrilineal descent, on the other hand, is narrowly focused in terms of exclusion from or belonging to a corporate patrilineal segment (see Crandall 1991). It is through membership in a patrilineal segment that one gains access to God, to patri-ancestors specific to oneself, to ritual, to manhood, to a mature position within the perceived order of things and to sacred cattle and other ritually charged objects.

Himba live in small settlements of extended patri-households, comprised of fathers, sons and their wives and children, that I term homesteads. A circular homestead is composed of individual houses grouped around an *okuruwo* (ancestral fire) (see Fig. 2.1 – chapter 2). The entrance to a completely fenced homestead is traditionally on the west, though sometimes the entrance faces the nearest major footpath, making it a practical rather than a symbolic entrance. The most important homesteads are headed by the eldest living male of a patrilineal segment, and he it is who officiates as both keeper of the ancestral fire and head of the homestead. As patrilineal descent is the primary focus of a homestead, all persons residing in a homestead are directly related to him and residence is based upon direct attachment to an ancestral fire that represents patrilineal ancestors specific to oneself. But domiciled in many homesteads are several households of persons matrilineally related to the head of the homestead who live with him because they possess rights in usufruct to his matrilineal cattle. These two sets of kinsmen occupy different halves of the homestead – patrilineal on the left, matrilineal on the right, with the ancestral fire acting as the reference for the division of space. All Himba patricians (with the exception of two) locate the ancestral fire at the most easterly point of the circular homestead, situated between the central livestock enclosure and the 'big house' in which the fire-keeper lives. Though the ancestral fire is located at the most easterly point of a homestead, according to Himba reckoning, a homestead 'looks' west. The hearth of stones directly in front of the fire (i.e. east of the fire), and curling slightly round to the south-east of the fire, is the locus of most ritual – the place where the living stand or kneel to face the ancestors. Thus, as one stands at the fire, one faces west, while one's back is to the east; and it is from this vantage point that the homestead is divided into two halves: patrilineal/left and matrilineal/right.

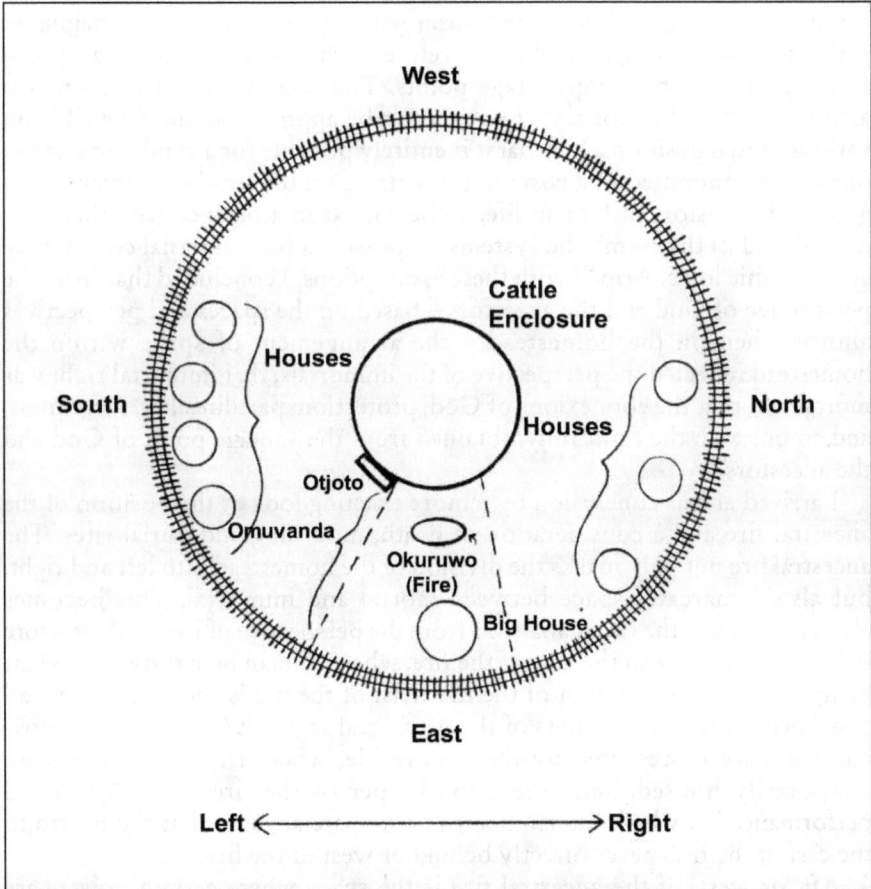

Figure. 2.1. The homestead of Wamesepa Ngombe, 1991.

Despite the fact that Himba call the right arm 'the strong arm' (*okumanene*) and the left arm 'the weak arm' (*okumuho*), and associate the former with maleness and the latter with femaleness, the many ritual and ceremonial elements of a Himba homestead take place on the left-hand side of a homestead. Thus, ancestors, God, patrilineality, safety, goodness, maleness, and so on, are connected with the left-hand portion of the homestead, while the right is associated with matrilineality, strangers, the absence of ritual and ancestral protection, and other forms of potential danger. Given the fact that beyond the confines of this setting Himba associate maleness, strength, God, the ancestors, ritual protection, and so on, with the right, and femaleness, weakness, evil, danger, and so on, with the left, the arrangement of space – and objects in space – within the homestead is a curious puzzle, and in my earlier paper (Crandall 1996) I attempted to resolve this matter.

This sort of symbolic reversal is hardly unknown in the literature (see Granet 1933; Needham 1960 and 1967), yet every case requires its own distinctive approach. In my paper, I proposed to solve the Himba dilemma by carefully connecting Himba symbolism with a pattern of mirror imaging in order to find a single mediating referent that functioned as a spatial convergence of opposing vantage points. This analysis was based on two assumptions: 1) that not only can symbols be approached and viewed from various spatial positions, but that it is entirely possible for a symbolic system, one richly committed to a cosmology centring on the steady involvement of gods and ancestors in human life, to be rooted in a perspective other than mortal; and 2) that symbolic systems do possess a basic internal consistency and systemic logic. Armed with these assumptions, I concluded that from the perspective of God and the ancestors – based on the spaces and perspectives allotted them in the homestead – the arrangement of space within the homestead reflected the perspective of the immortals, that immortal right was mortal left, that the connexions of God, protection, partilineality, sacredness, and so on, with the right fully obtained from the vantage point of God and the ancestors.

I arrived at this conclusion by a more exacting look at the position of the ancestral fire and a consideration of death, mourning and burial rites. The ancestral fire not only marks the division of the homestead into left and right, but also demarcates space between mortal and immortal. This becomes clearer still when the fire is analysed from the perspective of fore and aft – fore being in front of or to the east of the fire, where human beings dwell, and aft being behind or to the west of the fire. East of the fire is the space where all ritual occurs, where members of the patrilineal segment (whose direct patri-ancestors are represented by the fire) reside, where ritual candidates are temporarily housed, and where the keeper of the fire lives. All sacred performances in which human beings participate are staged at the hearth to the east of the fire, never directly behind or west of the fire.

Aft, or west, of the ancestral fire is the space where certain objects are placed that directly represent the ancestors. (Though I am not aware of this being done currently, in earlier days, Himba have told me, the men of a homestead were actually buried behind, or aft of, the fire.) The most common among these things are sturdy limbs from ironwood trees that have been lopped off and carried to this site after a special remembrance rite is performed. Each branch in this often considerable stack of limbs directly represents the ancestor for whom the remembrance rite was performed. Mingled among these branches are other items representative of the ancestors: animal horns, milk pails, small wooden objects, and sometimes ornaments – things that belonged to a man in life and now represent him in death. Behind the ancestral fire, at the very centre of the homestead, stands a circular cattle enclosure that houses all the cattle of the homestead, many of which are sacred, consecrated cattle belonging to and representing specific patri-ancestors. Their milk and their meat may only be consumed by direct patri-kinsmen, and only then after the keeper of the fire has tasted it, thereby making it safe to drink. From these and other clues, it becomes clear that mortals and mortal concerns are represented in the space to the east of the fire, while the immortals are represented in the space to the west of the fire, and that the ancestral fire itself is the mediating point between these two spaces and their corresponding perspectives.

The realisation that the ancestral fire is the meeting place of mortals and immortals who belong to the same patrilineal segment is key to understanding the Himba context of symbolic parallax. It is the idea of symbolic parallax that allows one to account for the apparent change in position of an object, a symbol, or referent that actually results from a change in the direction from which it is viewed. Within the Himba cosmos, mortals symbolically view life from east of the fire. As a man stands at the fire, his gaze is toward the west, where the sun goes down. Human life – mortal life – is associated with the perspective of the dying sun and the darkness of night. Immortals, on the other hand, symbolically view human life from aft of the fire, from west of the fire, with a view toward the east. There are many ethnographic evidences of this, but perhaps the opposing spatial perspectives of ancestors and human beings are more clearly demonstrated in death, mourning, and burial practices than anywhere else.

That sunrise and daylight are associated with the immortals, and, in fact, symbolically constitute the perspective from which they view the world, is best illustrated in Himba funerary practices. When a Himba man dies he is buried in a graveyard, often at quite a remove from the homestead, beside his father and brothers. Females are normally buried near their husbands, though as ancestresses, they are mostly inactive. Himba inter their dead in a methodical and deliberate manner. The corpse is placed in the grave in a sitting position, with the knees drawn up almost beneath the chin, and the body covered in a leather blanket. The direction of the grave and the position of the body within it are critical. Himba dig their graves along the east-west axis and position the body in the grave so that 'the soles of the feet and the eyes face east' – the direction of the rising sun. Thus, upon death, a Himba undergoes a transformation of position: the direction a person in life faces – west – is no longer emblematic of his ancestral position in the cosmos. The dead 'leave their graves' to become ancestors – immortals whose directional perspective of the world is exactly opposite that of mortals.

This transformation is symbolised not only by the placing of the body but also through *okuprika* (mourning practices). Himba do not mourn a kinsman in a general way, but as either a member of one's patrilineage or matrilineage. The clear and obvious indication of whether it is a matri- or patrikinsman one in mourning is manifested by the removal of jewellery from either the left or the right half of the body. While a patrilineal relation throughout life is represented by the left, in death that person is symbolised by the right; and one mourns the death of a patrikinsman by the removing the jewellery from the right side of one's body. The opposite obtains in the case of the death of a member of one's matrilineage. Thus, the rites of mourning spatially/directionally symbolise, from a human perspective, the transformation from mortal to immortal; from the position of fore of the fire to aft of the fire; from viewing the world according to the direction of the setting sun to viewing the world from the direction of the rising sun. The deceased has turned and taken his place among the ancestors as the closest link to the living.

The resolution of this puzzle, as I articulated it, rests on the inclusion of a dual perspective – mortal and immortal – focused on the ancestral fire as *the* spatial referent that allowed the concept of symbolic parallax to bring clarity to this matter. The directional/spatial logic and consistency of the Himba symbolic system demonstrated very clearly that immortal right equalled mortal left, that Himba conceptualised the living and the deceased as forming a single patrilineal unit, that the meeting place of mortal and immortal is the ancestral fire, that living and deceased meet face-to-face and view the world, and one another, from opposing spatial perspectives, and that immortal strength, greatness and blessing is unbrokenly symbolised by the use of mortal left.

From a 'System of Ideas' to 'Shreds and Patches'

In many ways, this bit of anthropological knowledge is derivative of a rather typical sort of structural analysis – though in a very odd manner. I freely admit that I have found such analyses not only intellectually pleasing, but aesthetically appealing as well. Reflecting on it now, I believe the ethnographic data are correct and that something in their eventual understanding is sound. But I do not think there was truly a puzzle here at all. All of these data were clearly present before the Himba, many of whom had been involved with left/right issues for fifty and sixty years, yet to them there was no puzzle, no mystery, no bother, and not because they were unthinkingly going about things (obviously, some people are more thoughtful and contemplative than others), but, as I have come to understand since, their basic intellectual structure for apprehending things is different from the formal analysis that I used. Had I explored this issue fully and come to an understanding of the nature of that ordering, my analysis of this data would have been different. The eventual understanding may have had some broad similarities with the solution I proposed, but they would have followed a different train of thought and more accurately depicted the flow of Himba cogitation. Instead, I transposed the Himba world into a highly systematised formal analysis that more or less required the Himba world to shed its less rigid form of intellectual organisation for one of extreme rigidity. The true impediment here was the idea of a system – a system of thought. In our common understanding, a system is comprised of a number of fully integrated, fully interrelated, and fully interdependent elements (*OED*, Compact Edition, 'system'). It is a learned conception that emanates from a particular kind of cultural and intellectual tradition, but it does not follow that this manner of ordering things is part of every intellectual tradition. It is deeply embedded in the minds of students of virtually every academic discipline – indeed, it is something tacitly as well as explicitly learned from the earliest days in school onward – and though we fully expect the world and our patterns of thought to disclose themselves to us in this manner, we must not assume that tight systemisation is *the* universal form of intellectual ordering. As a concept, system may be a useful analytical tool in some settings, but our traditional understanding of system can likewise be gravely distorting.

At present, anthropologists are fond of 'cultural paradoxes' and 'cultural contradictions'; but might it not be the case that such appear to us as paradoxes and contradictions primarily because of our specific way of being in the world? Our traditional understanding of system allows us to identify seeming contradictions and to be bothered by them; yet this does not mean these contradictions actually exist. If the people one is studying do not recognise a supposed contradiction or paradox, one ought to be exceedingly careful in labelling it as such; for what we come to recognise as a contradiction or cultural puzzle is a reflection of a mode of thinking we thrust upon the world. Thus, in the creation of anthropological knowledge, it is important to ascertain whether or not such a contradiction or paradox or puzzle is 'real', or if it is simply the analytical conclusion of the anthropologist.

From the vantage point of day-to-day life, of individual human pathways through life – whether Himba or my own – I am not in the least convinced that any pattern of human thought or human action conforms to a high and consistent degree with our traditional understanding of system. Because of this conclusion, I argue that the concept of system may be a poor intellectual tool in the creation of anthropological knowledge, that it offers very little resemblance to life as lived. I am not arguing that the concept of system be entirely banished from anthropological analysis, only that it be thoroughly modified to reflect a much more accurate depiction of human thinking and human action.

That human beings desire some sort of coherence in their various strands of thought is not only an ancient idea, but a fundamental underpinning of anthropology. Drawing on a modernised Aristotelian model, Iris Murdoch reasserts that the notion 'of a self-contained unity or limited whole is a fundamental instinctive concept ... Intellect is naturally one-making. To evaluate, understand, classify, place in order of merit, implies a wider unified system; the questioning mind abhors vacuums' (1993: 1). It would be difficult indeed to argue to the contrary, and I have no intention of doing so, yet I wish to draw attention to the ease with which Murdoch equates 'one-making' with 'system'. The two are certainly not synonymous, but it is the deeply assumed synonymy between them that makes it difficult to see things otherwise. This very synonymy is implicit in virtually all modern anthropological definitions of culture, from Tylor's 'that complex whole' (1871), to culture as 'learned sets of ideas and behaviors that are acquired by people as members of society' (Lavenda 2002: 14). When applied to specific cultural domains, such as Geertz's well-known definition of religion, religion becomes 'a system of symbols which acts to ... ' (1973: 109). My point here is that the idea of a system comprising fully interrelated and mutually coherent elements saturates anthropological thinking.

The tradition of assuming 'system' to be a most basic and elemental pattern of mental organisation obviously antedates modern anthropology by millennia. Yet I find it curious that at least two widely known and influential ideas in anthropology – ideas that present an alternative to the prevailing understanding of system – were never properly fostered as alternatives, least of all by their respective originators. When Lowie writes that 'cultures develop mainly through the borrowings due to chance contact' (1920: 441) and describes culture and civilisation as 'that planless hodgepodge, that thing of shreds and patches' (ibid.), he is reacting in Boasian-style against Victorian-age theories of unilineal social evolution. The very notion of culture as a thing of 'shreds and patches', as a 'planless hodgepodge' of ideas and behaviours stands in the starkest possible contrast to current sentiments of culture as a *system* of ideas. It is a very intriguing proposition and suggests a rather different approach to understanding how human beings order their essential ideas about the nature of reality. Ruth Benedict, a contemporary of Lowie, further articulates this idea in a passage from her book, *The Concept of the Guardian Spirit in North America*:

> It is, so far as we can see, an ultimate fact of human nature that man builds up his culture out of disparate elements, combining and recombining them; and until we have abandoned the superstition that the result is an organism functionally interrelated, we shall be unable to see our cultural life objectively, or to control its manifestations. (1923: 84)

The assertion that disparate elements can be combined without being functionally interrelated is a consequential one, yet it was never quite transposed into a category of human intellectual ordering by either Lowie or Benedict. Instead, the idea was given catalytic value in the processes through which cultures come into being and change over time. In their work, culture as ideas was simply treated by recourse to typical systemisation. Apparently, neither one of them wondered precisely how disparate elements without a functional interrelationship suddenly became putatively functional and interrelated as ideas in the minds of the peoples they studied.

Lévi-Strauss acknowledges a critical link between the Boasian ideas taken up by Lowie and Benedict, and his own work (1966: 21), particularly as they relate to his concept of the bricoleur. Here, Lévi-Strauss proposes to explore a method human beings use in organising their intellectual worlds, which he contrasts with those employed by scientists and engineers – though bricolage represents what is prior to science (ibid.: 16). The bricoleur is a handyman, a Jack-of-all-trades and master-of-none, an odd jobs man who, with his limited bag of tools and general knowledge, is able to mend just about anything. The repairs of a bricoleur, however, are always a bit on the rough side, never do they dovetail with any real precision; the job is done, but it lacks the exactitude, the dexterity and perhaps even the aesthetic ingenuity that a true engineer-craftsman – one who is not limited to the tools at hand but is capable of creating new ones – could have brought to the repair. Lévi-Strauss ' bricoleur is an intellectual handyman. On the disparate ideas, experiences, and new propositions that confront him in day to day life, he must impose order, but can only do so within the confines of a limited grouping of tools. It is not within his purview to create new tools or methods; instead, he must work with what he already has to fashion some sort of order among the elements of his intellectual world. The bricoleur's repairs and additions to an intellectual world are made with the same rough fit and inexactitude that characterise the bricoleur's repairs to furniture or stone walls or plumbing. Still, this mode of reflection and ordering 'can reach brilliant unforeseen results on the intellectual plane' (ibid.: 17). Bricolage is not an intellectually complacent way of being, but a mode of apprehending, ordering and drawing meaning out of the world that differs from the modus operandi of science and engineering.

To a significant degree, bricolage represents everyday thinking, the kind of thinking that even the scientist and engineer are obliged to participate in to some degree once they have left the confines of their specialised worlds. In everyday life, human beings play the part of the bricoleur, fashioning out of a 'planless hodgepodge' of ideas, out of the disparate 'shreds and patches' of life's experiences, some sort of order – not an order of exact precision and overlapping continuities, but a slightly bumbling order well-suited to the demands of everyday life. It is unfortunate, however, that in developing his structuralist theory (in which the bricoleur features as a continual though mostly unmentioned background character), Lévi-Strauss entirely leaves behind the 'subtle' roughness and inexactitude of the bricoleur's ordering, and opts instead to fully systematise human thinking – whether the bricoleur's or the scientist's – according to, among other things, a leitmotiv of binary opposition. This, he carries to a degree of intellectual artistry that no one else in anthropology (or beyond anthropology, for that matter) has ever done. Yet by so doing, Lévi-Strauss has, in my mind, deprived a potentially useful alternative concept of mental organisation of further development.

On the closely related topic of polythetic classification, Rodney Needham (1975) challenges the deeply held assumption that a conceptual class of elements must hold certain properties in common. Drawing on the work of Vygotski and Wittgenstein, he contends that there is no logical necessity in determining a class of objects or ideas by a single defining property, 'and once it is admitted that the common-feature definition of a class need not be the only possible method, the hypothetical number of "ways" in which things can be classified is multiplied over and over again' (1975: 349–50). This clearly runs counter to established opinions and methodologies in most fields, but there are compelling reasons for taking polythetic classification seriously, not the least of which is the deep resonance it has with the 'shreds and patches, the planless hodgepodge' of ideas that constitute a culture, as well as its peculiar fit with the work of the intellectual bricoleur as he cobbles together the ideas of his world in a rather rough and inexact manner. Polythetic classification is a considerable stride forward in more accurately depicting the manner in which human beings actually do order the elements of their intellectual worlds.

In the following passage, Needham describes key ideas about the nature of polythetic classification:

> Now we know experimentally from Vygotsky that classificatory concepts are not in practice formed by children in the way traditionally supposed in formal logic (Vygotski 1962, ch. 5); and we have been shown analytically by Wittgenstein that verbal concepts are commonly not constructed on that pattern either (Wittgenstein 1953; 1958). Instead, classes can be composed by means of what Vygotsky calls complex thinking: specifically, in a 'chain complex' the definitive attribute keeps changing from one link to the next; there is no consistency in the type of bonds, and the variable meaning is carried over from one item in a class to the next with 'no central significance,' no 'nucleus' (1962: 64). In a remarkable parallel, Wittgenstein, writing in the same period as Vygotsky, resorted to the image of a rope (later, in the *Philosophical Investigations*, a thread) in order to convey the same constitution of a concept: the rope consists of fibres, but it does not get its strength from any fibre that runs from one end to the another, but from the fact that there is a vast number of fibres overlapping' (1958: 87). Among the members of such a class there is a complex network of similarities overlapping and criss-crossing; sometimes overall similarities, sometimes similarities of detail. These features Wittgenstein termed, in a since famous phrase, 'family resemblances'. (Needham 1975: 350)

Murdoch may be correct that the 'intellect is naturally one-making', but that the intellect's chosen pattern for one-making is 'the system' is indeed open to grave doubt. Vygotsky's work clearly demonstrates that children order objects and ideas, but not in a manner that could possibly be described by the term 'system' in its conventional meaning. Coupled with the work of

Wittgenstein on language usage (which is not child specific) – particularly his observation 'that concept words do not denote sharply circumscribed concepts, but are meant to mark *family resemblances* between the things labeled with the concept' (Audi 1995: 858) – the intellect remains 'naturally one-making', but the human mind is not 'naturally' systematic. Systemisation appears to be a learned pattern of organisation, and Wittgenstein's conclusions suggest that systematising is not the standard means of mental organisation, rather, that systematising is the work of the specialist and done only on special occasions.

If polythetic classification bears a much closer resemblance to the ordering of human intellectual worlds in day to day life, it also upsets the neatness and elegance of systematic analyses – a consequence not lost on Needham:

> 'We should not rest content until family resemblance predicates, admittedly intelligible, have been banished from our sciences' (Campbell 1965: 244). This is exactly the aim of my 'Remarks,' to which this essay forms a sequel, though I do not think that such (polythetic) predicates can ever be eliminated from practical description in the field or from academic discourse about ethnographic reports. Where they can deliberately be dispensed with is in the contrivance of a formal theoretical terminology. (Needham 1975: 366)

I believe Needham is quite correct that the decreased simplicity associated with polythetic predicates is ill-suited to typical formal analyses, but if a formal theoretical terminology is created that sidesteps the facts of the matter, then the effect of the same is nothing less than a systematic distortion of the nature of the intellectual worlds within which human beings live – the very difficulty I am addressing in this paper. Any potential difficulty due to the increased complexity that arises from the use of polythetic classification is more than offset by the increased fidelity to the object of study.

A final suggestive idea that bears a family resemblance to polythetic classification (and is worthy of a more detailed consideration than I am able to make here) is Lofti Zadeh's concept of the fuzzy set (1965: 338–53). Mathematically based, Zadeh's fuzzy set is an attempt to deal with the issue of vague predicates, to understand the basis upon which a group of elements without one common, uniformly strong feature can be said to belong together. A fuzzy set is a set in which membership is based on a matter of degree. The characteristic that binds the elements together into a defined set is not uniformly manifest in each element. One element may exhibit that characteristic to a degree of 90 per cent, while another element of the set does so to a degree of 15 per cent.

> In classical set theory, for every set S and thing x, either x is a member of S or x is not. In fuzzy set theory, things x can be members of set S to any degree between 0 and 1, inclusive. Degree 1 corresponds to 'Is a member of' and 0 corresponds to 'Is not'; the intermediate degrees are degrees of vagueness or uncertainty. (Example: Let S be the set of men who are bald at age forty). (Audi 1995: 290)

Continuing with the example of the set of men who are bald at age forty, there are three criteria for membership in this set: being a man, being at the age of forty, and being bald. The first two elements may exhibit some tiny degree of vagueness, but it is the element of baldness that is most troublesome because baldness may encompass everything from moderate recession of the hairline to the complete absence of hair. To conclude that 35 per cent of men at age forty are bald is to create a set of men who are at the age of forty, who exhibit some degree of baldness ranging from 0 to 1. It is necessarily a vague statement. The set itself can be said to be vague or fuzzy because one of the mutual characteristics that link together the elements of the set is not uniformly manifest to the same degree in each element. Still, there is a recognisable fit among the elements of the set, fuzzy though it may be. 'All these books have indecent content', 'The ancestral fire, cooked butter-fat, ancestral fire-drills, and mopane limbs have ritual value among the Himba', and 'All Himba men and women recognise the authority of the ancestors', are statements that partake of vagueness. Fuzzy set theory is an attempt to understand the inexact and unequal relationships among the component parts of the sets we human beings create by combining and recombining the disparate elements of our cultural worlds.

Though the traditional concept of system holds an honoured and key position in virtually every form of anthropological analysis, I have argued that its usefulness in understanding the organisation of everyday human thinking is truly questionable. My objection to system as an analytical tool is that as we use it, we forcibly impart to human thinking a strict formality that it does not have; we raise the expectation of normalcy for a near absolute mutual coherence among the constituent elements of a 'system of thought' that simply is not there; and we are eagerly disposed to finding paradoxes, contradictions and puzzles whose actual 'existence' may be located solely in the mind of the analyst. I have also proposed that taking seriously the idea of shreds and patches, that seeing the suggestive importance of the intellectual bricoleur and his inexact method of cobbling ideas together, and that recognising the greater resemblance that polythetic and fuzzy approaches bring to an understanding of the organisation of human thought will lead to the establishment of a far more useful and accurate intellectual toolkit for grasping the fundamental ordering of everyday human thought than traditional systematic approaches provide.

Conclusion

The process of creating anthropological knowledge always draws upon the subjectivity of the anthropologist as well as the subjectivities of informants, yet within this endeavour it cannot fall too far off the mark to suggest that anthropologists prefer greater fidelity to lesser fidelity in their accounts of other peoples and their worlds. Based on this, I have argued that the creation of anthropological knowledge is inherently fraught with difficulties, some of which stem from the basic and unchanging fact that we are situated beings and engage the world as such, and that all forms of translation – cultural or otherwise – take place within a situated human mind. These are basic facts of life we cannot change, yet there are certain things within the process of creating anthropological knowledge that we can change, namely, our intellectual/analytical tools. Tools we find distorting can be left behind so that we may employ others in the hope of producing a better, perhaps more accurate, understanding of human beings and human society. I have further argued that one of the most prominent analytical tools of the anthropologist – the traditional concept of system – may bear little resemblance to the actual arrangement of human thought in day to day life, and that the uncritical use of system can distort our descriptions, analyses, and basic understandings of human beings; likewise, the concept of system can fundamentally misrepresent the organisation of human thinking, the cleavages between cultural ideas and cultural practices, and the inner workings of societies. In so doing, I argue that human cultural ideas do have some type of organisation, a structure that is not merely a trope, that beyond the chemical and electrical reactions of the brain there is an ascertainable linkage of ideas crucial to ordering and holding together human intellectual worlds. I have also introduced several alternative ideas – promising ideas – that I believe hold good potential in offering a greater 'accuracy' to our work.

As I myself have learned that being doctrinaire can lead to unintended distortions of other peoples' worlds, I urge those of us involved in the creation of anthropological knowledge to not only take these ideas seriously, but to explore and foster them as we analyse the thought of other peoples. In so doing, we should be able to ascertain whether or not a greater fidelity between how people actually organise their thoughts and our analyses of their thinking can be achieved. Finally, I urge a general flexibility in our approaches to creating anthropological knowledge and a willingness to place ethnographic 'accuracy' above any anthropological tradition.

References

Audi, R. (ed.). 1995. *The Cambridge Dictionary of Philosophy*. Cambridge: Cambridge: University Press.

Benedict, R. 1923. *The Concept of the Guardian Spirit in North America*. Menash, WI: American Anthropological Association.

Campbell, K. 1965. 'Family Resemblance Predicates', *American Philosophical Quarterly* 2(3): 238–44.

Clifford, J. and G. Marcus (eds). 1986. *Writing Culture*. Berkeley: University of California Press.

Crandall, D.P. 1991. 'The Strength of the OvaHimba Patrilineage', *Cimbebasia* 13(2) 45–51.

_____. 1992. 'The Importance of Maize among the OvaHimba', *Journal of the Namibian Scientific Society* 43: 7–17.

_____. 1996. 'Female over Male or Right over Left: Solving a Classificatory Puzzle among the OvaHimba', *Africa* 66(3): 327–48.

Derrida, J. 1997. *Deconstruction in a Nutshell*. New York: Fordham University Press.

Evans-Pritchard, E.E. 1976. *Witchcraft, Oracles, and Magic among the Azande*. Oxford: Oxford University Press.

Fabian, J. 1991. 'Culture, Time, and the Object of Anthropology', in *Time and the Work of Anthropology*. Chur, Switzerland: Harwood Academic Publishers, pp. 191–206.

Foucault, M. 1973. *Madness and Civilization*. New York: Vintage Books.

Geertz, C. 1973. *The Interpretation of Cultures*. New York: Basic Books.

Granet, M. 1933. 'Right and Left in China', reprinted 1973 in R. Needham (ed.), *Right and Left*. Chicago: University of Chicago Press, pp. 43–58.

Grene, M.G. 2004. *The Philosophy of Biology: An Episodic History.* Cambridge: Cambridge University Press.

Junod, H. 1966. *The Life of a South African Tribe*. Hyde Park, NY: University Books.

Kuhn, T. 1962. *The Structure of Scientific Revolutions*. Chicago: University of Chicago Press.

Kuper, A. 1989. *Anthropology and Anthropologists*. London: Routledge.

Lavenda, R. and E. Schultz. 2002. *Core Concepts in Anthropology*. New York: McGraw-Hill.

Lévi-Strauss, C. 1966. *The Savage Mind*. Chicago: University of Chicago Press.

Lowie, R.H. 1920. *Primitive Society*. New York: Boni and Liveright.

Marcus, G. and M. Fischer (eds). 1986. *Anthropology as Cultural Critique*. Chicago: University of Chicago Press.

Murdoch, I. 1993. *Metaphysics as a Guide to Morals*. New York: Allan Lane.

Needham, R. 1960. 'The Left Hand of the Mugwe', *Africa* 30(1): 20–33.

_____. 1967. 'Right and Left in Nyoro Symbolic Classification', *Africa* 37(4): 425–51.

_____. 1975. 'Polythetic Classification: Convergence and Consequences', *Journal of the Royal Anthropological Institute, Man (N.S.)* 10(3): 349–69.

Oxford English Dictionary (Compact Edition) 1981. London: Oxford University Press: 321–314.

Tylor, E.B. 1968 [1871]. 'The Science of Culture', in M. Fried (ed.), *Readings in Anthropology*, Vol. 2: *Cultural Anthropology*. New York: Crowell, pp. 1–18.

Vygotsky, L.S. 1962. *Thought and Language*, ed. and trans. by Eugenia Hanfmann and Gertrude Vakar. Cambridge, MA: MIT Press.

Wittgenstein, L. 1953. *Philosophical Investigations*, trans. G.E.M. Anscombe. Oxford: Blackwell.

_____. 1958. *Preliminary Investigations for the 'Philosophical Investigations', Generally Known as The Blue and Brown Books*. Oxford: Blackwell.

Zadeh, L. 1965. 'Fuzzy sets', *Information and Control* 8: 338–53.

Chapter 3

Knowing without Notes

Judith Okely

Writing Methods

When I first conducted anthropological fieldwork there were few if any formalised discussions about the practice. Certainly there were no courses on fieldwork. This does not mean that the gap should be filled by some of the very instrumental text books which are now emerging. The move from action and participation to knowledge is a profound intellectual problem (Marcus 1998). The most rewarding fieldwork is when the anthropologist is open to what comes and what the people often consider significant. Thus the anthropologist may find herself changing emphasis and topic. This openness and disponibility (Breton 1937) means that research practice is not a formulaic recording of answers to predetermined questions and what might risk becoming a mechanical collection of unproblematic data.

The act of writing notes is a mnemonic device, making an act of remembering. The opportunity to write notes varies remarkably. My supervisor Godfrey Lienhardt, recalling his fieldwork among the Dinka, said the problem with writing notes when involved in a ritual is that they may be blurred by the libations. My former colleague, David Brookes, was astonished by the sight of my pages of notes for each day. He had followed the annual migration of the Bahktiari – a very hazardous journey across mountains and icy rivers with goats and sometimes on mule or on foot. Field notes for him were scarce jottings. His experience was more bodily and memory dependent than most.

In the early 1970s, there was no guidance as to how field notes might be written, just as the practice of fieldwork had to be gleaned from stray appendices (Whyte 1955; Hannerz 1969). I had to find a satisfactory way through trial and error. Being at first employed on a policy-oriented project directed by a seconded civil servant unacquainted with ethnographic methods, I had to justify the latter with difficulty since there was little published material on this method. It was only after the project that I obtained a doctoral grant for independent research. Meanwhile, the priority for my research centre was a multi-page questionnaire – something which I instinctively knew was inappropriate for Gypsies as a non-literate group, used to deviating from outsiders' interrogations. Question asking was associated with interfering officials such as the police, health inspectors and local councillors. It was not even acceptable for either a Traveller or the anthropologist to ask anyone's name when first meeting.

In the policy project, there were few if any plans for detailed note-taking. Moreover, I had already had extensive pre-anthropological participant experience in Western rural Ireland with my former partner (Brody 1973; Okely 2002). I had learned how much that approach revealed wider material and crucial insights. By contrast, it was presumed by my director, for example, that the only way to gain credibility was to 'have a statistical table on every page'. I do not underestimate the value of field notes. They were always crucial in my research. Recently, other anthropologists have explored their value and varying meaning to anthropologists in different cultural contexts (Sanjek 1990; Emerson, Fretz and Shaw 1995). I have explored in detail the process of making and analysing field notes in the research process (Okely 1994a).

Thanks to my former anthropology tutor, I obtained the best, most workable advice. This was to write down everything without predetermined ideas of relevance, all in a narrative stream (Okely 1994a: 23). In this way I did not consciously exclude aspects of the experience. However, I was explicitly looking for some themes and foci. Alongside the daily narrative of events, I occasionally recorded emergent theoretical questions and musings. Inevitably those emergent themes were in part governed by my previous ideas and reading in anthropology.

Unwritten Experience

Despite the indispensability of field notes, writing down experience is insufficient on its own. Agar was later to note: 'Since you do not yet know what is significant, you don't know what to record' (1980: 112).

Fieldwork as total experience is more than a cerebral exercise. There linger other events and other concerns. Indeed, persons who were present may appear in the notes but without apparent theoretical and conceptual significance. With some surprise, I came to recognise that, although I had notes on a range of events and daily sequences, which I later identified by themes, there were entire areas which lay dormant or just hinted at in passing.

Since the initial research had been driven by policy issues concerning the official provision for Gypsy sites and their own wishes, some very explicit themes were ever present, for example travelling patterns, the Gypsy economy, experience of housing and of schooling, as well as criteria for ethnic membership and identity. Kinship and marriage patterns were obvious anthropological concerns.

Women and Gender

It was thanks to Shirley Ardener, who first suggested that I write a paper on Gypsy women, that I realised that my original focus was incomplete, indeed inadequate. The suggestion came like a thunderbolt. Yet having finished my policy-oriented project, I was being prepared for this in attending an all-women anthropology seminar as a doctoral student. Hitherto I, a feminist already transformed by Simone de Beauvoir (1949), had not paid any specific attention to women, let alone gender. I had not highlighted them by gender in notes but women were there everyday in my notes. They were my main companions and confidantes but I had not thought of them as a category. Incongruously by today's academic debates, I had not fully problematised and theorised gender. In the highly gender divided Traveller society, I had been more concerned with the need *not* to spend all my time in the company of women. I had to reach out to and gain access to the Gypsy men as well. I was more concerned with obtaining a gender balance of as many different Travellers as possible and absurdly saw my own gender only as problematic (Okely 1996: Ch. 2).

Once I recognised the importance and challenge of considering women as a category, I had to find the material, concepts and theoretical frames. But I had not highlighted these in the narratives. When I first embarked on fieldwork, the new feminism had not hit anthropology in a very visible way. Earlier women anthropologists, for example Mead and Kaberry, had looked at gender in some key contexts, but their publications had not featured on the reading lists at Cambridge where I had completed a postgraduate anthropology course before the policy project.

In the 1960s, my reading of de Beauvoir had already converted me to feminism (Okely 1986b), but her theories had not as yet been applied to anthropology. It was only later that the feminist cross-cultural publications emerged (Oakley 1972; Reiter 1974; Rosaldo and Lamphere 1974, including the very volume which Shirley Ardener had instigated and in which my article on Gypsy women appeared (Okely 1975). Even in the late 1970s, when I became a university lecturer, I was subsequently to learn that my attempts to introduce an anthropology course on gender would still be seen as controversial (Okely 2007).

The intellectual breakthrough, in order to approach the subject of Gypsy women, came when I recognised that the ideas and 'data' did not inevitably have to be traceable on paper and in notes. I had momentarily and naively thought that I should be able to point to a stack of evidence in files and my filing cabinets. Such an approach may now be labelled 'evidence based research' and risks being a resurgence of positivism. But I was to realise even more fully that anthropological practice brings other knowledge embodied in the fieldworker's being.

I did indeed have hundreds of pages of typed notes. After seeking advice from a number of social scientists, these had been meticulously copied, classified, then cut and pasted according to the emergent themes. A subsequent article on 'qualitative' methods (Okely 1994a) is concerned to prove to quantitative sceptics that 'hard' material is collectable and then analysable through participant observation. In a couple of paragraphs I had already declared that the analysis of fieldwork was more than a mechanical set of procedures and that the anthropologist is a 'walking archive'. I addressed the way in which interpretations are reached. These passing observations now form the core of this article:

> Interpretations are attained not only through a combination of anthropological knowledge and textual scrutiny, but also through the memory of field experience, unwritten yet inscribed in the fieldworker's being. The ethnographer, as former participant observer, judges the authenticity of his or her conclusions and interpretations in terms of that total experience. (Okely 1994a: 31)

I had been provoked into this realisation in part because my former research director, trained in the then civil service research procedures, had suggested that my material should ideally be written up by someone else, drawing on my written data. In this way it would apparently be truly objective and 'scientific'. I intuitively questioned this. But there was no language and no one to articulate my scepticism. Anthropological approaches in publications were then officially methods-free. Despite my uneasiness about the alleged scientificity of having someone else writing up 'the data' which another person, the fieldworker, had written down, I had inadvertently absorbed a reductionist empiricist belief when first confronted with the invisibility of gender concerns in my notes. I worried that perhaps I might be 'making it all up' if I wrote about Gypsy women when I had not already written down this 'data'. I was still a closet empiricist.

The liberation came when I realised the knowledge about Gypsy women and indeed other aspects were in my head and in my memory. Jean Jackson has since recorded Ottenberg's concept of '"headnotes" (remembered observations)' (1990: 5). Several anthropologists whom Jackson interviewed recognised the continuing link between fieldworker and field notes: 'it's dead data without me' (ibid.: 10) and 'It took a while for me to be able to rely on my memory. But I had to, since the idea of what I was doing had changed, and I had memories but no notes. I had to say: "Well, I saw that happen" I am a fieldnote' (ibid.: 21).

Knowledge through the Body

As I have suggested (Okely 1992), participant observation brings non-cerebral knowledge. This was visually demonstrated in a photograph of myself and a Gypsy woman. I have unknowingly empathised with her mood willingly but defensively posing for a photographer known to me. She has her arms in a barrier pose. I had unknowingly imitated her (ibid.: 18). This is one graphic example of how fieldwork can lead to the wider empathetic comprehension of the anthropologists' day to day companions and co-residents. Certainly, I also consciously imitated in a mimetic process of participation. I adjusted my clothing, posture and speech. From outer performance to eventual internalisation, I came to understand otherwise elusive perspectives. Nothing of this could have been acquired through the dreaded but fortunately abandoned questionnaire and clipboard research procedures. I acquired a newly created intuition, something which was not written down but which nurtured the eventual writing up.

The vulnerability of the sexed body came in an unexpected way. Since I felt under pressure to write against the stereotypes of tabooed sexuality among the outsiders' constructions of Gypsies, especially of women, I avoided turning any discussion towards sex and reproduction. I acted dumb and as an apparently single woman, I needed to act innocent: an honorary virgin. The image of the easy virtue gorgio/non-Gypsy woman among the Gypsies might bring trouble. Well into fieldwork, I was used as a target for sanctioning a Gypsy man who had a womanising history which had ended in someone's death in the ensuing feud. A rumour was fabricated that he had got me pregnant. I extricated myself through acting out an absurd charade. By then, my in-depth and practical knowledge gave me the confidence to turn the joke around. In front of key witnesses, I claimed I had given birth to his baby and presented him with a doll wrapped in swaddling clothes and demanded paternity support. The Gypsies loved the joke. But such an action could only have been risked after in-depth knowledge of the group dynamics (Okely 2005a).

From the outset, I had acted virginal. This was unexpectedly nearly put to the test. One day I was sitting in a trailer with a cluster of Gypsy women who were discussing conception. One woman argued that the sex of the baby depended on the position in intercourse. I sat quiet. Suddenly a very dominant woman asked how much I knew. When I feigned ignorance, she said 'There's only one way to find out. Get her up on that bed'. Fortunately, one of my closest Gypsy woman friends skilfully diverted the conversation. But again the potential risks of such violation of bodily privacy ensured even greater caution on my part. Thus my gendered and sexed bodily vulnerability also diverted my research focus. Much later in the 1980s, as with gender, anthropologists showed detailed interest and documentation on ideas of reproduction. I had written few notes on the matter but in contrast to other imbibed knowledge, I merely learned that curiosity held too many risks.

Nevertheless, although excluded from discussions of sexual intercourse and conception, I was able to record birth practices and their association with pollution. Offers of transport in my motor vehicle proved a useful resource for taking women to hospital for checkups. Such visits were at first not recognised for their gender research potential. They came to make sense in the context of wider beliefs later when writing up and thinking through my hitherto unacknowledged field experience in the dominant culture(s).

Representations

A new twist occurred when I realised that I had to engage also with representations which floated far from fieldwork. I was drawn back into a study of my own or the larger culture, and this included Culture with a capital C. Whereas a policy-oriented research brief had engaged with the politics and economy of the dominant society, such a focus had not free ranged in the world of representations and ideologies, although I had already begun to question the so-called 'hard data' in local and national government reports. My employer set me such reading at the outset of the research project. But I soon found them as more informative of the dominant society's stereotypes of Gypsies who were labelled 'pure blooded', 'half castes'. 'didikois', tinkers [*sic*] – Irish drop-outs (Okely 1983: 16–19). Some local authorities actually gave specific numbers of these allegedly separate subgroups.

Nevertheless, in this exercise I was being challenged to respond to these outsiders' near fantasies and racist overtones with contrasting empirical factual realities. It was important to find out how the Travellers classified themselves. With the inspiration of Barth (1969), these were obvious anthropological questions which were pursued all the time in the field and which were regularly recorded in field notes. In addition, I was increasingly open to themes from beyond the ethnic group. The study moved to integrate the ethnic group into the hegemony of the surrounding society.

Thanks to the policy priorities of the research, I had already been made familiar with council and parliamentary facts and figures – matters which had been read as relevant even before fieldwork. I was also living the difference on a day to day basis on the encampments and on the doorsteps of house dwellers when out calling with Gypsies. I was forced to confront unexpected ethnographic knowledge also in the political spaces with officials 'dealing with the problem'. Much of the official printed material I did indeed collect. But I did not record the discussions and encounters with officials in the same systematic narrative of a field journal. Moreover, my director considered it sufficient to record the officials' perspectives in formal and preordained questionnaires (Okely 1986a).

All this seemed a long way to stereotypes, opera, songs, poetry and free-floating associations. The anthropologist's own amorphous Culture became an ethnographic resource. Unexpected icons, inchoate knowledge and suggestions became gloriously relevant. Thus, another field experience of the imagination and iconic symbols were to be drawn upon. This contrasts with the classical circumstances of fieldwork where the anthropologist crosses the globe to study a group of peoples with only secondary sources for the wider context, although Orientalism has been a significant filter with which anthropologists might have engaged (Said 1978).

As I have explored elsewhere (Okely, in press), by being open to the classical psychoanalytical form of free association, I was confronted with unpredictable material from a long incorporated cultural knowledge. I could draw on my past readings, which covered the stereotypes through centuries. I had seen the first production of Bizet's *Carmen* in Paris when it was recognised as good enough for the main opera theatre rather than being sidelined in the Opera Comique. I had even seen an amateur production in the Isle of Wight in the 1950s on a school outing. The Gypsy woman was portrayed as sensual, powerful and non-social. Bizet, inspired by a Merimée short story, never visited Spain. Carmen was a classic example of projection: the tabooed sexual and uncontrolled passion accredited to the outsider/other. Subsequent literary studies have explored more fully those representations (Bardi 2004).

When commencing my policy-oriented project, inevitably the *local* context was included. The unexpected was the experiential use of my own and others' broader non-Gypsy culture as perceived in relation to the Traveller-Gypsies. I was drawing on unanticipated fieldwork in the supposedly familiar. This use of my 'own' culture was grounded by interconnections of difference lived both in and outside the camps, and through several years together with retrospective relevant long past knowledge.

This study of creative cultural interconnections also goes against the nineteenth century and ongoing stance which has argued for the reconstruction of a once pure and isolated Roma culture centuries back, partly through linguistics. The Roma/Gypsies are thus treated merely as passive receptors of non-Gypsy cultures. Such an approach fails to examine the inner logic and coherence of the Gypsies' current and indeed long-term adaptations, as creatively selective cultural forms with constructed differences (Okely 1997a).

Western anthropologists who have only done fieldwork beyond the West tend to contrast 'their' village/island with 'the West', which in their massive comparative generalisation can include not only Britain, but Europe and even the USA. The West is thus treated as an unproblematic whole, which the anti-Europeanist anthropologists are under no intellectual obligation to interrogate. It is homogenised and taken for granted, especially by those who declare that the West is already 'known' at least to the Western anthropologist (Barnes 1988; Bloch 1988). Way back in the 1970s, the study of Northern Europe was considered suspect precisely because the ideal group, islands or villages studied by 'real' anthropologists were supposed to be isolates 'untouched' by modernisation, despite the history of colonialism.

Others' Lived Representations and Vacuities

The wider Western cultures with floating representations of the Gypsies in others' imagination, inevitably affected the perceptions of the non-Gypsies whom I encountered locally, if not nationally. Gradually, it became apparent that the repeated comments I listened to and the ubiquitous questions I was asked by a wide range of people whom I encountered when outside the camps, in social events, academic exchanges and the most banal fleeting moments, were all research material. Through the very questions I was asked by incredulous non-Gypsies who heard that I was living with or had lived with the Gypsies, I was led to the preconceived notions which long intrigued my interlocutors. On some occasions I was never once asked about my field experiences, but instead subjected to extended monologues of authoritative projection from these strangers. These non-Gypsies vehemently asserted views based on scant or almost no contact with Gypsies. I was also presented with intriguing stories of Fortune Tellers and ones which revealed the non-Gypsy clients' belief in the Gypsies' magical powers. The non-Gypsies were less interested in learning from my fieldwork, but seemed compelled to offload their own fractured expertise. Eventually I was to recognise this material to be significant ethnography of the inter-relations between the Gypsies and their clients (Okely 1996: Ch. 5).

The power of any association with the Gypsies was exposed surprisingly with acquaintances, associates and even friends of friends. My visit to Kansas City and the parents of my American partner revealed the unexpected spoiled identity which travelled with me. At a large Mid West family dinner party, some American relatives were intrigued about my research among the Gypsies. Before I could answer, my hostess declared to my horror: 'And she hates them'. This woman feared that some stigma from her son's partner would spill over. Naturally, I vehemently denied this outrage, but I learned the Western prevalence of anti-Gypsy racism at the heart of a supposedly separate private life, although, fortunately, not in my own anti-racist natal family. All this experience, even in far Kansas City, at the heart of America and the West, nevertheless became grist to my analytical mill. Again, I was unknowingly doing another but equally significant fieldwork, yet did not write up these non-Gypsy interventions. At first I thought these were misconceptions merely to dismiss in contrast to the 'real' empirically based knowledge.

Wherever I have travelled from India to Africa, throughout Europe and North America, people seem to have ideas about Gypsies. They are not an anonymised isolate of a people. The name is a password for a range of preconceptions whether or not my listeners have ever met such individuals bearing that name.

Gypsies' Acquaintance with Othering

I came to recognise that it was all the more important that such representations be studied as part of the Gypsies' own history, however they might wish to be free of them. While today their access to the media is now even more sophisticated, already in the 1970s and indeed the 1960s, the Travellers had televisions in their trailers, with power supplied by dynamos. Often these were flickering in the corner all the time, with the sound turned down. But the moment a Gypsy theme appeared, word went round the camp and the volume was turned up. I recall someone rushing to the door one evening telling the inmates in the trailer where I was also sitting that Sid James, the comic actor, was talking about Gypsies or addressing one. Thus, through the mass media, despite their non-literacy, and across doorsteps, at the scrap yard, in shops and at cinemas, in public houses, Gypsies were confronted with the indigenous non-Gypsies' views of Gypsies, as well as non-Gypsies' values and priorities. I naively refrained from taking notes on this barrage of representations unless in the company of Gypsies. Despite myself, I carried the representations within me and I was also confronted with them in face-to-face encounters, through the media. Although the vast majority of Gypsies I knew were non-literate, such representations were conveyed to them in almost intangible ways.

The Gypsies themselves were likely to have seen a range of films in which they were represented. In addition to having televisions, they went to the cinema, indeed I accompanied a group of young Gypsy women to the local cinema.[1] The Gypsies loved specific pop music songs and some had wind-up record players. When I was getting to know some Gypsies on a brief field trip to Hull in the 1970s, one teenager mentioned Cher's hit song, 'Gypsies, Tramps and Thieves'. I had a copy of the record and gave it to her and received a happy hug in return. The lyrics were indeed a wonderful confrontation of the stereotype as lived by someone claiming that identity.

Beyond the Fact/Falsity Division

Gradually it transpired that my analysis, indeed my fieldwork, would move beyond what appeared in the painstaking field notes. Away from the field, on a visit to my partner or when having a break from 'writing up', I found that an anticipated 'break' from research did not come easily. I could not compartmentalise the fieldwork/personal life divide. I was doing fieldwork in my 'own' culture, whether or not I chose it or knew it in advance. A chance television showing of the film 'Gypsy' after a dinner party with friends became for me more than mere fiction against the 'reality' of fieldwork. The actress/dancer labelled Gypsy was embodying something beyond the people I had lived with. But she represented a reality with which the people I had known had to engage. There was a requirement for the anthropologist to engage with those lived representations and, more specifically, the interrelation of these with the Gypsies' own experience.

In my encounters with curious non-Gypsies I regularly witnessed a projection based on fantasy not empirical reality. The final twist in my analysis came when I recognised that the clash between fantasy or projection and fact, was not the project. This fact/fantasy dichotomy was a positivist mirage. The facts might have appeared as part of the field notes, but the fantasies were part of the reality with which the Travellers had to negotiate. I had ready sources for these fantasies all around me.

Unwritten Fieldwork in the Familiar
1. Space and Pollution

Thanks to the existing social science literature on Gypsy/Roma pollution beliefs in the US and in the UK (Acton 1971; Miller 1975 and Sutherland 1975), I was already alerted to these aspects. When my research moved beyond immediate observation and note-taking in the field, it was my grounded knowledge of lived contrasts between the minority and the larger society which emerged as unexpectedly but wholly appropriate. For example, the local and national newspaper coverage of Gypsy issues were also windows into dominant beliefs. Especially prominent were the media's aesthetic criteria concerning encampments and continuing emphasis on alleged uncleanliness. This locked straight into Mary Douglas' suggestion that dirt was matter out of place (1966). The contrasting notions of cleanliness were a supreme example of interconnecting differences rather than a fact/fantasy division. I did indeed have in my notes a statement by a Gypsy about what house dwellers only see from the outside in contrast to what is inside (Okely 1983: 87). This helped unlock the theme of constructed contrast. But, at the same time, it only resonated further because I was observing and reading newspaper headlines about the visible 'dirt' of Gypsy encampments. The very month when I was preparing a paper for a postgraduate seminar convened by Rodney Needham, I was confronted by a local Oxford paper article about a Gypsy camp. Thus, public discourse in the mass media reflecting non-Gypsy priorities led me to comprehend the Gypsy values by contrasts and dissonance. The sensationalist local news article became a key text in my presentation (Okely 1983: 79).

The hysteria which as recently as 2004/5 was revived about the alleged dirt and disorder of Gypsy camps was never modified with any suggestion that the Gypsies had their own priorities (Okely 2005b). My earlier text emphasised these (Okely 1983). Inevitably, I did not focus on occasions when individual practices may have been inconsistent with the ideal practices or when less visible rule breaking occurred. Strangely, a recent doctorate has now used some occasional examples of encounters with individual Gypsies as evidence that such pollution beliefs are questionable and that boundaries either do not exist or are flexible and 'more complex' (Buckler 2003). But, as with the (universal) existence of the incest taboo, individual flexibility and rule breaking, in many instances, does not mean that the taboo is non existent nor merely performative. In any case, the strongest validation for my early analysis came from a literate Gypsy who wrote in to praise my article on pollution beliefs in *New Society* and asked for more like it. He certainly did not deny boundaries. There are also similar examples among the Roma elsewhere (Miller 1975; Sutherland 1975; Ni Shuinear 2003).

2. Animal Categories

The analysis of the general pollution beliefs in relation to the body, eating, domestic camp space, then unexpectedly lead to the analysis of animal categories. Little if anything of the system was explicitly articulated in the narrative of field notes. Indeed, there was almost nothing in the existing publications on Gypsies around the world. The analysis and interrogation of a range of scattered material came to full fruition some months and indeed years after my initial fieldwork. It grew out of knowing in a highly complex and not easily articulated process. It could never be a mechanistic exercise but a creative, holistic condition. The insights are so grounded that they offer possibilities for interpreting future ethnographic contexts.

From thence my lived but unwritten knowledge of gorgio/non-Gypsy beliefs and practices at local and often national levels were also utterly relevant in describing the contrasts in animal classifications. I knew from years of house dwelling in a British culture that gorgios valued cats, in part because it was noted that they cleaned their bodies by licking them. The clue to the Gypsy system of classification came through a footnote in the writings of a scholar Gypsiologist, T.W. Thompson, who visited English Gypsies and published in the 1920s (Okely 1983: 236; 1994a).

The Gypsies' classification I came to recognise, was inter-related by selected contrast with that of the non-Gypsies. Here I should have made this original perspective more explicit. I was pursuing the necessary interconnections of the system. This was a development from the work of Lévi-Strauss (1966), Leach (1972) and Tambiah (1973), who had analysed animal categories where the symbolic focus was usually self contained *within* rather than interconnected with others' categories. The major exception was Lévi-Strauss who had in *Totemism* (1963) emphasised that people used the difference between animals to make or create differences between themselves. Where I moved further was to incorporate the Gypsies' selective *ideas* or *stereotypes* about the gorgios' beliefs to affirm their own beliefs.

I had also to be acquainted with *both* in order to explain their power on both sides of the ethnic divide. My interpretation was crucially interdependent with long-term knowledge of the local and national cultural context of gorgios or non-Gypsies which I, as non-Gypsy, had inhabited for decades without ethnographic reflexive awareness. To understand the interconnections, I resorted to that unwritten knowledge. It was not a facile contrast between an amorphous 'West', as the orthodox anthropologists would still have it, but a connection with one's own culture paradoxically othered in contrast with the original other group among whom I had lived. I did not doubt aspects of my own cultural knowledge when I recognised its contrast with that of the Gypsies and in some case their selective perception of gorgio culture.

Unconscious Premonitions and Fragments

Years later, I recognise that the themes in the surrealist André Breton's *L'Amour Fou* (1937) can be transposed to the experience of my anthropological fieldwork and subsequent interpretation and recognition. While Breton's book is about love and premonition and the ultimate encounter with the loved one, there are imaginative parallels in the encounter between cultural formations or the interrelationships of difference (cf. Okely 2005a). Breton records a poem he wrote involuntarily some years before his encounter with his future partner. Retrospectively, he suggests that the poetic images, objects and selected locations were premonitions of the events to follow. His surrealist, near automatic writing, allowed ideas and fragments to flow in a seemingly non-rational sense.

As a student studying in Paris, I was captivated by Breton's approaches, especially his notion of *disponibility*: being ever open. Such approaches from Breton can be transposed to the experience of fieldwork and its knowledge resolution. The anthropologist also has to be disponible to whatever comes her way. This is very different from the positivistic approach still privileged in some social sciences. Recently, I watched an economics professor rebuke an anthropologist postgraduate. She was supposed to sharpen her hypothesis before embarking on fieldwork, otherwise she would be in danger of 'drifting'. Yet it is that very drifting which brings unpredicted and grounded knowledge.

All those fragments and representations of 'the Gypsy' I carried with me or later confronted. They emerged beyond prediction and control during and after both bounded and amorphous fieldwork came to make sense. I was not and could not cut my fieldwork into a geographical and spatial isolate. The sites (both literal and figurative) where I lived alongside the Gypsies were embedded in the wider outside. That included all those non-Gypsy others and other cultural forms. Breton, in a poem he wrote by free association, offers a narrative of events as detailed poetic prediction – in his case, a passionate meeting with a great love. Unlike Breton, I had not been inspired before the event to write a poetic text to decipher subsequently. Instead, I carried and remembered, without intention, the unwritten flotsam and representations which I was to disentangle through thinking and writing only long after the encounters. The bits and pieces about the dominant society's practices and notions about a different, ethnic group, such as the Gypsies, gradually fell into a reformulated comprehension. Again, it had not initially been written down. It was in my body, head, being, past and ever unrolling present.

The fragments, like the surrealist poem of Breton before the encounter, were advance clues. Breton's book was about mad romance but also about sensuality and the body. Fieldwork is also for the anthropologist a total participation but not so much Breton's eroticism. The analogy is multi-faceted, not a domesticated partnership, but a long-term relationship between the anthropologist and a people or cultures. The anthropological encounter is more than the bounded and timed event of fieldwork but, especially when located in the geography and context of the anthropologist's 'own' culture(s), it is infused with years of ideological representations, flotsam and fragments which are carried as internal baggage. These, like the disjointed poems in the surrealist's imagination, may come to fruition and make sense years and dreams and events later. This is what happened in my encounter with understanding the Gypsies' perspective in relation to their surroundings.

Pursuing Contrast through Subconscious Knowledge

A reflexive and autobiographical awareness is now acceptable in the analysis of fieldwork and writing. But it was airbrushed out in those early days (Okely 1992, 1996: Ch. 2). The link between the personal and the theoretical or substantive may enhance and drive the writers' and researchers' enthusiasms (Okely 1986b; Okely and Callaway 1992; Reed-Danahay 1997; Okely 2003a). In his opening paragraph of his study of death rituals among the Manouches in France, Patrick Williams (2003) is intellectually generous in stating that he was influenced by reading my own work on English Gypsies (Okely 1983: Ch. 12) and the work of Leo Piasere (1984) among Yugoslav Roma in Italy. Otherwise he suggests he had not thought through the ethnography of death.

Thanks to Williams' comment, I in turn began thinking why I had devoted so much to the treatment of death among the Gypsies. First, although both Williams and I have experienced the same setbacks in being seen as a 'real' anthropologist, because we had done fieldwork in Europe, I had emerged from a postgraduate course steeped in Malinowski. The latter's functionalist approach, for all its historical and political limitations, encouraged an holistic approach. I felt it important to write a monograph which, like Malinowski in the Trobriands, covered ritual, kinship, politics and economics as essential (1922). Thus, mortuary rites described and interpreted in detail by Malinowski (1929), should in turn be scrutinised among the English Gypsies. To be taken seriously, to write up anthropological fieldwork in Europe, it was vital to show that such research could be as thorough and all encompassing as that done beyond the West. In his earlier publication on marriage (1984), it may be that Williams enthusiastically focused on marriage partly because it resonated with his biography. He has married into a Roma family. When writing on Gypsy death rituals, I believed I was merely following through the Malinowski inspired project. Again, there were other concerns not recorded on paper, not explicitly thought through.

My own focus had additional and autobiographical explanations, although I did not consciously realise it at the time of fieldwork, analysis and indeed when writing my chapter. True, I was deeply impressed by the fact that Gypsy children, indeed babes in arms, attended the funerals. Young boys and girls were encouraged to scatter earth on the coffin. Children were witnesses to the shrieks of kin who were carried, fainting from the graveside. Again, in both the banal and dramatic ritual, Gypsy cultural practices may counter some of those of the dominant society. Unaware of any subconscious motives, I lovingly reproduced a photograph of two little girls relaxed in the company of their fathers (Okely 1983: 160). I did not reveal in the text that one of the fathers had been or was about to be diagnosed with a brain tumour and died within the year. Some photographs in the last chapter are of his funeral which I attended. I was especially keen to include a picture of a young Gypsy girl next to her small brothers staring into the open grave at the funeral (Okely 1983: 221).

Many years later, I realised the momentum of my focus on death and choice of images. This was unconscious, as opposed to the very conscious recognition by Renato Rosaldo (1989) in his reanalysis of headhunting after the death of his wife. My father died when I was about the same age as the happy little girl photographed with her father. But, in accord with the bourgeois British culture in which I was nurtured (Okely 1996: Ch. 8), both my sister and I were kept ignorant of our father's fatal illness and death. While isolated in a boarding school, we were told nothing of his funeral, let alone allowed to attend it. We learned of his death and cremation weeks later when our mother visited the school to inform us. She returned to London the day we were told.

The institution made no allowances for our bereavement. That first night, aged nine, as I sat on my dormitory bed, the matron asked me why I was crying. I told her that my daddy had died. In that grim regime, she said she knew, but that I was not to cry because I would keep the other girls awake. To make any noise 'after lights out' was the ultimate sin in that prison of alleged privilege. At that moment I learned the stark horror of the British upper middle class culture and its stiff upper lip values which I soon learned to reject. Hence the making of the anthropologist as willing participant observer of other cultures, an elsewhere, yet even within one's own geographical territory and polity (Okely 2003a).

Without fully recognising the intensity of my personal interest in Gypsy mortuary rites, I engaged with them with exceptional intensity. It was at the funeral that I witnessed the wondrous and admirable cultural contrast with my own culture.

From the outset, I learned how Gypsy children are not screened by adults from any sudden tragedy. It is only the facts of sexuality from which they are ritually and ideally sheltered. Death and illness are matters which they are permitted to confront from infancy. They learn to be human not by guessing in exclusion, but through participation. There is no adult silencing in that and most domains.

By contrast, in my past non-Gypsy British culture, from the very *outset*, awareness of death was made a non-subject for children, if not adults. The silence began before the approach of death and continued through the burial and beyond (Okely 2003a).[2]

Thus, an unconsciously motivated focus by the anthropologist was unknowingly linked to a specific topic related to biography. The positionality of the anthropologist was an unpredicted and unwritten resource. A negative experience of the anthropologist's own culture raised appreciative and empathetic questions elsewhere. The focus on death rituals in one cultural domain became an unconscious resolution in another. Using past tragedy as a hidden search for an alternative to one's own culture, my analysis of Gypsy death rituals was written up some years after the original project. The sensitivity and minutiae in interpretation as contrast with the anthropologists' own ethnic/class experience came from within. Thus, the contrasting knowledge from the field fell into place, without intellectualising in advance.

Another Theme from Inside towards Elsewhere

In my appreciation of the Gypsies' alternative socialisation and education, again something of the anthropologist's biographical experience pinpoints the focus. My unfolding engagement with the Gypsies' education was in stark and admirable contrast with that of the anthropologist's own schooling and cultural history. My subsequent distinction (Okely 1997b) between gorgio schooling and education among the Gypsies, hitherto designated by policy makers as the 'most deprived' children in the country (Plowden 1967), came again from the anthropologist's lived cultural experience within the same nation. A rejection of aspects of the anthropologist's own schooling and its cultural and class trappings opened the way to appreciating a positive elsewhere (Okely 1996: Ch. 8, 2003b).

Again, a negative experience and grounded knowledge of the anthropologist's own culture inspired an enhanced sensitivity to difference. Whereas the ideology of the dominant non-Gypsy culture has emphasised 'illiteracy' and deprivation of schooling, the anthropologist's fieldwork revealed an alternative education and different way of thinking, free of the bureaucratic burdens of literacy. This specific focus on children emerged through the thinking and only from fragments in field notes. Like the lack of a problematisation of gender and women in my notes, I also edged away from infants and children. Since women had to prove themselves as 'honorary men' in the anthropological academic field (Okely 1996: Ch. 2), I was not going to be doing the conventional academic division of labour. Where couples went into the field it was presumed the woman did one thing, usually child care, and the man did the other. We knew only too well that this gender division of academic labour had a male hierarchy. But there were already some advance exceptions, namely Charlotte Hardman who was indeed looking at children in an original and imaginative way (1973).

Thus, the positionality of the anthropologist affects the focus and interpretation. It unknowingly seeps through the being of the experience and moves from the particular to the group.

Knowingly Written Down but Not Written Up

There are vast areas of my field notes which have of necessity deliberately been excluded from publication, although their content is crucial. Writing anthropology in Europe and about fieldwork in the geography of publication, there are greater obligations and risks attached to identification. I have addressed the need to cut out the narratives and persona of rounded identifiable individuals. As I have explained elsewhere,

> I hesitated to give too graphic a portrait of specific individuals because I could not predict the possible problems. I deliberately split the attribution of quotes … Sometimes quotations from one person were attributed to more than one individual. Statements by different individuals were attributed to just one individual. It was a deliberate strategy of leaving no easy traces. (Okely 1999: 62)

This deliberate practice has been entirely misinterpreted as a theoretical bias towards massive and allegedly dogmatic generalisations, without individual agency and flexibility (Buckler 2003). Buckler has ignored the risk of identifying and detailing individual Gypsies in an ever vulnerable context, especially when, unlike classical anthropology, the publications are produced and more widely circulated in the country of the anthropologist's fieldwork. My decision to withhold identifiable details about individuals was thoroughly vindicated, given that a linguist mischievously published the location of my field-site on a website. This would have done no harm to the anthropologist, but could harm the Gypsies still travelling in that location. Indeed Buckler disingenuously admits that she herself faced negative responses from the Gypsies she encountered and wrote about in the early 1990s. They considered that their detailed and easily identifiable individual stories had been appropriated in her thesis (ibid.).

Granted, by the mid-1990s, there was a more explicit emphasis in anthropological writing on the value of individuals (Herzfeld 1997). I would have liked to have explored that creativity earlier but had ethical and self-imposed publishing constraints. In future, now that the individuals have grown up, moved away or indeed passed on, the notes could be mined for that detail. It is only some decades after my fieldwork and my monograph and articles, that I have felt able to publish some specific and individualised ethnography concerning disputes and conflict (Okely 2005a). But again the names and key features are disguised. There are other stories which hang together in the memory and which are not necessarily in field notes. The fieldworker may be the most suited to convey the narrative and stream of events.

Conclusion

My fieldwork possibly depended more than most on participant observation rather that linear information elicited by direct questions and answers. Knowledge came, as it is generally for anthropologists, through bodily knowledge and lived events, although some anthropologists may not always acknowledge this. Coherence emerged from remembered and re-configured experience. Bodily and subsequent unpredicted knowledge is not visible in the inscribed evidence of written scripts and field notes, however useful the latter are in the process of understanding.

By definition, the focus on gender and women before the new articulation and publications in feminist anthropology was not an advance focus in my earlier fieldwork. Thus, accumulated confidence in the knowledge from participant fieldwork brought unexpected and grounded knowledge which only the fieldworker could produce.

Having been a long-term inhabitant of the surrounding non-Gypsy culture(s), rather than just passing through, on the way to a bounded 'field', my other cultural knowledge became an unexpected resource. This contrasts with a continuing tendency for Western anthropologists who have done fieldwork outside 'the West', and not within cultures in which they have lived, to make sweeping contrasts between 'their' village, island or people elsewhere with 'the West'. Since the Gypsies have to know and deal with non-Gypsies on a daily basis for survival, their perceptions of the gorgio 'other' are crucial interconnecting material for analysis. I was thus in a position to contrast and compare the Gypsies with the local and dominant cultures as lived by both the anthropologist and the Gypsies. Fieldwork was a continuing process in unpredicted places. When non-Gypsies often felt compelled to inform *me* about the Gypsies, they were unknowingly giving me insights into themselves and the dominant ideologies with which Gypsies have to contend. That I had lived the other non-Gypsy culture came to be vital for understanding the constructed and actual contrasts.

Part of the non-Gypsy dominant culture with which the Gypsies have daily engagements politically, economically and ideologically includes representations. Thus, the anthropologist moved from 'facts' to representations. Writing up demanded the analysis of interconnections of difference. Representations included cultural idioms from opera, folklore, fiction, to art and film. This approach draws on imaginative knowledge alongside that lived as practice.

The study and analysis of pollution and animal classification pivoted on the disjunction between the Gypsies' beliefs and practices and what they have perceived and selected as non-Gypsies' beliefs and practices. The anthropologist as native of the surrounding hegemony and whose fieldwork was continuous both inside and outside the encampments was in a position to decipher the contrasts and present a coherent way of viewing the world. The unconscious focus on specific topics could in some instances be traced to the biography of the anthropologist. The positionality of the fieldworker was again an unpredicted resource. Negative experiences raised appreciative and empathetic questions elsewhere. Ultimately, only some of the fieldwork experience and holistic knowledge were explicit and retrievable in the narrative of field notes. The analysis and interrogation of a range of material came to full fruition months and sometimes years after the initial fieldwork. Writing up could never be a mechanistic exercise since I drew on more than what had first been written down.

Notes

1. Much later I appreciated the brilliance of Powdermaker who wrote down individual spectators' comments in the cinema during her African fieldwork (1967).
2. After the death of Princess Diana, the emotional public response took the stiff upper-lipped British royalty and their courtiers by surprise. It marked one transformation in the hegemony of ruling class culture.

References

Acton, T. 1971. 'The Functions of the Avoidance of Moxadi Kovels', *Journal of the Gypsy Lore Society*, Third Series, 1(3–4): 108–36.
———. 1974. *Gypsy Politics and Social Change*. London: Routledge and Kegan Paul.
Agar, M.H. 1980. *The Professional Stranger*. London: Academic Press.
Bardi, A. 2004. 'The Roma as Trope: Representations in Early Twentieth-Century Literature', Paper presented at the *Annual Conference of the Gypsy Lore Society*, September 3–4 Newcastle: Newcastle University.
Barnes, B. 1988. Discussant comments at the *ASA Annual Conference on Ageing*, London: School of Oriental and African Studies, University of London.
Barth, F. 1969. 'Introduction', *Ethnic Groups and Boundaries*. London: Allen and Unwin, pp. 9–38.
de Beauvoir, S. 1949. *Le Deuxieme Sexe*. Paris: Gallimard.
Bloch, M. 1988. 'Interview with G. Houtman', *Anthropology Today* 4(1): 18–21.
Breton, A. 1937. *L'Amour Fou*. Paris: Gallimard.
Brody, H. 1973. *Inishkillane: Change and Decline in the West of Ireland*. London: Allen Lane.
Buckler, S. 2003. 'Fire in the Dark: Telling Gypsiness in North East England', Ph.D. thesis. Durham: Durham University.
Douglas, M. 1966. *Purity and Danger*. London: Routledge and Kegan Paul.
Emerson, R.M., R.I. Fretz and L. Shaw. 1995. *Writing Ethnographic Fieldnotes*. Chicago: Chicago University Press.

Hannerz, U. 1967. *Soulside*. New York: Columbia University Press.

Hardman, C. 1973. 'Can There Be an Anthropology of Children?', *Journal of the Anthropology Society of Oxford (JASO)* 4(1), 85–99.

Herzfeld, M. 1997. *Portrait of a Greek Imagination: An Ethnographic Biography of Andreas Nenedakis*. Chicago: University of Chicago Press.

Jackson, J. 1990. '"I am a fieldnote": Fieldnotes as a Symbol of Professional Identity', in R. Sanjek (ed.), *Fieldnotes: The Makings of Anthropology*. Ithaca: Cornell University Press, pp. 3–33.

Leach, E. 1972. 'Anthropological Aspects of Language: Animal Categories and Verbal Abuse', in P. Maranda (ed.), *Mythology*. London: Penguin, pp. 39–67.

Lévi-Strauss, C. 1963. *Totemism*. Harmondsworth: Penguin.

_____. 1966. *The Savage Mind*. London: Weidenfeld and Nicolson.

Malinowski, B. 1922. *Argonauts of the Western Pacific*. London: Routledge and Kegan Paul.

_____. 1929. *The Sexual Life of Savages*. London: Routledge and Kegan Paul.

Marcus, G. 1998. *Ethnography through Thick and Thin*. Princeton: Princeton University Press.

Miller, C. 1975. 'American Rom and the Ideology of Defilement', in F. Rehfisch (ed.), *Gypsies, Tinkers and Other Travellers*. London: Academic Press, pp. 41–54.

Ni Shuinear, S. 2003. 'Irish Travellers: Ethnolect, Alliance, Control', Ph.D. thesis. London: University of Greenwich.

Oakley, A. 1972. *Sex, Gender and Society*. London: Temple Smith.

Okely, J. 1975. 'Gypsy Women: Models in Conflict', in S. Ardener (ed.), *Perceiving Women*. London: Malaby Press, pp. 55–86.

_____. 1983. *The Traveller-Gypsies*. Cambridge: Cambridge University Press.

_____. 1986a. 'Fieldwork up the M1: Policy and Political Aspects', in A. Jackson (ed.), *Anthropology at Home*. London: Tavistock, pp. 55–73.

_____. 1986b. *Simone de Beauvoir: A Re-reading*. London: Virago: Pantheon.

_____. 1992. 'Anthropology and Autobiography: Participatory Experience and Embodied Knowledge', in J. Okely and H. Callaway (eds), *Anthropology and Autobiography*. London: Routledge, pp. 1–28.

_____. 1994a. 'Thinking Through Fieldwork', in R. Burgess and A. Bryman (eds), *Analysing Qualitative Data*. London: Routledge, pp. 18–34.

_____. 1994b. 'Vicarious and Sensory Knowledge of Chronology and Change: Ageing in Rural France', in K. Hastrup and P. Hervik (eds), *Social Experience and Anthropological Knowledge*. London: Routledge, pp. 45–64.

_____. 1996. *Own or Other Culture*. London: Routledge.

_____. 1997a. 'Cultural Ingenuity and Travelling Autonomy: Not Copying, Just Choosing', in T. Acton and G. Mundy (eds), *Romany Culture and Gypsy Identity*. Hertford: University of Hertfordshire Press, pp. I88–203.

_____. 1997b. 'Non Territorial Culture as the Rationale for the Assimilation of Gypsies', in *Childhood* 4(1): 63–80.

_____. 1997c. 'Some Political and Intellectual Consequences of Theories of Gypsy Ethnicity: The Place of the Intellectual', in A. James, J. Hockey and A. Dawson (eds), *After Writing Culture*. London: Routledge, pp. 224–243.

_____. 1999. 'Writing Anthropology in Europe: An Example from Gypsy Research', in *Folk* 41: 55–75.

_____. 2002. 'Written Out: *Inishkallene* Revisited', Unpublished paper presented at the *Association of American Anthropologists Annual Conference*, Washington DC. November 2002.

———. 2003a. 'Deterritorialised and Spatially Unbounded Cultures within Other Regimes', *Anthropological Quarterly* 76(1): 151–64.

———. 2003b. 'The Filmed Return of the Natives to a Colonizing Territory of Terror', *Journal of Media Practice* 3(2): 65–74.

———. 2005a. 'Gypsy Justice and Gorgio Law: Interrelations of Difference', *Sociological Review* 53(4): 691–709.

———. 2005b. 'Traveller-Gypsies and the Politicised and Cultural Construction of Difference', Keynote paper. *The Future of Multicultural Britain: Meeting Across Boundaries.* Cronem Conference. Roehampton University.

———. 2007. 'Gendered Lessons in Ivory Towers', in D. Fahy Bryceson, J. Okely and J. Webber (eds) *Identity and Networks*, pp. 228–46. Oxford: Berghahn.

———. In press. 'Free Association and Free Passage' in M.Melhuus, J. Mitchell, and H. Wulff (eds), *Ethnographic Practice in the Present*. Oxford: Berghahn.

Okely, J. and H. Callaway (eds). 1992. *Anthropology and Autobiography*. London: Routledge.

Piasere, L. 1984. *Mare Roma: Categories humainese structure social: Une contribution a l'ethnologie Tsigane*. Paris: Etudes et documents balkaniques, no. 6.

Plowden, Lady B. 1967. *Children and their Primary Schools*. Report for the Central Advisory Council for Education, vol. 2. London: H.M.S.O.

Powdermaker, H. 1967. *Stranger and Friend*. New York: Norton.

Reed-Danahay, D. 1997. *Auto/ethnography: Rewriting Self and Society*. Oxford: Berg.

Reiter, R. 1974. *Toward an Anthropology of Women*. London: Monthly Review Press.

Rohrlich-Leavitt, R. (ed.). 1975. *Women Cross-culturally: Change and Challenge*. The Hague: Mouton Press.

Rosaldo, M. and L. Lamphere (eds). 1974. *Woman, Culture and Society*. Stanford: Stanford University Press.

Rosaldo, R. 1989. *Culture and Truth: The Remaking of Social Analysis*. Boston: Beacon Press.

Said, E. 1978. *Orientalism*. New York: Pantheon.

Sanjek, R. (ed.). 1990. *Fieldnotes: The Makings of Anthropology*. Ithaka: Cornell University Press.

Sutherland, A. 1975. *Gypsies: The Hidden American*. London: Tavistock.

Tambiah, S.J. 1973. 'Classification of Animals in Thailand', in M. Douglas (ed.), *Rules and Meanings*. Harmondsworth: Penguin, pp. 127–66.

Thompson, T.W. 1922. 'The Uncleanness of Gypsy Women among English Gypsies', *Journal of the Gypsy Lore Society*, New Series 1(1–2): 15–43.

Whyte, W.F. 1955. *Street Corner Society*, appendix in 2nd edition. Chicago: Chicago University Press.

Williams, P. 1984. *Marriage Tsigane*. Paris: L'Harmattan, Selaf.

———. 2003. *Gypsy World: The Silence of the Living and the Voices of the Dead*. Chicago: University of Chicago Press.

Chapter 4

To Know the Dancer: Formations of Fieldwork in the Ballet World

Helena Wulff

'If I could tell you what it meant, there would be no point in dancing it', Isadora Duncan famously said.[1] Not only is dance elusive, it is also non-verbal.[2] There are certain moods in dance that cannot be adequately translated into text. In my study of career and culture in the transnational world of ballet my ambition was 'to know the dancer from the dance' to paraphrase W.B. Yeats, even though the dance played a part too, and thus had to be understood in anthropological terms.[3] Anthropologists of dance tend to look for what dance conveys about its society, and this ranges from direct reflection to critical commentary, even suggestions for future scenarios (Wulff 2001).

In this chapter I have the opportunity to re-consider how my knowledge about dancers and their dance in the ballet world was constructed. This process first started when I learnt to dance as a child and teenager, and continued in elaborated forms when I was doing fieldwork in the ballet world. Here I will detail how the process was shaped by reactions from my fieldsites to my presence there (cf. Halstead 2001; Jacobs-Huey 2002), as well as from colleagues to my study both during informal conversations and seminars where I gave papers. Even though my fieldwork is completed and has found its way into a number of publications, mainly Wulff (1998), but also Wulff (2000, 2002a, 2004, 2005a, 2006), I still have a relationship to this field both as an ex-native and an anthropologist. I keep up with performances and major events, also with the careers of some of the dancers. Obviously, the knowledge construction reached yet another level when I transformed my field notes into academic texts. Writing this article has pushed me up on yet another level of analysis in this knowledge construction of dancing and researching ballet. My ballet fieldwork built on experiences from earlier fieldwork I had conducted.[4]

In what follows here, I will briefly bring in my most recent fieldwork for comparative purposes as it also focussed on dance, this time in Ireland. That study was framed theoretically in terms of memory and mobility (see mainly Wulff forthcoming 2007, but also Wulff 2005, 2002b, 2003a, b, c).

Woven into this chapter are ideas about representation, reflexivity and memory. This means that I will discuss representations of ballet and the ballet world as data and in text, and the implications of the fact that I used to dance ballet in relation to the reflexive turn in anthropology which includes my bodily memory of dancing ballet, my body hexis of ballet, but also my visual memory of learning and dancing ballet.[5] I will argue that my memory of dancing was useful when I was doing fieldwork as I was not able to participate in the dancing anymore by then. My main method for data collection was thus observation. I did a lot of hanging around, spending time with dance people, talking and interviewing. I was a participant *observer*. As Grimshaw (2001: 172) notes, 'vision is central to modern anthropology', which makes us rethink the consequences of the fact that participant observation is central in the discipline. According to the visual theory of John Berger (1972) in his celebrated little book *Ways of Seeing*, we negotiate what we see with what we know, watching is structured by knowledge and belief. The reasons for watching as well as the ways of watching are also prominent aspects of how knowledge comes about through observation in the field.

I would like to dwell for a moment on the fact that I was trained in a relatively new anthropological tradition. A small country outside major colonial and postcolonial systems, Sweden is often left out of political or economic analysis. Our welfare with extensive employment laws has, however, attracted a certain attention, especially in transnational comparison. This was one point of comparison in my transnational ballet study. Sweden was the odd case in point, offering permanent positions to dancers and long parental leaves – also to male dancers who were new fathers. The Royal Swedish Ballet is mostly state-subsidised, a circumstance which impacts on company culture and repertoire Apart from a very small percentage of funding, the Royal Ballet in London, the American Ballet Theatre in New York and Ballet Frankfurt in Frankfurt-am-Main depended on funding from corporate and private sponsors.

In the social organisation of global anthropology, language skills are paramount. At the Stockholm department we were taught mostly in Swedish as undergraduate and graduate student, but the reading was on the whole in English. As Swedes learn English from the age of ten at school, and many spend time in English-speaking countries, most of us are fluent already as teenagers. This is probably the main reason for a stronger Swedish involvement with British and American anthropology rather than with the French. Contrary to Norway and Denmark, where British anthropology has had a more pronounced impact than American anthropology, Swedish anthropology has related to both traditions to about the same extent when it comes to conference participation and publications.

I will soon elaborate on the importance of the fact that my knowledge construction of ballet and the ballet world started already in my childhood and teens when I was dancing and was being enculturated into the ballet world. Of equal importance is obviously my enculturation into the anthropological world. For one thing, reputations of departments and supervisors certainly matter for anthropologists, too, as do interests and knowledge (!) of supervisors and themes of programmes in the department where one is trained. Anthropological knowledge construction is indeed shaped by departmental milieu against a backdrop of national traditions (see Gerholm and Hannerz 1982). National and transnational networks as well as imagined communities based on theoretical and regional interests also matter. Some of them are linked to circles around journals or publishers. Given that research and writing are the main modalities where knowledge construction takes place in anthropology, the bottom line is really research councils' politics and programmes as well as other funding issues, including salaries during sabbaticals. Time, money and different research strategies intertwine in making the construction of anthropological knowledge happen.

Back to Ballet: Re-re-revisiting

Dancing in a circle with other children in a light room, I remember feeling happy and safe, my mother waiting outside. This is my earliest memory of dancing, a practice which would develop into an extensive engagement in classical ballet for many years to come – until a back injury put a sudden end to it. The physical pain was excruciating. It confined my normal movement pattern to careful walking. Dancing was out of the question. I was seventeen years old, and felt like my main expression had been taken away from me. In a sense, I did not quite recover until I came back to the ballet world about twenty years later to do fieldwork and started writing about it (Wulff 1998). By going back home to the ballet world I also found my home in anthropology: dance, aesthetics and visual culture.

When I was dancing I was watching a lot of ballet, both rehearsals and performances. Thinking back, there were three junctures of ballet revelation that stand out in my memory. The first one occurred at a children's Christmas ballet, *Little Peter's Journey to the Moon*, at the Opera House in Stockholm: on stage I discovered an alluring world of glittering tutus and movement to live music. I can still recall the feeling of being totally mesmerised. A few years later, my father and I were watching *The Moon Reindeer* by Swedish choreographer Birgit Cullberg. In the intermission we talked about the piece and I suggested that the dancers should wear horns on their heads as they were portraying reindeer. My father disagreed and pointed out emphatically: 'That's the whole point with ballet! They *dance* the horns!' (Wulff 1998: 4). And with this piece of verbal explanation, he had given me the key to ballet literacy. That was when I learnt how to watch ballet. My third most momentous memory of ballet took place when I was a young teenage girl and Russian dancer Rudolf Nureyev was coming to Stockholm with his English partner Margot Fonteyn. A true top team in ballet at the time, they were going to dance *Giselle*, one of the major classical ballets. From my seat, I saw Fonteyn do a delicate Giselle, but for me she was overshadowed by Nureyev's charismatic Prince Albrecht, danced with virtuoso technique and very high jumps. The audience went wild, uncharacteristically so in Stockholm, and would not let Nureyev go until after the sixteenth curtain call (Wulff 1998).

Watching ballet in the studio is a prominent part of learning this dance form for the young ballet student, and it is a way to learn new roles for the professional dancer. Like other bodily skills, ballet is learnt through mimesis, at first as an imitation, and later the dancers will add their own distinct interpretations. There are national and choreographic dance styles that are expected to come through in how ballet is executed, as is the training of legendary teachers and coaches. Yet another important part of watching ballet for the ballet student as well as the professional dancer, is obviously to watch performances, both live and on film and video in order to see what they are working towards.[6] A male dancer, a principal with the Royal Swedish Ballet, told me in an interview that he spent a lot of time watching from the wings at the Opera House in Stockholm when he was a ballet student. One night, during a performance of *The Taming of the Shrew*, he suddenly saw 'how the steps you learn in the studio can be used!' (Wulff 1998: 2). The steps in different combinations were not only technique, they could be put together in all kinds of combinations and, most importantly, express an array of feelings. This was the heightened moment when he made the decision to become a dancer. It is also common that ballet students participate in classical ballet performances dancing children's roles, and later as dancers get to dance one role after another in the same productions (Wulff 1998).

When I was learning ballet, it never occurred to me that our teachers were too old and stiff to be able to show the steps like we were supposed to do them. Contemplating this circumstance both in the field and later at my desk, I realised that this is a very unusual circumstance in an educational context. Most training is organised around the teacher showing the student explicitly how to perform a particular task, even though this may occur over a long period of time and include repetitions, trial-and-errors and an accumulation of smaller information pieces into a larger entity. During my fieldwork, ballet teachers told me that they have an inner image, which is a visual memory, of what the steps should look like. But they also remembered what it felt like to execute them. The steps were in their 'muscular memory' as they said. I observed teachers having the best dancers do the steps in front of the rest of the company. There was also a lot of *peer-coaching*, dancers in different casts, or who were friends, showing each other or finding out together how to do steps and connect with other dancers, not least in a way which would prevent injury (Wulff 1998: 72). Learning from one's peers among apprentices, is put forward by Lave and Wenger (1995) as one aspect of what they call situated learning, which refers to how learning is shaped by its social context, by apprentices spending time with 'masters', but also by stories and lore among practitioners. Lave and Wenger address the non-verbal aspect of knowledge and learning, especially in relation to apprenticeship. Roy Dilley's (1999) inspiring article about the importance of mimesis in fieldwork enculturation also reveals indigenous ideas about learning. Dilley writes about mimesis among Senegalese Tukulor weavers. As he (1999: 37) points out, 'knowledge in the main is not verbalised, but apprentices are expected to copy the work of their master'. This, again, also applies to the ballet world.

Yet most training includes verbal instructions. But then how does a teacher verbalise a non-verbal bodily activity such as ballet? First of all, there is a special vocabulary of indigenous ballet terms that refer to steps and their expression, some invented by individual coaches, others used more generally. The terms often take the form of metaphors such as 'Be like a pencil!' when a back needs to be straight, or 'Go up! Be like an elevator', or 'Dance as if the floor is on fire!' to get a dancer to do small, quick steps across the stage (Wulff 1998: 61).

Not only were the 'masters', that is teachers, coaches and choreographers, unable to demonstrate the steps sufficiently, but I was also unable to do them the way the dancers did them. It did matter, however, to all of us, and for my knowledge construction, that I, just like the teachers, used to be able to perform them. I too, had an inner image of what the steps were supposed to look like and what they felt like to dance.

In a critical discussion of the notion of 'native' anthropologist, Kirin Narayan's (1993: 678) draws on fieldwork in her native India and argues that the meaning of 'pre-existing experience' changes with time in the field. Also Seteney Shami (1988) has done fieldwork in her native country, Jordan, on Circassians. Shami found that she was aware of certain circumstances already when she started working there, but was to acquire new knowledge. Coming back after twenty years to the ballet world as an ex-native, I found it strikingly unchanged with regard to old-fashioned ballet pedagogy and decorum. But I was to learn more about ballet as a career and art form than I had known when I left, still a ballet student at the time. I had, for example, been ignorant about the fact that the majority of dancers do not make a lot of money. And with very little performance experience, I had not understood fully the excitement, the implications of the possibility of ballet art to spring up on stage, or the risk of injury or performance failure. I remember being aware of ballet's historical and contemporary links to court life, after all, Swedish Princess Christina was in our ballet school and our Russian teachers taught us how to thank the Tsar for the applause (!). But I had no idea that the ballet world was considered a closed world, both from the inside and the outside. This became clear to me as I was moving in and out of the ballet world during my fieldwork: both ballet people and people outside talked about it in such terms. Ballet people tend to keep to themselves because of odd and long working hours and the sensitive nature of the process of learning a performance practice back stage. There are instances of this practice that have to take place without outside spectators. And from the outside, the ballet world back stage is often looked at as inaccessible, even among ballet goers, let alone people who have never been introduced to ballet. To the latter even the public part of ballet, the performances at grand theatres and opera houses, may appear out of reach, part of a closed world.

Building a Ballet Study

As a young lecturer at the Department of Social Anthropology, Stockholm University, I discovered the wonder of seeing students grow in front of you. I found, and still find, students fascinating people. And I tailored my teaching along my research interests as much as I could, which was rewarding intellectually. Yet, I was craving for the intellectual challenge to do new research and get into a major writing project again. Having a long-standing engagement in literature, I had been playing with the idea to study writers, Third World novelists especially, but saw this as a field with few opportunities for observation of their work practice (Wulff 1998). At the Stockholm Department, a number of research projects were underway on the transnational networks of occupational cultures. The research was conducted by way of multi-sited fieldwork (cf. Hannerz 2003a, b), such as Christina Garston's (1994) study of Apple computer employees, Tommy Dahlén's (1997) on so-called interculturalists who train businesspeople to deal with cultural difference, and Ulf Hannerz's (2004) work on foreign correspondents.

I entitled my research proposal 'A Transnational Ballet World: Network and Subculture in Stockholm, London and New York', thus from the beginning covering classical ballet only. But as I got into my fieldwork I realised, both from my own observations of the dancers and the dancing, and comments by key informants, that it would be useful to include a contemporary company in the study. With the three ballet companies, in a global perspective, I assembled ethnography from a ballet periphery (Stockholm), an old ballet centre (London), a new ballet centre (New York) and with time, following my interlocutors' good advice, I added a contemporary experimental ballet company (Frankfurt-am-Main). The latter was a particularly illuminating case in point as back stage culture in contemporary companies are defined by a cutting-edge ambition. This is quite different from the conservative cultivation of ballet heritage in classical companies, yet there are connections both artistically and socially: contemporary choreographers make use of classical references in their dance productions and dancers move between the two types of companies from one country to another. Transnational network was thus one of the central notions from beginning to end: it was in the outline of the research proposal and also in the final publications. Not so subculture. This concept did not make it out of the research proposal. As my fieldwork unfolded transnational connections between the different national sites took precedence over the idea of one ballet company or a national ballet world as a subculture embedded in a larger entity.

Observering Observer

It was the annual spring party of the Royal Swedish Ballet at the Opera House in Stockholm. This marked the conclusion of the season, and also of my year with the company. The party had been preceded by great excitement and recollections of past pranks, such as the traditional sketch where dancers in a review of the season make fun of the ballet management and choreographers that they depend on for their careers, as well as successful colleagues that they envy. In a structural ritual of rebellion (Gluckman 1955) the dancers are temporarily allowed to release their frustration with the intensity and ranking system of their career, and feelings of lack of influence. The sketch started by featuring the director of the opera house and the ballet director, and events from the tour to Japan. Then 'the fieldworker' came on stage. A male dancer was acting me, wearing trousers and jacket, and a wig resembling my hairstyle and colour: I saw myself hanging around in the background trying to look inconspicuous, but being very visible. As the sketch unfolded by way of a series of stories, 'I' emerged in many of them, usually unexpectedly, but slowly making friends and finally being included in the central circle of the company (Wulff 1998).

Totally unprepared, it was at first a funny feeling to watch the dancers comment on my presence in their daily life, but I was very pleased to note that they showed that they had accepted me. Another instance of the observer being observed was when I realised that not only did I make use of the big mirror in the studio by watching dancers through the mirror without them noticing, but they were watching me in the same way! These covert gazes took place before I had spoken to most of them. After a while they would disclose that they had been checking me and my views of their dance, and that they had also identified my background in dance from my movement pattern, which was important to them. My dancing experience would ensure that I represented them in a fair way, they said. It is common that dancers feel misunderstood by non-dancers since their extensive bodily training makes them move more, and more expressively, than other people, also when they are not dancing. And they have usually not had a lot of time to develop their verbal or writing skills. When I was well into my fieldwork I caught some of my own expressions about social and artistic aspects of the ballet and dance world reappearing in dancers' conversations both among themselves and with me. Somehow I had provided the dancers with words, which indicated that I had got things right from their point of view (Wulff 1998).

My acceptance process contained the usual situations when the fieldworker is regarded as a threat, a supporter and a confidante. The threat was that I was taken to be a dance critic who would evaluate them, or that I would write (in newspapers or in my book) about famous dancers' career setbacks or family problems. There was also an assumption that I was there to hire dancers on behalf of other companies. Some sensitive issues concerned drugs, eating disorders and AIDS. I did learn about them quite early in my fieldwork, but it was not until the end that I got to hear about how dancers with wealthy parents provided some of the companies with large sums of money, thereby buying their children fame. It did not take long, however, before I became a staunch supporter, someone who was around when bad reviews hit or performances did not go well. I was to become a confidante over issues ranging from promotions and declines in careers to broken hearts and homesickness (Wulff 1998).

Comments from Colleagues

When I had made the momentous decision to do a major study of the transnational world of ballet, and also while I was conducting fieldwork, I had some striking comments, both disturbing and poignant, by colleagues in Europe and the United States. There was the sexist reaction by a male American anthropologist who asked if he could 'help with observations' as if all dancers were women, and the European anthropologist, also male, who felt called upon to make sure in an insinuating tone of voice that I was aware that dancers 'are gay'. Even though male homosexuality has been and still is a feature of the ballet world, it is not as pronounced as it used to be. It is more common in contemporary dance companies, both among the dancers and in the dance stories on stage (Wulff 1998: 7). Such prejudice was, however, balanced by some remarkable reactions from other colleagues. These were people I had known for almost twenty years, some quite well, and when they heard about my study they were completely overwhelmed. A whole new landscape opened up for me in the anthropological community. I remember how someone would stop, and look at me, changing a professional expression of efficiency into a relaxed posture radiating personal warmth. And then spin a startling story about harbouring a secret passion for dance, music or the arts. A leading American anthropologist confessed that he was an amateur musician and that he could not do anthropology if he did not get to play his instrument regularly. A number of women anthropologists revealed that they had once had dreams about becoming dancers, but had not made it or had been prevented by parents who found dancing a dubious career. There was also the senior woman colleague whose son was a dancer with a major company in the United States, a circumstance she normally felt academic colleagues did not appreciate. This dancer became one of my introductors into the American ballet scene.

When I had been doing fieldwork for a few months, and even been on tours (which is especially useful as circumstances are uncovered that are not visible in everyday life in the theatre back home), I gave my first seminar reporting on its early phases. Two comments in particular were to have an impact on my continued knowledge construction of the project. Having had a good start, re-engaging with ballet, and now being heavily involved in the field and the native's point of view, I was arguing that in order to do fieldwork in the ballet world, in order to reach an understanding of the closed, highly specialised world of ballet – you must have been dancing. This provoked a heated discussion initiated by someone for whom music and dance do not really matter, nor any particular body activity. The discussion moved into the issue of whether not everyone can do any fieldwork, and why the ballet world might be different from other fields in this respect (see also Merton 1972). It now seems to be increasingly accepted that certain fields are more suited for some fieldworkers than others because of parameters such as personality, age, gender, race, national identity and personal history (cf. Okely and Callaway 1992), which can help both when it comes to access and accommodation in the field. What matters here is really that in order to study a bodily activity, or people whose life is work which is a bodily activity whether dance, music, sports or anything else, it is very useful for a fieldworker to be able to do this activity, perhaps by learning it, or to have been doing it in the past. The reason is that:

there is knowledge in the *practice*.

Now I know that virtually every dance scholar from the first dance anthropologists and dance sociologists to dance historians have danced. Many have some training in classical ballet, but it is even more common that dance scholars started out as contemporary dancers on some level. For methodological reasons, it has been expected that dance anthropologists learn the dances or sections of the dances they study. As these dances, ethnic and folk dance, often consist of types of movements that are quite different from earlier movement practice, this must be considered quite an achievement (Wulff 2001).

Phases of Fieldwork, Phases of Knowledge

It has been suggested that there are three phases in fieldwork (Agar 1980; Wulff 2000), as in any stay, away or abroad. And they seem to be more or less inherent, a necessary part of adapting temporarily to a new setting, no matter how many times we have been away nor in that particular place. I have gone through them in all my field studies, both the traditional ones: a year in South London in the early 1980s and a year with the Royal Swedish Ballet in Stockholm in the mid-1990s, and my three months each with ballet companies in London, New York and Frankfurt-am-Main, as well as my 'yo-yo fieldwork' on Irish dance which took me back and forth between Stockholm and Ireland on week long trips. I spent thirty-three weeks in the field, in all more than eight months starting in 1998 (Wulff 2002b). I should emphasise that in all these different types of fieldwork: traditional, multi-local, mobile and yo-yo fieldwork, my relationships with my informants have been of the same nature: I have known some of them quite well, others less well. There is also a certain kind of confidentiality to be gained from short but regular visits in multi-local, mobile and yo-yo fieldwork.

The first, of the three phases in fieldwork, is the 'honeymoon' or 'tourist' phase when we have just arrived and everything is new and exciting for the researcher. With formal access, the fieldwork has started well. After handling the occasional lie from locals and the attention of hangers-on who are marginal in the group and thus not really reliable as representatives of the people that are being studied in the long run, things move on. This happy beginning lasts for about a month until we get into a bad patch. Suffering from homesickness and a feeling of alienation in the field, the fieldwork does not go anywhere. A common strategy is then to do an interview series, since that is a way to collect a lot of data in a short time. It is often towards the end of this first phase that a dramatic event occurs, which throws the fieldworker into the next phase and informal acceptance (Wulff 2000). This event usually involves some emotional outburst leading the locals to conceptualise the fieldworker as 'a real human being', 'someone who is just like us'. This is the longest phase, with a lot of time for participation and 'going native'. This phase is approaching its end when the fieldwork will soon be over. Here is then another stressful moment since this is the point when the fieldworker often starts to worry about the quantity and quality of the data. Do I have enough? Is it of the right kind? Another interview series is a good strategy to deal with the separation anxiety and transition into the last short but intense phase before going back home.

We all know that first impressions in the field are crucial, and should be written down in order to compare what and how we write about things later on, when with increasing cultural competence we start thinking more like the people we study. First impressions are also illuminating to read later when some time has passed, and the field notes are there as an entity. When I was writing my book on the ballet world, I remember reading my early field notes not only as a fresh testimony, but also like nodes that I now could connect in a net which kept growing denser: having accumulated so much data over the course of nearly two years, I was able to see circumstances and make connections with later events that I could not do when I took the first notes. Clearly, the nature of our knowledge changes with different phases in fieldwork, but it keeps changing also afterwards during the writing up.

Fieldwork into Field Notes

I did participant observation on an everyday basis with three national ballet companies, beginning with the 1993/4 season with the Royal Swedish Ballet in Stockholm. Then I went on to spend three months each with the Royal Ballet in London, the American Ballet Theatre in New York and the contemporary ballet company, Ballett Frankfurt in Frankfurt-am-Main.[7] I was watching morning class, rehearsals in the afternoon and performances in the evenings both from the wings and the auditorium. I joined the dancers on tours: most noteworthy was the major three-week tour to Japan with the Royal Swedish Ballet, when I helped out as a dresser. I took field notes every day when I came home, or back to the hotel when I was on tours. My field notes had the form of a diary, where I was reporting and commenting on the day, sometimes one day took up many pages, sometimes just a few lines. Occasionally, when I came back very late tired after some post-performance party or event, I just wrote down some key words before going to bed. The day after I would write out what was in-between them. Once or twice when I forgot to write down even key words, I would be shocked by how little I remembered from the day before after one night's sleep.

If this forgetting happened because of a bodily state, that of sleeping, my memory operated selectively when I was awake filtering away certain data that I did not find useful: one evening in the depths of winter, two years after I had finished my fieldwork with the Royal Swedish Ballet and one year after I had finished the whole fieldwork, I was busy writing at home in Stockholm. The phone rang, and there was one of the dancers on the line, a colourful male soloist who had just retired. With his talent for story telling, he had been a great informant. A bit of a jester, not only on stage in such roles, but also back stage, he was, like many comics, a sharp observer of life. The story of his own breakthrough which happened completely unexpectedly was one of my best cases in my field notes, which would later go into the book. His breakthrough illustrated how chance and individual will power can launch a career. The dancer had asked the ballet director if he could dance the Jester in *Swan Lake*, but had been denied. Then he sneaked into the studio where his colleague was learning the role, and learnt it unobtrusively at the back of the room. The day before the opening night his colleague became sick, so now the ballet director begged him to do the role, which he did to great acclaim (Wulff 1998). This was what I remembered when he called me. But he went into a long and complicated story about something he had told me when I interviewed him, and wanted to make sure that I would not write about this in my book. Nor mention any names. This was not difficult to promise. I had no idea what he was talking about!

While writing field notes, I organised them around the theoretical, ethnographic and indigenous themes (that sometimes overlapped) of my study, the ones I had outlined in the research proposal such as transnationality, career, body and mind, gender, time and culture, performance, and also some new ones that emerged as the fieldwork progressed, such as new technology. When these themes, or concepts, occurred in the text, I obviously highlighted them in order to be able to find them easily afterwards. I distinguished among them, making some of them major themes, others minor ones. Later as my writing progressed, I would move some minor themes into major, and vice versa. I would discover new themes as I went along. I sorted the themes with their data in alphabetical order, and made a contents list of them which indicated major and minor themes, and whether I had a lot of data about them, or not so much – even though a theme with many pages in my field notes would not necessarily be more important than one with just a few pages, or a few lines of a pithy portrait of a dancer. Altogether I was working with 199 themes ranging from 'age' to 'working day' across 299 single-spaced pages. I also made use of other qualitative combinations by juxtaposing data from ballet programmes, leaflets informing about companies and ballet schools, dancers' biographies that often are authored by dance journalists, dance reviews from daily papers, dance historical sources in the form of popular and academic articles and books, and of course videos and photographs. Some dancers even gave me a couple of the many fan letters they received, and I also collected Good Luck cards that dancers give to each other before opening nights or when someone is doing a role for the first time (Wulff 1998).

I avoided taking notes in front of the dancers as I was worried that they would be self-conscious and not act in a natural way, but pretend certain things and conceal others that they believed I should not see (whether they were a part of my study or not). But it happened that I sneaked into the Ladies toilet to jot down some particularly striking comment or a dialogue in a small notebook I carried with me in my pocket, sometimes an odd piece of paper, the back of a performance ticket or a napkin from the canteen would have to do. It was important for me to get the wording right, not least in order to be able to make correct quotations. On a rare occasion, I did write down a piece of information in front of a dancer, such as a name or a concept which came up in a conversation I was having with someone. This was also an opportunity to get the spelling right, even though in general not having very much formal training in foreign languages, the dancers did not always get it right either when I asked them to write down something for me. The names of dancers of other ballet people in my study ranged from Russian and Swedish to English, French, German and American. Dancers who had moved to England or the United States (especially from Russia) had in some cases anglicised their names in order to make them easier to pronounce and remember in their new countries, and also sometimes as a part of upward social mobility (even within the same national context that is Britain).

When I had finished my fieldwork, I had assembled a daunting heap of notebooks, small and big ones in different shapes and colours. There were also the many odd pieces of papers that must not get lost. And of course the close to 120 interviews I had done with dancers, choreographers, coaches, directors, musicians, critics and other ballet people. I had written them down by long hand while the interviewee had been talking. As soon as I had a moment to myself, I would go through what I had written in order to make sure that I could read my own handwriting, and also fill in pieces of information where I still remembered something that had been lost. As I had to write really quickly while the interviewees spoke, in a few cases parts of sentences remained undecipherable. But then, this happens with tapes too.

Some of the interviews were complemented with tapes, but most of the time I did not use a tape-recorder. The reason was not so much that interviewees can be uncomfortable by those machines or that the settings such as the theatre canteen where we were could be noisy,[8] but rather the enormous amount of time it takes to transcribe notes. As I was not doing a linguistic study, I did not think I needed every interview on tape. But when I was writing my book, listening to the voices of informants was a good way to get back into the atmosphere of the ballet world, as was watching videos of performances and rehearsals where I had been present. Just like key words on a paper can bring back material about the spaces in-between them, the sound and sight of the dancers reminded me of the details in the social and artistic organisation of the ballet world. As the time distance to my fieldwork grew, I also went on to discover new aspects, aspects I had not been aware of while I was still immersed in the field. This joy of discovery happens of course also when reading, organising and re-organising field notes after fieldwork and during the writing process. Then new connections and insights are likely to rise out of the material, also because of the head notes (cf. Sanjek 1990) that are not written down anywhere, but get activated at this stage.

After Fieldwork: Writing Up

It was in the summer of 1995 that I found myself with the heap of notebooks and the stretch of time to write a book manuscript in front of me. I did not yet have a deadline with a publisher, but was driven by a strong urge to get down to writing. For me, it is crucial to be a *writing* anthropologist. We need publications in order to get and stay in jobs, and get grants, but I think that for those of us who become compulsive writers, the meaning of writing goes beyond those requirements. It becomes a second nature, and a way to breathe. A labour of love, which continues no matter what is going on around us in terms of life crises or just everyday logistics. We keep writing.

Getting my handwritten field notes into my computer was, however, a question of sheer will power, not any romantic writing away there. It took three months. As always, the beginning was the hardest. As this was mostly mechanical work, I thought I might as well start early in the mornings in order to get it over with. So, completely against my nature, I was at my desk at seven o'clock in the morning, barely awake. The light Swedish summer mornings, which are especially clear in the country where I was, helped. And I was gradually beginning to enjoy the monotony of getting more and more material into neat files in my computer. In fact, I was discerning a structure for the book. I was not only copying the notes, but organising them along the themes of the study. After a while I saw with great pleasure that my computerised field notes were turning into a first very rough draft of the book!

I did not cut off my fieldwork overnight, at least not the Stockholm site which was connected to the other ones. Even though the exit was a bit of a sad drama (Wulff 2000), I went back to visit there also when I was in my writing phase, both back stage watching rehearsals now and then, and meeting key informants for dinner and coffee, and of course attending performances. Gradually though, as I would get to know the senior critic of the largest newspaper in Sweden, *Dagens Nyheter*, and join her at performances she was going to review, I knew dancers who saw me from stage and those I met in the foyer would think that I had moved over to the other camp, that of dance critics. This is actually untrue. I do not see it as an anthropologist's job to evaluate the people we study, not even when a study has been concluded (Wulff 2004).

Conclusions: Knowing How to Know the Dancer

I want to return to the quote by Isadora Duncan, which set the tone of this chapter. How can the quality of dance that I, with Isadora Duncan, claim is out of reach of words, at least in the form that is experienced at a live performance, be constructed as anthropological knowledge? To know the dancer from the dance might mean on one hand to separate the dancer from the dance (if this is possible), and on the other hand that the dance will give us information about the dancer. And if the dance is difficult to capture in words, and this is the whole point with it, then my anthropological text will say so in relation to reactions to the dance as a part of the social organisation of the dance world. There is also the prevalent unease with textual and visual representations of dance in the ballet and dance world. The only exception was the suggestion by a dancer and choreographer that poetry would be the best way to convey dance.

John Blacking (1977, 1988), ethnomusicologist and anthropologist, saw limitations in how language can express feelings. He often talked about the problems of translating an experience of dance into words. This did not mean that Blacking was interested in ideas about the subconscious in relation to dance. He rather identified 'another kind of reasoning' which was in line with the non-verbal form of dance: 'It is not that people abandon reason for emotion when they dance', he said, 'but that they often introduce another kind of reasoning, whose grammar and content are most effectively, though not exclusively, expressed in non-verbal language' (Blacking 1988: 67). This points to the issue of whether such 'grammar and content' match ideas about reason and emotion as we know them, or if dance has the power to find new experiential categories. Working with 'an open form that generates new possibilities', this is what choreographer William Forsythe is attracted to. There is no doubt that Forsythe's dance productions create new atmospheres of fright and fun, as well as parody, always changing guise. If all dance is difficult to represent in text, Forsythe's work is harder than most. A full Forsythe experience is multi-layered and mobile, and very complex (Wulff 2006).

In this chapter I have been re-considering yet again how my enculturation into the ballet world as a child proved useful for my knowledge construction of ballet and ballet dancers when I was doing a study of this highly specialised world. I have explained how I built my ballet study on fieldwork consisting of participant observations, interviews and other qualitative combinations such as ballet programmes, reviews, fan letters and videos. The dancers' view of me also shaped my study, especially in the form of a dancer acting me in a sketch, as well as prejudiced and enthusiastic comments from colleagues. They all gave me different type of data about the ballet world. I have also made account of how I wrote and organised my field notes, and got going on my book manuscript.

Although postmodernism and the reflexive turn in anthropology made us sharpen out methodological tools and declare the process of knowledge construction for particular studies in greater detail than what had been regarded as necessary before, things did go out of hand for a while. This spurred Adam Kuper (1999: 223) to write about 'a paralysing effect on the discipline of anthropology'. Not only did the fieldworker appear to be more important than the people studies were supposed to be about, but I remember thinking somewhat irritated to myself that in the endless auto-critique of our methods and deconstruction of texts, we seemed stripped of our anthropological authority, as if we did not know what we were doing. 'Based on an ethos of trust', as Moshe Shokeid (2001: 5630) says, our discipline has 'never been able to implement a procedure of testing the accuracy and truthfulness of field notes reported by colleagues and students'. But there is a cultivated shared sense of good versus bad ethnography. At the height of the postmodernist movement, anthropologists became vulnerable and were often seen as not quite credible by scholars from other disciplines with positivist agendas or aspirations. This period is over now, and we can finally put these worries to rest. With the wide-ranging critique came a new awareness of how knowledge construction takes place in anthropology and a confidence in knowing how to know – in this case, the dancer.

Notes

1. For a reference, see Middleton (1988: 165).
2. There are words, however, in some contemporary dance usually in the form of an occasional monologue, dialogue, exclamation or song. Words and sentences are also projected on screens or posters, thereby connecting to the rest of the dance performance by moving around, either on the screen, or on a moving screen.
3. My study of career and culture in the transnational world of ballet and dance was funded by the then Swedish Research Council for the Humanities and Social Sciences (now The Swedish Research Council).
4. My very first fieldwork, which was for my Ph.D. thesis on youth culture and ethnicity in an inner-city area of South London (see mainly Wulff 1988, and also Wulff 1995) lasted for fourteen months in 1981/2. Then I did a small six-month study in 1989 of young Swedes and cultural moratorium on Manhattan (Wulff 1992).
5. The concept of body hexis was of course coined by Pierre Bourdieu (1977).
6. Now DVD is a major technology for watching recorded ballet and dance. It was not yet in use in the ballet world when I was doing fieldwork in the mid-1990s.
7. Ballett Frankfurt folded in 2004 and began a new life as the private The Forsythe Company in 2005.
8. With new digital recording technology, noisy setting is not a problem.

References

Agar, Michael. 1980. *The Professional Stranger: An Informal Introduction to Ethnography*. New York: Academic Press.
Berger, John. 1972. *Ways of Seeing*. Harmondsworth: Penguin.
Blacking, John. 1977. 'Towards an Anthropology of the Body', in J. Blacking (ed.), *The Anthropology of the Body*. London: Academic Press, pp. 1–28.

_____. 1988. 'Movement, Dance, Music, and the Venda Girls' Initiation Cycle', in P. Spencer (ed.), *Society and the Dance*. Cambridge: Cambridge University Press, pp. 64–91.

Bourdieu, Pierre. 1977. *Outline of a Theory of Practice*. Cambridge: Cambridge University Press.

Dahlén, Tommy. 1997. *Among the Interculturalists: An Emerging Profession and its Packaging of Knowledge*. Stockholm Studies in Social Anthropology, 38. Stockholm: Almqvist and Wiksell International.

Dilley, Roy. 1999. 'Ways of Knowing, Forms of Power', *Cultural Dynamics* 11(1): 33–55.

Garsten, Christina. 1994. *Apple World: Core and Periphery in a Transnational Organizational Culture*. Stockholm Studies in Social Anthropology, 33. Stockholm: Almqvist and Wiksell International.

Gerholm, Thomas and Ulf Hannerz (eds). 1982. The Shaping of National Anthropologies, *Ethnos*, special issue. No. 47.

Gluckman, Max. 1955. *Custom and Conflict in Africa*. Oxford: Blackwell.

Grimshaw, Anna. 2001. *The Ethnographer's Eye: Ways of Seeing in Modern Anthropology*. Cambridge: Cambridge University Press.

Halstead, Narmala. 2001. 'Ethnographic Encounters: Positionings within and Outside the Insider Frame', *Social Anthropology* 9(3): 307–21.

Hannerz, Ulf. 2003a. 'Being There ... and There ... and There! Reflections on Multi-site Ethnography', *Ethnography* 4(2): 201–16.

_____. 2003b. 'Several Sites in One', in T. Hylland Eriksen (ed.), *Globalisation*. London: Pluto Press, pp. 18–38.

_____. 2004. *Foreign News: Exploring the World of Foreign Correspondents*. Chicago: University of Chicago Press.

Jacobs-Huey, Lanita. 2002. 'The Natives are Gazing and Talking Back: Reviewing the Problematics of Positionality, Voice, and Accountability among "Native" Anthropologists', *American Anthropologist* 104(3): 791–804.

Kuper, Adam. 1999. *Culture: The Anthropologists' Account*. London: Harvard University Press.

Lave, Jean and Etienne Wenger. 1995. *Situated Learning*. Cambridge: Cambridge University Press.

Merton, Robert K. 1972. 'Insiders and Outsiders: A Chapter in the Sociology of Knowledge', *American Journal of Sociology* 78(1): 9–47.

Middleton, John. 1988. 'The Dance among the Lugbara of Uganda', in P. Spencer (ed.), *Society and the Dance*. Cambridge: Cambridge University Press, pp. 165–82.

Narayan, Kirin. 1993. 'How Native is a "Native" Anthropologist?', *American Anthropologist* 95(3): 671–86.

Okely, Judith and Helen Callaway (eds). 1992. *Anthropology and Autobiography*. ASA Monographs, 29. London: Routledge.

Sanjek, Roger (ed.). 1990. *Fieldnotes: The Makings of Anthropology*. Ithaka: Cornell University Press.

Shami, Seteney. 1988. 'Studying Your Own: The Complexities of a Shared Culture', in S. Altorki and C. Fawzi El-Solh (eds), *Arab Women in the Field*. Syracuse, NY: Syracuse University Press, pp. 115–38.

Shokeid, Moshe. 2001. 'Fieldwork in Social and Cultural Anthropology', in N.J. Smelser and P.B. Baltes (eds), *International Encyclopedia of the Social and Behavioral Sciences*. Oxford: Elsevier, pp. 5628–32.

Wulff, Helena. 1988. *Twenty Girls: Growing Up, Ethnicity and Excitement in a South London Microculture*. Stockholm Studies in Social Anthropology, 21. Stockholm: Almqvist and Wiksell International.

———. 1992. 'Young Swedes in New York: Workplace and Playground', in R. Lundén and E. Åsard (eds), *Networks of Americanization*. Stockholm: Almqvist and Wiksell International, pp. 94–105.

———. 1995. 'Inter-racial Friendship: Consuming Youth Styles, Ethnicity and Teenage Femininity in South London', in V. Amit-Talai and H. Wulff (eds), *Youth Cultures*. London: Routledge, pp. 63–80.

———. 1998. *Ballet across Borders: Career and Culture in the World of Dancers*. Oxford: Berg.

———. 2000. 'Access to a Closed World: Methods for a Multilocale Study on Ballet as a Career', in V. Amit (ed.), *Constructing the Field*. London: Routledge, pp. 147–61.

———. 2001. 'Dance, Anthropology of', in Neil J. Smelser and Paul B. Baltes (eds), *International Encyclopedia of the Social and Behavioral Sciences*. Oxford: Elsevier, pp. 3209–12.

———. 2002a. 'Aesthetics at the Ballet: Looking at "National" Style, Body and Clothing in the London Dance World', in N. Rapport (ed.), *British Subjects*. Oxford: Berg, pp. 67–83.

———. 2002b. 'Yo-yo Fieldwork: Mobility and Time in a Multilocal Study of Dance in Ireland', *Anthropological Journal on European Cultures*, Issue on 'Shifting Grounds: Experiments in Doing Ethnography' 11: 117–36.

———. 2003a. 'The Irish Body in Motion: Moral Politics, National Identity and Dance', in N. Dyck and E. Archetti (eds), *Sport, Dance and Embodied Identities*. Oxford: Berg, pp. 179–96.

———. 2003b. 'Steps and Stories about Ireland', *Choreographic Encounters* 1(1): 70–74.

———. 2003c. 'Steps on Screen: Technoscapes, Visualization and Globalization in Dance', in C. Garsten and H. Wulff (eds), *New Technologies at Work*. Oxford: Berg, pp. 187–204.

———. 2004. 'The Critic's Eye: Ethics and Politics of Writing Dance Reviews', in E. Anttila et al. (eds), *Making a Difference in Dance*. Helsinki: Theatre Academy, pp. 281–97.

———. 2005a. '"High Arts" and the Market: An Uneasy Partnership in the Transnational World of Ballet', in D. Inglis and J. Hughson (eds), *The Sociology of Art*. Basingstoke: Palgrave pp. 171–82.

———. 2005b. 'Memories in Motion: The Irish Dancing Body', *Body and Society*, Special Issue on 'The Dancing Body', edited by Bryan S. Turner, 11(4) 45–62.

———. 2006. 'Experiencing the Ballet Body: Pleasure, Pain, Power', in Suzel Ana Reily (ed.), *The Musical Human: Rethinking John Blacking's Ethnomusicology in the 21st Century*. Aldershot: Ashgate Press.

———. 2007. *Dancing at the Crossroads: Memory and Mobility in Ireland*. Oxford: Berghahn Books.

Chapter 5

Knowledge as Gifts of Self and Other[1]

Narmala Halstead

Introduction

This chapter considers the negotiations of access in the field by moving beyond an idea of access as gaining entry into field-sites. It looks at access as a process which mediates research encounters to become part of knowledge construction. Anthropologists have dealt with the issue of access in fieldwork plans by involving local assistants, networks and offers of gifts. The need to gain physical access to the people anthropologists study co-resides with the emphasis on obtaining the confidence of research participants and privileging their perspectives on their lives. What the emphasis obscures is that access is not just about what anthropologists can know about these 'others', but also what they give to the process. The fieldwork encounter is located and informed by different trajectories of knowledge construction. The trajectories constantly position the issue of access as shaped by varied understandings of self and other through debates in the academic setting, and through fieldwork interventions and negotiations. Thus, I locate the issue of access in practices of gaining knowledge, and explore the unfolding of these practices between persons as self and others which are intertwined in the various kinds of scrutiny of knowledge construction in the academic and the research sites.

At one level, the paper considers access as ways that I come to know through particular encounters in the different sites. At another level, it probes the connections in the different sites by drawing on specific thematic issues and analytical focus through my efforts to access research participants. The paper examines material on fieldwork interactions in Guyana to illustrate access as a two-way process, inclusive of how research participants also gaze at the researcher. Thus, 'being there' is also shaped by what research participants make of the anthropologist's project/presence (see Rabinow 1977: 48–49; Brettell 1993; Halstead 2001). The experience of 'being there'[2] is the reference for anthropologists' positioning. It is a point from which anthropologists can return. The anthropologist's reliance on 'being there' in order to know is also about her/his positioning in and by the academic and explicit research sites. His or her reflections on all this as an ongoing process of discovery also constructs the ethnographic present. These reflections extend the notion beyond dualistic understandings of a positioned present. The term, 'ethnographic present', has to be understood beyond 'ordinary historical categories', as Kirsten Hastrup (1990) has noted. But it is also a category given meaning through various moments of discovery as particular kinds of access into what we come to know (see Strathern 1999).

In this paper, I explore the intertwined forms of access, beyond physical access to the field-sites, as a gaining of confidence and in some cases not gaining it, and as *knowing* the 'field' and field-site before entering it, which allowed certain themes to emerge in my research. This led to an overarching mode of difference and scrutiny from which I made sense of the material by also probing the preoccupation of anthropology with the boundaries between self and other and the interfaces between these boundaries. I had to understand the different ways I was both insider and outsider, how my research participants wanted me to occupy these positions in different contexts, and how all this replayed into academic debates. While my initial efforts to gain physical access relied on certain strategies that also drew on 'insider' understandings, access in the research sites became ongoing, embodied as the *research*. In these exchanges my positioning as both insider and outsider relied on negotiating the boundaries between self and other, learning anew what was familiar both as academic theory and fieldwork material and piecing together a multitude of conflicting accounts interspersed with fragments and seemingly unconnected bits (see Crandall, this volume Ch. 2).

As a researcher of Guyanese East Indian origin, I learnt that my insidership was contextually allocated according to my participant-hosts' status concerns (see Halstead 2001). But I also learnt to make use of this insidership and its repositioning as starting points for finding out that which I knew in different ways where the boundaries and assumptions of this knowledge extended the bases for scrutiny. Virangini Munasinghe (this volume, Ch. 9 & 2001) identifies how the literature positioned East Indians in the Caribbean region, where they could never be Creole, as people who were culture-carriers rather than creators of culture. Brackette Williams in her 1991 study on Guyana suggests the unsoundness of this culture carrier position in her exploration of their movements across identities and borrowings of cultural forms (see also Jayawardena 1963; Drummond 1980). However, her argument, despite the emphasis on slippage of boundaries, *also* allows for a boundary-focused position. She discusses East Indians' distinctiveness as a tenuous construct: as an argument against the need for racial tensions, this over-relies on describing their forms of distinctiveness as flawed by multiple impure sources and thus obscures the ways this multiplicity constitutes Indianness. East Indians demonstrate awareness of the various aspects of their identities: they carry out intra-group scrutiny of the performative spaces of Indianness and, in doing so, they themselves challenge the boundaries of their *Indian* and *non-Indian* identities as ways of being Indian. By considering the emergence of these identities in the research encounters I also engage with my research participants' understandings of themselves as knowledgeable people where they privilege their competence in managing different cultural settings. This engagement, in turn, provides for particular kinds of access into these multiple identities and knowledge settings.

I look at these encounters as access which allows for nuanced interfaces of knowledge construction: there is constant negotiation between difference, sameness and their boundaries. I consider these negotiations as endeavours for empathy. Knowledge emerges through the gifts that are offered between the researcher and her participant-hosts. It is transacted through objects and intervenes in the constructing and representing of others.

The Field: Context, Indianness and Gifting

I began my research in the mid-1990s in Guyana in Georgetown and on predominantly East Indian villages on the West Bank Demerara.[3] I was immediately visible as an East Indian woman of educated status who was also a migrant. This was where the term 'East Indian' had different meanings/visibility vis-à-vis various perceptions about these categories. My contextual positioning brought out the notion of 'East Indian' as a problematic, which was also viewed through distance by East Indians. This suggested a shared platform for the encounters, which was, however, based on *shifting ideas of our insidership*.

The term 'East Indian' is used in the Guyana[4] census to identify an ethnic group: it refers to East Indians' collectivity and demarcates them as separate. The categorisation is recognised through their self-description of being Indian, which embraces multiple contexts of Indianness across religions and through their notions of sharing a culture and of acting against this identity.[5] East Indians demonstrate their *Indian identity* through certain public, religious and/or social activities, and where they publicly affirm 'being Indian' through these activities. Public distinctiveness[6] is framed around an idea of an Indian collectivity and the need to render it visible in intra- and inter-group settings. However, East Indians also act in contradiction to this publicness in other contexts.

This partiality encompassed my presence and project on the West Bank Demerara, where I became visible as insider and outsider. I variously gained access by negotiating my prior understandings of status and hospitality. In several instances, I gained access by just turning up and 'explaining' myself. Initially, I visited East Indians in their homes and this would subsequently extend to meetings in social settings such as weddings. I turned up in a couple of instances with a local guide, but without any gifts. This related to my own understanding of how I expected to be received and greeted as an 'educated person', where this also conferred status. In the early stages of my research there were various occasions when someone suggested or indicated their expectations that I should offer a gift. I was bemused and perplexed by these expectations. This was already drawing on how I thought I knew the *field* to be embedded with status interactions which excluded gift requests: this meant that people would not initiate *requests* for gifts. What they did initiate were *offers* of gifts. These gifts were offered to me at various stages in the research.

In exploring the *gifts* exchanged between me and my participant-hosts, I go beyond the offer and expectation of gift items. The notion of gift[7] is discussed in terms of the hospitality and welcome extended to me, the expectations of my presence and what occurred through our encounters as hierarchical exchanges and status transactions (see Mauss 1967; Raheja 1988). Here, the gift emerges as a status and/or knowledge transaction. This is reliant on what I give of myself as a 'loss of particular status' or a sharing of narratives. I also negotiate and/or participate in encounters where my hosts are able to give or demonstrate themselves in status-enhanced gifting capacities and/or as particular knowledgeable persons.

East Indians emerged as knowledgeable persons which, in some instances, provided for a scrutiny of my project. Further, their efforts to know me and my study were contextualised in their own concerns. Several strands emerged around our knowledge concerns: emphasis on global networking activities, cultural transformations and status. In some instances, as both insider and outsider, they constituted me as someone who would listen or who would construct a particular account of how they wanted to be represented. This meant that they saw me in selective ways which variously privileged my gender, my Indian identity and my researcher status. Our subsequent interactions brought out issues of respect and status in different cultural contexts and revealed connections between global networking, their knowledge concerns and their visibility as modern persons. These interactions were both explicit and implicit, and eventually emerged as constructions of different kinds of space. I came to understand these forms of Indianness also through my various positioning by my participants-hosts. My presence and project also intervened in the construction of the research. I had to appreciate explicitly (as against my implicit understandings) the different forms of Indianness with regard to respect notions[8] and respect relations. This was further contexualised in terms of various transformations occurring, particularly so in relation to an an external outside imagined as, and in relation to, America (see Halstead 2002 and 2005).

Partial Persons and the Researcher: Respect and Place

I carried out fieldwork on the West Bank Demerara on several sites which were in proximity to each other. Two were 'proper villages' whilst one was a squatting area where residents had just turned up, and built houses as their primary claim to the land. These sites were visible as *impoverished*, framed by political neglect for rural areas by a past dictatorship, but also by the major ongoing outward migration which affected the country as a whole. Outward migration has led to an extended chain of overseas relatives for many. Guyanese, in general, have also become involved in global networking activities. These activites and people's overseas family connections allow for new forms of income and intercede in the visibility of impoverishment so that the physical conditions are poor indicators of levels of prosperity. The material is drawn largely from a main village, renamed for the purposes of the research as 'Better Prospects'. The renaming is also meant to reflect the efforts of residents to transcend local conditions[9] or to extract a home from the environment where this is conceived as *wild*. This is generally the case in these Guyanese villages, where place emerged as a problem: this environment, has to be distanced to achieve or maintain respect. Further, people generally enacted distance to local conditions through their involvement in an external imaginary. Guyanese saw America variously as a desired destination. Those who were able to achieve outward migration obtained immediate status on this basis, although there was also talk of 'American decadence'[10] (see Halstead 2005). This notion of decadence resonated with local understandings of wildness: East Indians would often speak of people being wild or modern. The physical conditions of the sites on the West Bank Demerara exemplify the idea of wildness.

The presence of the young, in street corner *limes*[11] or behaving badly 'pon (upon) the dam', rendered this wildness visible. The dam is a long, winding, muddy road punctured with holes created by vehicles. The holes turn into puddles following rain. The dam separates the houses from rice fields, but it also represents a site *without respect* so that those standing for any lengthy periods on it also become persons who are without respect. This is in contradiction to the houses, where persons by remaining within the confines of the houses can be seen as maintaining respect (cf. Bourdieu 1979: 89–92). People 'talk name' (identify negatively through gossip) of those on the dam: I initially became aware of this when during one of my visits to the home of an extended family, several women told me unprompted about the wild behaviour of a neighbour's daughter who was *walking out* on the dam. 'Walking out' meant that she was displaying herself inappropriately and, thus, inviting advances from the opposite sex – the physical space of the dam was complicit in this visibility. By walking out, this 'wild person' became someone who was uncaring of being seen to engage in conversations with men and, thus, uncaring of maintaining respect. The women made gestures to indicate where she lived and also to distance themselves from her.

As a researcher, my presence on the dam was in order to gain access to the houses rather than as someone who was just liming. Their knowledge of my researcher status interceded in possible interpretations of my presence. I met with people on the dam who were also willing to stop and talk with me. Thus, despite the interactions around respect in terms of the *public* and *private* conduct of the residents, I achieved a certain leeway in presenting myself and my research project in 'research conversations'. My occupation of conducting research on the dam meant that I occupied a different space from that occupied by the young woman mentioned above. But there were other factors which 'assisted' in my positive visibility. In particular, my educated and migrant status, which helped to alter my visibility as an East Indian woman *within* respect relations, to that of a migrant researcher with possible status-enhancing global connections (see Halstead 2001).

In some of the conversations which emerged between me and various persons on the dam, I was asked questions which privileged my overseas residence and the networking possibilities this offered: for instance, could I help with overseas migration, did I know of a potential bridegroom overseas? It was in my visits to the houses that the focus on my outsider status altered. Further, the concerns about the properties of the dam as a respect 'saboteur' demonstrated the *community* through notions of respect. Thus, it was also about the different ways my presence – or how the absence of my presence was imagined in relation to particular spaces – could be transformed into gifts to provide status and satisfaction, that informed these interactions.

Access Through and Beyond Prescribed Indianness: 'Naked-skin' Women and Respect

I entered into roles that brought out the issues around respect and status, and came to understand these issues through the intra-group scrutiny carried out by my participant-hosts in different cultural contexts. In all of this, I had to be *known* as a listener in specific ways by my participant-hosts. One woman, Anjie,[12] offered to tell me her story on tape as an account of how she had been a victim of 'Indian culture'. She had been forced into marriage by her parents after her sister had been seen talking to a man on the Ferry; she felt that Indian culture was to blame for the loss of her further education, which she had to forego. However, this blame became selective in those instances where she saw other aspects of Indian culture that were desirable and to which she subscribed. Another, a grandmother, Sati, in an extended household in a nearby village, told me a story about her marriage that was a secret. This disclosure came after I told her about my deceased grandmother, and showed that this relationship and her loss had meant much to me.

As a conventional woman, Sati *had to* participate in her own secret Hindu wedding rites on the day of her son's marriage. This was because she had decided not to go through with a 'bamboo wedding' (Hindu rites) in order to avoid what she thought was a family curse: her belief in this curse emerged after her sister had died following *her* wedding ceremony and Sati believed that she too would die shortly after a similar wedding ceremony. However, to participate in her son's ceremony, she had to wear *sindhoor*, a red dot on her forehead, which symbolises her married status and which is first placed by the groom during the ceremony. As Sati had never carried out the rites, she could not wear sindhoor. She consulted with the *pandit* (Hindu priest) who was already present to officiate at her son's wedding. He brushed aside her fears of a family curse and advocated an immediate and secret ceremony to precede her son's wedding. Sati's granddaughter learnt of this secret wedding for the first time when Sati told me about it during one of my visits. She narrated this story after I had visited her and her extended family on a number of occasions. But on this visit she became curious about my involvement in my research. She wanted to know how it was that I could visit so often to listen to other people. At that stage, I told her about my maternal grandmother who had had many interesting accounts to tell me about herself and others.

By itself, Sati's account was interesting and added to accounts of specific forms of *being Indian*. However, other insights emerged through my connecting of the conventional Sati (who emerged in the above) to the present-day woman who was uncaring of certain other conventions; these insights allowed me to piece together understandings around respect and its transformations. This also drew on various other interactions with women, men and children. The second account is around Sati's television viewing of an American soap opera, *The Young and the Restless*. Sati's husband had expressed his displeasure with her viewing it. He told her she would turn into the 'half-naked man and half-naked woman' who were featured on the soap opera. This meant that Sati could become 'naked-skin' not by losing clothes but by losing respect. Despite the respect due to him in terms of 'wifely duty', Sati did not listen to him, but continued to view the soap opera.

The soap opera is deemed to be highly immoral generally among Guyanese, but is also highly popular. One woman noted that women were so immersed in the soap opera, they 'nah kay if picknie dead', that is, they could not be dislodged from viewing even if their children were dying. Among East Indians, the open viewing of the programme by women contradicts certain conventions of how women are meant to uphold the 'culture', and breaches notions of respect. The association of women with the soap opera unveils them outside of their traditional role as upholders of culture. The practice of viewing this 'immoral' soap opera in a communal space affects the dynamics of these respect displays where women can contextually 'invite' shame by watching 'shameless programming' openly. The concern of how women appear is also about the communal loss of respect which ensues – that is to say, women do not appear in gendered isolation, but are visible in a representative capacity to maintain the family's respect and guard against shame. Men would support women in this role by displaying expressions of uneasiness to sexuality as public attitudes of respect. They are conscious of the possibilities of shame in their attitudes to women and generally in their behaviour in a communal or prescribed public space.[13] In the efforts to safeguard against this loss which may occur vis-à-vis the open viewing of the *Young and the Restless,* some men publicly deny that the women in their household would view such a programme; efforts by some men, women and children discourage others from viewing it.

In one extended household, a young boy would turn off the set so that his grandmother would not view 'naked-skin' (people both scantily-dressed and without respect) white people. Another grandmother surreptitiously watches this and other 'English' (American) programming in a communal space which includes her grown children. Similarly, young girls negotiate how others see their viewing of this soap opera and similar programmes in the communal space. If they are present in this space, they demonstrate various forms of avoidance and embarrassment when certain scenes are featured – such as 'bending my head', as one young woman noted, or by looking away. While there are generational issues here on respect, the interactions are not limited to young people and grandmothers. Rather, the roles of women and men feature centrally in notions of respect and in its negotiations: the open viewing of the soap opera by many women of various age groups is met with dismay by men, some women and children.

The emphasis here is on the word 'open', which raises various kinds of publics. There is, first of all, the public as constituted by the *communal space* in the domestic setting. In this space, respect has to be negotiated against the activities of the 'open viewers'. How this space is negotiated relies on the ascribed attitude each person present in this space is *meant* to have in terms of respect around the central narrative of women as cultural upholders; it also relies on a public absence of women's sexuality. As noted, men support the expectations of women in this role through their public demonstration of uneasiness, which allows them to express respect to women. Other persons such as children or grandparents in this space are expected to add to respect through their expressions of deference or duty and through emphasising proper behaviour: this is demonstrated in the attitudes of the young people above to deter the communal viewing of the soap opera. But the contradictions which also emerge in this space demonstrate that it is also constituted through behaviour which goes against *respect*, and where the emphasis on a selective Indian identity is shown as contextual and partial.

Knowing the Researcher through Different Kinds of Public

To gain an appreciation of these contrasting attitudes to respect in this communal space and the ways these emerge under my gaze, I have to consider how I am also constituted as a *particular public* in terms of how my participants position me. This publicness is also complicit with my understandings of my academic agenda as one implicated in current approaches to fieldwork and anthropological knowledge construction (see Nencel and Pels 1991; Brettel 1993; Narayan 1993; Gupta and Ferguson 1997; Bunzl 2004, Linger 2005). I do not appear in isolation as the researcher, but in my various guises which are also constructed and embedded in local forms of constituting publicness. These local forms emerge through the negotiations of respect and display of Indian distinctiveness in communal settings within the home, through public gatherings and in the way the environment is separated from these settings and seen as part of *wildness*, the 'other' of respect. My efforts to access East Indians in these various spaces are also about my varying appearances in different guises of knowing. My need to understand and to *access* becomes an exchange of gifts where my hosts position me as both self and other. Their positioning brings out their negotiations of different kinds of visibility.

When a woman with her daughter stands at the doorway of their kitchen and gestures to me that they view the *Young and the Restless* contrary to what the woman's husband is saying to me in their living room *simultaneously*, their disclosure assumes my complicit understanding of these contradictions. I have a different kind of access to this woman and her daughter than to that of the host. The woman's husband endeavours to manage the knowledge I gain of those activities:what I (come to) know may demonstrate for him a loss of respect.

As a woman, I am privileged in the communication with the women standing by the doorway to the kitchen, which goes beyond my host's public statement. Our silent and subversive communication acknowledges my presence as East Indian woman: I am expected to understand the dualism which constructs the East Indian woman publicly outside of 'bad behaviour'. The women's readiness to admit knowledge of this 'decadent Western soap opera' also has to be probed in terms of their possible positioning of my presence as researcher. Further, my visibility as a 'Western researcher' is encompassed in my participants' understandings of the West as part of Indianness. These women are visible through the ways they are both *Indian* and *non-Indian:* this encompasses their inhabiting of a redefined West (see Carrier 1995; Clifford 1997; Trouillot 2003).

In this household, I am constituted as two different kinds of public at the same time – one who *can* know and one who *must not* know. The husband's denial of the women's viewing constructed me as a public who must only observe a confirmation of respect in this communal setting. The husband is keeping at a distance the 'audience' who has to be provided with a specific knowledge of Indianness through notions of respect: this is particularly so in this setting, where the women's propriety has to be upheld to maintain his respect. In this emphasis on women's roles, he separates them from an everyday setting, where women act in contradiction to respect, but also he separates me from my likely knowledge of these contradictions as East Indian; he does so by locating/isolating me as an external public. This management of my *access* is partly about guarding against shame as a result of being seen to lose respect publicly. But given the construction of Indianness through these contradictions and where there is knowledge within the community of how people will behave against respect, this is also an attempt at maintaining a particular image of being Indian under the gaze of a public seen as other – *someone who cannot be allowed to share his space for shame.*

Insider and Outsider Positioning in Indian Distinctiveness

In appreciating the different displays simultaneously provided by the husband and wife above, I have to consider that insider and outsider are differently constructed within this communal space in the home, as compared with that of the public communal space. This is demonstrated in the home through a different emphasis on demonstrating respect. The negotiations of respect are the domain of the private communal setting and reflected, for instance, in the ways spaces within the house are arranged in contrast to a wild outside, such as the dam.

In the public communal setting, which includes 'wedding houses' and '*jandhi* houses' (Hindu religious occasions), the emphasis is on the display of culture and its correct performance, which are already embedded in understandings of respect. In this setting, the emphasis on performing culture as a duty, assumes the role of and inscribes women as cultural upholders. There are no *prescribed* spaces for discussing/condemning wildness of women – people will 'talk-name' in these and other forums. However, these discussions of who may have lost their good name through particular conduct/shameless behaviour are carried on 'privately' rather than as a public part of the proceedings.

There are, however, acknowledged spaces for contra-traditional behaviour by women in 'women only' forums, despite the emphasis on duty and women as cultural upholders. This is particularly so in ceremonies which precede weddings, which allows for the *dig dutty* (a Friday night ceremony preceding the main Hindu wedding ceremony), which also becomes the women's night (see Halstead 2001). The inclusion of this contra-traditional women-only space acknowledges the way women act contrary to their prescribed roles. It is incorporated as a private event within the public communal setting, but explicitly outside of a *shared*, particular public gaze. The incorporation of the event also shows how distinctiveness is constituted through management of the multiplicity of Indianness.

The public communal setting as a display of distinctiveness shifts the emphasis on women and respect to that of culture and of performing culture in the 'correct' manner (see Halstead 2000). However, women remain central to the process of upholding respect although their adherence to duty and respect is assumed to be present. The women-only forum as an acknowledged space outside respect achieves and identifies a public dualism that is present mainly through uneasiness in the private communal setting. But the presence of this forum in the public setting also demonstrates that these displays of distinctiveness have to accommodate and are constituted through multiple understandings of Indianness.

Thus, in the public communal space, the concern is with performing Indian culture where knowledgeable persons emerge: those who *know* what is *correct* and those who reflect on the 'correct' as a construct. As Indian, I am explicitly positioned as someone who will endorse these displays. As an insider within the display of Indian distinctiveness, I am inscribed with the task to *represent* Indian culture in positive ways: In this context, I occupy an apparently unquestionable position as the person recording Indian culture. But as a researcher seeking to understand how these different displays construct knowledge, I become complicit with those who also question the construct of distinctiveness as ways of understanding their own identities – that is, I become various particularised kinds of knowledgeable person. In these guises, I experience the displays of distinctiveness as an emphasis on demonstrating Indian culture, but one which also emerges through efforts by me and others to understand it as a construct or to demonstrate other identities alongside the display.

Whilst the literature identifies the erosion of boundaries, East Indians also reflexively engage with the reformulating and altering of these boundaries in and through the construct of distinctiveness. This reflexivity is present through the efforts of those who attempt to understand the contradictions and have *roles in the* processes of constructing distinctiveness. The processes can be encountered and shaped by intra-group scrutiny and derision, where persons become critical of women and men who redirect attention to specific notions of respect and those women and young people who are seen to go against it. In contrast to this space for mockery, various other persons emerge: the reflective person who is also a cultural leader, the reflexive person who engages beyond culture as part of global networking, and those who are able to manage their involvement in the different cultural settings without having an explicit need to show themselves through culture loss or as culture-restricted. Their various activities demonstrate different spaces of being Indian within the construct of distinctiveness. This is where they also form a collectivity in order to display distinctiveness.

Knowing the Performative Spaces of Being Indian

Various individuals who also occupy public roles reflect on or demonstrate other aspects of themselves in specific ways, even while they have to carry out certain activities to orchestrate or maintain distinctiveness in the public communal space. At public ritualistic ceremonies, there are usually various 'knowledgeable persons' who occupy roles of advice and instruction in the 'proper' enactment of the rituals. Within the mode of distinctiveness my presence is immediately visible as someone 'recording' Indian culture. However, my encounters with various individuals who assist in the display of distinctiveness and thus maintain Indian culture are encounters of the varied approaches to these displays and to their identities.

In previous publications I have discussed these contradictions through ceremonial activities, conversations with my participant-hosts and observations on the West Bank Demerara (Halstead 2000, 2001, 2005). I revisit some of this material to bring out further reflection on the data which helped me to understand my research-participants' forms of being modern as implicated in different kinds of knowledge and different visibilities of the persons. I consider one interpretation of my positioning by a food-sharer at a Hindu wedding known as a *Kanyadaan* (gift of the maiden). I had previously reflected on the food-sharer's comment that I videod myself whilst eating with my hand as an example of how he had positioned me as an insider and where, as an insider, I then had to provide positive representations of Indian culture (Halstead 2001).

This interpretation was still part of what was going on, but as I continued to reflect on this and other encounters, it became clear that there were other issues embedded in this positioning. As an invitee and visiting researcher at this particular wedding ceremony, I had moved among the guests with a video camera, entering into impromptu conversations at various stages, when someone suddenly pushed a leaf of food into my hand. I did not consciously switch role from researcher to invitee, which could be read as moving from 'outsider' to 'insider', when I took the leaf, put my camera down and began to eat with my hands as others were doing nearby, although I was trying to be part of the setting. But this must have been visible to the food-sharer who suggested I videod myself. Later, I realised that my task of researching Indians had produced for some who were 'observing' me a strange context as a result of my own East Indian origins. But what was also part of this strangeness was that my observation of this setting of Indian distinctiveness for academic purposes suggested an emphasis that might insufficiently account for East Indians' distinctiveness as a public display and insufficiently show that they were not bounded within it. Thus, the food-sharer's comment that I turn the camera on myself was also a redefining of our terms of understanding each other where he rendered himself visible outside of the display of distinctiveness by locating me more firmly within it. This switching of roles of who was self and who was other could also be considered in terms of the construction of distinctiveness as an assemblage of persons who can claim some visibility as persons while they are also acting as a collective: this allows for the distinctiveness to be constituted through acknowledgement and/or reliance on the partial visibility of persons.

My encounters with the officiating pandit at this ceremony add to this material. This pandit lives in one of the villages on the West Bank and in New York. He demonstrates a general involvement with 'the outside' which enters into the displays of Indianness: during the wedding ceremony, the pandit makes constant references to what was occurring in the New York East Indian migrant setting. He himself is a regular commuter between New York and his home in Guyana, as a US green card holder[14] and as a pandit who officiates at ceremonies in New York.

He necessarily has to re-state certain expectations with regard to notions of respect: thus, during the wedding ceremony, he tells the bride: 'You must obey your husband ... that is your duty'. At the same time, he is conscious of ways Indian culture is not being upheld outside of these public ritualistic settings and spends time reflecting on these 'changes'. He notes that *Indian culture* cannot really be found outside of the public settings of functions, that there are all kinds of different behaviour occurring outside of these settings which for him pose questions and problems of trying to understand what it means. His reflections do not focus on the changes around women and respect: rather, it has to do with understanding Indian culture as a construct, where, for instance, people do *Jandhis* (Hindu ceremonies of worship) and then behave outside respect (show themselves as explicitly wild, for instance), or have to be 'coerced' into wearing ethnic clothing.[15]

The ceremony mentioned above, at which he officiates, is an opportunity to reaffirm publicly what it means to be Indian. But it is also an opportunity for scrutiny and expressions of a complementary identity expressed in relation to the display of being publicly Indian. These contradictions come out through discussions by some of the guests among themselves, where ideally they are supposed to concentrate on the ceremony instead of carrying on conversations, on domestic matters or 'talk-name' about people's (wild) behaviour, for instance, as noted. The *nowa*, an old woman who is helper to the pandit brings the bad behaviour publicly into the ceremonial setting through her constant cursing which is ignored and where as the old woman who *knows* the correct traditions she transcends her gendered position of upholding respect (see Halstead 2001). The pandit finds opportunities when he is not officiating, but still present at the ceremony, to tell people how to 'behave', by telling them how not to behave or by commenting on the contradictions in a paternal way, which suggests that he has the right to offer these strictures by virtue of his pandit's role.

As a *person* who also reflects on all this, the pandit has to find a way to make sense of the contradictions outside of 'culture-loss' talk, which readily accompanies public distinctive settings, and as a suitable way of deploring this contra-behaviour which goes against this space. As a pandit, he emerges as knowledgeable about Indian culture. He then has to navigate how this category occupies different spaces, as someone who officiates and encourages Indians to be *Indian*, but also someone who *appreciates* the ways in which the contradictions constitute people's identities. As pandit he has the space to be knowledgeable. This concern with knowledge is common.

Within a reflective space, the pandit is more concerned with understanding the contradictions between Indian distinctiveness and the ways people act against this, generally, rather than the specific role of women who must uphold duty to their husbands. Notably, his wife exercises her freedom to be outspoken to the point where she rebukes him in my presence for disclosing certain information to me when I visit their home. He also 'gathers' together people with whom he can engage in conversation about these cultural contradictions, where, outside of his officiating role as pandit at various ceremonies, he is not prepared to make claims for notions of respect against what he sees going on. He can talk, for instance, about the way people are not upholding culture. He invites his neighbour with whom he chats regularly about these issues to come and meet with me and to tell me more about culture.

His acknowledgement of my research and my access is about how he positions me as someone who will write about Indian culture as part of an *institution*, something that needs to be documented and which attracts research. My access is also about my status as a researcher and migrant, where I am more visible as part of knowledge settings than in relation to gendered constructs around respect. This access is a positioning I have to understand by probing beyond the issues of respect and the co-residing narratives of 'culture loss' and wildness. This allows me to explore further the contextual (in)visibility of persons in settings of distinctiveness.

Distinctiveness and the Object of Research

As *East Indian*, I understood the strong sense of being distinctively Indian and the importance attached to this identity outside of an instrumentalist space. I was also aware of how people were critical of those with cultural pretensions, which provided for different kinds of Indianness outside of spaces for carrying out traditions. *As researcher, I had to extend a taken-for-granted frame around these understandings.* This was supported and directed by my observations and the emergence of ideas and visibility of 'knowledgeable people'. This was both in the public settings of Indian distinctiveness and in the ways these settings were used by persons to show themselves as knowledgeable by being part of or by distancing themselves from these displays.

I further consider the above in terms of the key literature by Chandra Jaywardena (1963, 1980) and Brackette Williams (1991), which looks at the issue of distinctiveness in Guyana through opposing frameworks.[16] Jayawardena is concerned with showing how certain activities reveal them as Indian whereas Williams points out that while their Indian activities are meant to render them distinctive these rely on tenuous boundaries,[17] as noted above. In both these works, the issue of authenticity is present, but again in different ways. Jayawardena focuses on the 'social significance of a custom' to show that it demonstrates an Indian identity and he does so outside of the issue of authenticity (1963: 24–25). However, Williams challenges their distinctiveness on the basis of this being inauthentic. In her study on a mixed coastal village in Guyana, Williams (1991: 252) notes that in the intensity of social and cultural interaction among these various ethnic groups, the claimed distinctiveness which demarcates ethnic cultures becomes 'increasingly difficult to sustain'.

Although Williams argues for mixedness and blurred boundaries, this over-relies on ideas of authenticity and purity in terms of these categories being the starting points which have to be and are readily disproved as the basis for distinctiveness. This reliance also shifts the emphasis from the actual emergence and maintenance of distinctiveness. This shift obscures how distinctiveness is constituted through the movements in different cultural settings: thus, rather than 'inauthentic Indians' becoming visible in these displays, *persons* (as culturally *un-marked* and thus not bounded in particular identities) become invisible and *Indians* appear.

The different understandings here of East Indians as distinctive, in one instance, and of this distinctiveness being readily challenged in terms of how they acted against this identity became a point of departure where I had the choice to collect material for and against distinctiveness: this was particularly through the proclaimed spaces for displaying distinctiveness and the emphasis on respect alongside loss of respect. However, I came to understand these forms of Indianness not as an argument against ethnic and cultural boundaries, but as an understanding of East Indians' belonging within and outside these boundaries. The contradictions embodied their identities and re-affirmed or allowed them to move across certain boundaries: this was demonstrated in terms of their visibility in different cultural settings and, in turn, my presence and positioning in these settings.

Conclusion

The paper examined access as practices informing knowledge construction. It considered the negotiation of self and other positions in the field-sites as a field also defined by academic theorising. It explored the interactions as an unfolding of particular forms of visibility and showed that as the researcher I was also located as insider and outsider. This both challenged and reconstructed my insidership and allowed for the research to emerge through encounters marked by our free and forced forms of symbolic and other exchanges.

By probing these encounters and the ways my participants-hosts also encountered 'Indian culture' and its other, I was able to appreciate that these cultural tensions fed into the constructions of Indianness through self and other understandings. This engaged not with defining boundaries and considering their authenticity, but with probing the construction and erosion of these boundaries vis-à-vis particular understandings of being Indian or acting against specific ideas of Indian culture. The material on respect and its perceived loss led me to consider how respect entered into intra-group scrutiny as debates about being 'real Indians' in relation to status bids. These authenticity issues were also about expressing understandings of the person in *Indian* and *non-Indian* contexts. Given the intensity of the interactions around notions of respect, the issue of access into the material and into 'systematising' knowledge construction inevitably had to be navigated through multiple accounts and constant efforts to understand the contradictions through this multiplicity.

In terms of constructing the account for the academe, it seemed important to extract 'sense' from all this as conclusive. In terms of understanding people from their local and various perspectives, it was about engaging with the 'problem' of establishing boundaries between these perspectives and others as potential culture-bound or academic-bound approaches. It became an issue of people demonstrating themselves in knowledge settings. This variously emerged through my presence as researcher, through their emphasis on knowing 'authentic culture' and through their ways of being modern, which also allowed them to be visible outside of cultural and ethnic identities. Access here emerged from my ability to listen, to empathise and to share and acknowledge the connectedness of our different kinds of knowledge. As East Indian, I too moved within and outside my prescribed East Indianness. In doing so, I entered into and experienced 'self and other' settings with my participant-hosts as an exchange of gifts.

Notes

1. A version of this paper was given as an invited lecture at Maynooth, NUI, in September 2005. I thank Lawrence Taylor for inviting me. I also thank James Saris, Chandana Mathur and other participants for their very helpful comments. I am grateful to Eric Hirsch for his comments on various versions of this paper. I remain grateful to my participant-hosts for their hospitality and gifts.
2. The idea of being there, once the 'authoritative' stamp for ethnographer and her/his claims has been subjected to much scrutiny and critique (Geertz 1988; Fox 1991: 6; see Hastrup 1990: 49, 1995: 19).
3. As an overseas researcher from a university in England, it was relatively easy to gain physical access to people's homes in the Guyanese field-sites. This ease was aided by a leisurely pace that was not present when I subsequently carried out research on the predominantly Indo-Guyanese locality in New York. When residents were at home, they were 'at home' in the Guyanese settings without the sense of urgency that their time was in demand elsewhere and, thus, they had a 'lot of time to spend' with visitors. Time, however, was differently managed in New York, where people were rarely at home during the day.
4. The term 'Indian' is in common use, however, and they are also known as 'Indo-Guyanese.
5. See Seecharan (1997) for a discussion of how Brahmans moved among the low caste to spread Sanatan Dharma, and Vertovec (1992), who notes the varied traditions of East Indian immigrants in Trinidad. More recently, Stephanides and Singh (2000) point to how *Kalimai* worship (of the Hindu Goddess Kali) moved across different strata from Madrassi to Sanatan Dharmists.
6. East Indians came to then British Guiana as indentured immigrants from diverse cultural backgrounds, and would construct a collectivity across religious, cultural and regional divides.
7. See Halstead (2001) for a discussion on a gift request by one of my hosts, and in which I was able to understand my contextual positioning as insider and outsider through these and other interactions. I also discuss how various hosts offered me gifts, in a paper, '*Mediating access and modernity through food*', presented at ASA 2003.
8. The issue of respect compares with the regional literature which has discussed notions of reputation and respectability as colonial-centric and which divided Caribbean society into two cultural poles (see Wilson 1969). These concepts have limited application in a focus which elided other cultural influences. The literature discusses how women following colonial influences were the maintainers and upholders of domestic life. Men were engaged in 'liming' activities such as gambling and drinking, as part of peer group activities. Olwig (1995: 69) points to the establishing of an egalitarian order by the Methodists in 1789 in the West Indies which saw notions of respectability modelled on eighteenth-century England. In this ethos, people were expected to be greatly restrained in their sexual behaviour. Being sexually tempted and idle was interlinked with poverty.
9. In 2005 there was much evidence of physical transformation, as residents had been granted titles to the land, roads were being built, a number of houses had been impressively renovated and some new houses were being built.
10. In my research on the migrant destination of New York, this notion of American decadence explicitly emerged to create *new boundaries* around Indian culture. This also contested decadent modernity as against that which was desirable: both forms of modernity were located by East Indians as American.
11. Limes are social gatherings of once disreputable activities of men, but which still have negative aspects, although no longer gendered – as located here in notions of place and respect (cf. Wilson 1969, Olwig 1995: 69).

12. All names are pseudonyms.
13. Daniel Miller describes a different setting in Trinidad, where sexual freedom is linked to the concept of bacchanal (scandal and confusion) and where men, including some East Indians, were known to have 'deputies', the term for lovers who supplanted wives in various social settings (Miller 1994).
14. Resident US status.
15. This is usually worn only on ceremonial and religious occasions.
16. Both of these works refer to particular histories in terms of the political setting and they also detail status interactions around the need of Guyanese to become somebody (Williams 1991) and of East Indians to prevent 'eyepass' (insult) against them (Jayawardena 1963).
17. See Cohen (2002) for a revised approach against the idea of community being constructed at its boundaries; see Amit (2002) for various discussions of what goes on within the boundaries.

References

Amit, Vered (ed.). 2002. *Realizing Community: Concepts, Social Relationships and Sentiments.* London: Routledge.

Bourdieu, Pierre. 1979. *Outline of a Theory of Practice*, trans. by Richard Nice. Cambridge: Cambridge University Press.

Brettell, Caroline B. (ed.). 1993. *When They Read What We Write: The Politics of Ethnography.* London: Bergin and Garvey.

Bunzl, Matti. 2004. 'Boas, Foucault, and the "Native Anthropologist": Notes toward a Neo-Boasian Anthropology', *American Anthropologist* 106(3): 435–42.

Carrier, James (ed.). 1995. *Occidentalism: Images of the West.* Oxford: Clarendon Press.

Clifford, James. 1997. *Routes: Travel and Translation in the Late Twentieth Century.* London: Harvard University Press.

Cohen, Anthony P. 2002. 'Epilogue', in Vered Amit (ed.), *Realizing Community: Concepts, Social Relationships and Sentiments.* London: Routledge, pp. 165–70.

Drummond, Lee. 1980. 'A Cultural Continuum: A Theory of Intersystems', *Man* 15(2): 352–74.

Fox, Richard G. 1991. 'Introduction', in Richard E. Fox (ed) *Recapturing Anthropology: Working in the Present.* New Mexico: School of American Research Press, pp. 1–44.

Geertz, Clifford. 1988. *Work and Lives: The Anthropologist as Author.* Standford: Standford University Press.

Gupta, Akhil and James Ferguson. 1997. 'Discipline and Practice: "The Field" as Site, Method and Location in Anthropology', in Akhil Gupta and James Ferguson (eds), *Anthropological Locations: Boundaries and Grounds of a Field Science.* London: University of California Press, pp. 1–46.

Halstead, Narmala. 2000. 'Switching Identities: Movements between "Indian" and "Non-Indian" in Guyana', *Anthropology in Action* 7(1–2): 22–32.

_____. 2001. 'Ethnographic Encounters: Positionings Within and Outside the Insider Frame', *Social Anthropology* 9(3): 307–21.

_____. 2002. 'Branding Perfection: Foreign as Self; Self as "Foreign-foreign"', *Journal of Material Culture* 7(3): 273–93.

_____. 2005. 'Belonging and Respect Notions vis-à-vis Modern East Indians: Hindi Movies in the Guyanese East Indian Diaspora', in Raminder Kaur and Ajay Sinha (eds), *Bollyworld: Indian Cinema through a Transnational Lens*. New Delhi: Sage, pp. 261–83.

Hastrup, Kirsten. 1990. 'The Ethnographic Present: A Re-invention', Cultural Anthropology 5(1): 45–61.

_____. 1995. *A Passage to Anthropology: Between Experience & Theory*. London: Routledge.

Jayawardena, Chandra. 1963. *Conflict and Solidarity on a Guianese Plantation*. London: The Athlone Press.

_____. 1980. 'Culture and Ethnicity in Guyana and Fiji', *Man*. (N. S.) 15(3): 430–50.

Linger, Daniel Touro. 2005. *Anthropology through a double lens. Public and Personal Worlds in Human Theory*. Philadelphia, P.A.: University of Pennsylvania Press.

Mauss, Marcel. 1967. *The Gift: Forms and Functions of Exchange in Archaic Societies*, trans. Ian Cunnison. New York: Norton.

Miller, Daniel. 1994. *Modernity: An Ethnographic Approach: Dualism and Mass Consumption in Trinidad*. Oxford: Berg.

Munasinghe, Viranjini. 2001. *Callaloo or Tossed Salad: East Indians and the Cultural Politics of Identity in Trinidad*. Ithaca: Cornell University Press.

Narayan, Kirin. 1993. 'How Native is a "Native" Anthropologist?', *American Anthropologist* 95(3): 671–86.

Nencel, Lorraine and Peter Pels. 1991. 'Introduction: Critique and the Deconstruction of Anthropological Authority', in Lorraine Nencel and Peter Pels (eds), *Constructing Knowledge: Authority and Critique in Social Science*. London: Sage, pp. 1–21.

Olwig, Karen Fog. 1995. *Global Culture, Island Identity: Continuity and Change in the Afro-Caribbean Community of Nevis*. Philadelphia: Harwood Academic Publishers.

Rabinow, Paul. 1977. *Reflections on Fieldwork in Morocco*. London: University of California Press.

Raheja, Gloria Goodwin. 1988. *The Poison in the Gift: Ritual, Prestation and the Dominant Caste in a North Indian Village*. Chicago: University of Chicago Press.

Seecharan, Clem. 1997. *Tiger in the Stars: The Anatomy of Indian Achievement in British Guiana 1919–29*. London: Macmillan Education.

Stephanides, Stephanos and Karna Singh. 2000. *Translating Kali's Feast: The Goddess in Indo-Caribbean Ritual and Fiction*. Amsterdam: Rodopi.

Strathern, Marilyn. 1999. *Property, Substance and Effect: Anthropological Essays on Persons and Things*. London: Athlone Press.

Trouillot, Michel-Rolph. 2003. *Global Transformations: Anthropology and the Modern World*. Hampshire, England: Palgrave Macmillan.

Vertovec, Steven. 1992. *Hindu Trinidad: Religion, Ethnicity and Socio-economic Change*. London: Macmillan Caribbean.

Williams, Brackette. 1991. *Stains on my Name, War in my Veins, Guyana and the Politics of Cultural Struggle*. London: Duke University Press.

Wilson, Peter. 1969. 'Reputation and Respectability: A Suggestion for Caribbean Ethnology', *Man* 4(1): 70–84.

Chapter 6

Knowledge from the Body: Fieldwork, Power and the Acquisition of a New Self

Konstantinos Retsikas

Over recent years there has been serious debate within the discipline about the nature of fieldwork – anthropology's centrepiece and distinct characteristic – and the constitution of knowledge that stems from such an intensive and transformative encounter with the Other, however the latter(s) is construed. The debate follows from the postmodernist critique of the 1980s and the interrogation of the claims to objectivity of traditional ethnography, according to which facts are always somehow out there, pre-existing and fixed, waiting to be discovered by inquisitive and impartial observers (Clifford and Marcus 1986; Haraway 1991). In place of such epistemological fictions, the postmodernist movement argued for the recognition of anthropological knowledge as being subjective and partial due to being conditioned as much by the cultural baggage the anthropologist carries in the field, and his/her specific positioning(s) during fieldwork, as by the historically specific textual strategies of what Spencer (1989) calls 'ethnographic realism'. As a result, a new epistemological paradigm was introduced. This was founded on the centrality of reflexivity, according to which anthropological knowledge is seen as the product of social interactions between the anthropologist and an array of multi-positioned informants in a field impregnated by constant negotiations and contestations, and a 'dialogic' mode of ethnographic rhetoric, itself based on democratic ethics and characterised by polyphony, discord and indeterminacy.

This kind of engagement with reflexivity has quite recently been subjected to further scrutiny. While there is a wide acceptance of the need to produce 'situated' accounts with the anthropologist's role as an active agent in the construction of ethnographic accounts being readily acknowledged (Okely and Callaway 1992), a certain uneasiness has emerged with respect to postmodernism's singular critical focus on techniques of textual representation as a remedy for anthropological ills. Such a focus, Turner objects 'has all too often constructed [the reflexive anthropologist] as a sentient consciousness reflecting on fieldwork without any consideration of the implications of his or her physical presence in the field' (2000: 52). This emphasis, thus, has reintroduced from the back door, as it were, one of the basic premises of Western epistemology that postmodernism itself tried to transcend, namely that of the body-mind dichotomy. Reflexivity is commonly portrayed as an activity that takes place after fieldwork has been completed, in the solitude of one's office when we self-consciously go about practising our profession, writing ethnographies (see Watson 1999: 4). Such a high degree of separateness between doing anthropology as predicated on living in close proximity with the Other, and writing with the Other-in-mind from afar, reproduces historical conventions about the nature of academic work and the workings of human cognition of a certain Platonic rather than Heraklitian persuasion. In this vein, textual reflexivity seems to me to reduce fieldwork as experience to an after-thought, implying that experience is important only to the extent that it comes to, or is brought to thought and linguistic expression. At the centre of this reduction lies a particular mis-acknowledgment of the realities of fieldwork as an endeavour, since it is always the anthropologist's totality of being, that is, his/her embodied and sensing, conditioned and situated self, which is the primary research vehicle for understanding, rather than his/her transcendent (is this constant?) analytical consciousness.

The privileging of the metaphor of dialogue as key to understanding the construction of anthropological knowledge, it has also been argued, rests on the relative priority of verbal communication and a view of culture as an assortment of public texts which, as Geertz writes, 'the anthropologist strains to read over the shoulders of those to whom they properly belong' (1993: 452). However, as Hastrup and Hervik demonstrate, 'language events or the eliciting of "information", are but a fraction of what constitutes the [ethnographic] material' (1994: 6) (see also Bloch 1991). Communication during fieldwork encounters is very much like interaction in more familiar, everyday situations where an array of elements ranging from gestures, postures, the pitch of one's voice, to place and overall context, provide such rich textures of meaning qualifying and conditioning as much as what is said as what is enveloped in silence. Incorporating the non-verbal field of communication and going beyond words and texts is for Hastrup and Hervik, as well as for Jackson (1983) and Csordas (1990), a project founded on a certain conception of culture that owes as much to Bourdieu (1977) as to the work of Merleau-Ponty (1962). The semiotic model of culture as a fragmented web of contested and ambivalent meanings is given way to a somatic model of constrained agency that focuses on the ways culture is lived by subjects who constitute it, by means of embodying and enacting it, linguistically as well as physically – that is, as skills and tastes, habits and proclivities of action. In this regard, the interrogation of the body as subject, its formation and deployment, and the thematisation of the condition of embodiment as the experience and perception of having or rather being a body have been highlighted as a privileged site of entry into culture.

In what follows, I attempt to bring together the analysis of culture as embodied practice and the anthropological enterprise of employing the embodied subject as the foundation of knowledge, in such a way that the one speaks to and qualifies the other. This attempt is undertaken with the explicit aim of formulating the rudiments of a new way of conceptualising fieldwork as grounded on the acquisition of a new kind of body by the fieldworker, which acts as the source of his/her always particular, incomplete and partial anthropological knowledge. My starting point is that commonly held analogies used to describe the process of learning in the field either as role-play (i.e. the anthropologist as a friend, a neighbour, or a fictive kinsperson), or as equivalent to the learning of a second language – equating fluency with knowledge of grammar, syntax, phonetics and vocabulary – are insufficient in accurately portraying fieldwork, or at least, the way fieldwork felt to me. Rather, my learning involved taking up new routines and habits and the cultivation of corresponding skills and sensibilities in the context of active encouragement by my interlocutors, who sought to reveal their world through instilling in me a sense of what it is to be a moral Muslim human subject. Instead of exegetical conversations and apprenticeships in the deciphering of actions, the answer I got to my insistent questioning about demographic movements and local identity (my Ph.D. topic) was muted. A reply was nevertheless provided. The multitude of avenues that my interlocutors deployed in incorporating and refashioning a foreigner in their midst is consonant with the ways the locality has historically dealt with the challenges – both political and conceptual – posed by migration and ethnic difference. What I term to be the acquisition of a new kind of body could not be further from now defunct romantic notions of 'going native'. This acquisition, and the related transformed sense of self it gave rise to, was embedded in particular historical conditions and specific cultural themes, and corresponded to what is for my interlocutors as much an historical as an existential reality in terms of which they make sense both of themselves and their Others.

Knowledge of my East Javanese others was founded on the careful and systematic re-configuration of my body by my interlocutors while living with them. Such a re-casting, I argue, was culturally and historically specific. In particular, it was based on indigenous modes of self-identification and the techniques my interlocutors have historically devised so as to deal with certain instances of ethnic difference, that is, their largely successful attempts at transforming the heterogeneity that marks Madurese bodies off Javanese ones into homogeneity. The area today consists mainly of descendants of local Javanese as well as migrants from Madura, an island off the north-eastern coast of Java, and from other places in Java, who have arrived during different times in the locality and have made their permanent homes there. These demographic movements have taken place over a period of two centuries and have resulted in the current self-identification of the locality as a 'mixed place' and of its people as a hybrid category, the 'mixed people' (*oreng camporan*, Madurese; *orang pedalungan*, Indonesian; *wong pedalungan*, Javanese) (see Retsikas 2003). Locals define themselves as neither Javanese nor Madurese, and, despite tracing their origins to different places, they all lay emphasis on being of mixed ancestry through intermarriage, and of having been socialised in a place of intermingled living. In this regard then, my bodily reconfiguration was one instance among many of the transformative processes locals have themselves undergone, the initial step towards a metamorphosis through intimate exchanges.

Reflexivity is not solely an anthropological, intellectual practice. It is part of the fabric of the social life, of recognising difference and coming to terms with it either through establishing institutional barriers, and living parallel lives, or through forcefully appropriating the other and turning him/her into part of the self. Either way, it is through everyday practical (dis-)engagement that a sense of identity is formed. Identity is not the product of contemplation but an emergent property of sociality. We and they are alike in participating in each other's lives. Such participation, though formally absent in the process of ethnographic writing, is, nevertheless, constant in memory. Remembering, though selective and partial, is both visceral and material, involving re-enactments and emotive responses.

Violent Uncertainties and a Friendly Gesture

I found myself in Java in October 1998 in the midst of the unfolding of a major economic and political crisis which, ten (2008) years later, Indonesia has managed to contain. The economic crisis was sparked by currency problems in Thailand the previous year and soon spread over East and South-east Asia in what was a rapid loss of investor confidence and capital flight to other destinations. Over the next year, the Indonesian currency lost much of its value against the US dollar, several factories seized operations, while inflation reached the unimaginable heights of 80 per cent. The economic crisis precipitated a political one as one of the basic supports of Soeharto's legitimacy, which was related to delivering development and prosperity, was severely undermined by global developments. Amid extraordinary scenes of student protests, anti-Chinese riots and looting in Jakarta in May 1998, Soeharto stepped down, only to hand power to his right-hand man, B.J. Habibie, who promised elections in the following year.

The 'little' revolution that was taking place all around me was not spared outbreaks of violence. Actually, violence was an integral part of the political landscape of East Java, my fieldwork area. In October 1996, death squads dressed in black-clad ninja fashion had incited serious rioting of an

anti-Chinese and anti-Christian character in the city of Situbondo in East
Java (Retsikas 2006). Ninja assassins re-appeared in January 1998 in the town
of Banyuwangi in East Java and again from July to December of the same
year, culminating in a killing spree of alleged sorcerers that engulfed the
whole of Java. Such killings were construed by both locals and the national
and international press as politically motivated and perpetrated by
paramilitary units under the orders of the remnants of the New Order state.
Elsewhere in the archipelago, in Aceh, West Papua and East Timor, demands
for independence were met by increased levels of military brutality, while in
Ambon and Central Sulawesi, violence between Christians and Muslims was
constantly in the news.

In all these cases, violence was articulated from within; it had to do with
internal divisions in the Indonesian polity. With the exception of East Timor,
Westerners like myself were construed as neither the instigators nor the
victims of violence. Yet, I was afraid and felt threatened. Nothing had
prepared me either for the loneliness, despair and fear I was experiencing, or
for the polite distrust, the alienating respect and constant surveillance which
my presence was met with. I was feeling threatened: my identity as an
outsider construed me as a potential source of danger. From a Muslim
perspective, I was a *khafir*, an infidel and, given the political history of the
West's domination of the archipelago, I was part of that history. As a
Christian, I was also closer to the Chinese-Indonesians local Muslims
despised for dominating the most lucrative sectors of the economy. From the
perspective of the disintegrating state, I also represented potential danger. As
the commander of the local garrison put it, I was to stay clear of any
involvement in NGO advocacy and student protest movements. Otherwise,
my research permit would be revoked.

The politeness and respect I was accorded were the flip side of the danger
I represented. Being from the West, I was associated with economically and
politically powerful states. I was also presumed to be rich beyond
imagination. In the local idiom, politeness, hospitality and help are to be
reciprocated. Though I tried my best in reciprocating, I am afraid that I never
came close to meeting expectations since I never managed to rebuild the local
sugar mill or distribute lucrative job contracts. My status as a Ph.D. student
was an added source of deference. According to my interlocutors, I was
supposed to be very clever and capable, with a ministerial post awaiting me in
Greece upon my return there.

I felt both threatened and privileged due to my particular position within
the wider context of societal change and violence. Though not a direct target,
had my intentions been misunderstood and had I become the victim of
violence – a possibility hinted at by several highly placed civil servants I met
– my position as my Other's Other would have only been reaffirmed. Had I
remained a respected stranger, the distance these very patterns of deference
imply would not have decreased and the familiarity and rapport I was taught
to seek as the basis of anthropological understanding would have continued

to be as elusive as ever. The need for finding a safe place away from violence was accompanied by an equally pressing demand of re-configuring my position in the field so that some degree of intimacy could be established. The opportunity of addressing both issues at once appeared two months into fieldwork when I visited the village of Alas Niser, a settlement at the periphery of the municipality of Probolinggo in the coast of East Java.

I had gone to Alas Niser to inquire about the possibility of taking up residence there. To this purpose, I visited the offices of the village headman and the houses of several Islamic scholars for it was obvious from the regional literature that the ones wielding influence were the latter, not the former. It was in once such occasion that I met *kyai* Saiffudin, a 35-year-old scholar who was married with two children. *Kyai* Saiffudin, who was well educated in Islamic theology and law and was interested also in Western sociology and political science, headed the district's largest Islamic boarding school. He was a member of *Nahdlatul Ulama*, Indonesia's largest Islamic organisation dedicated to religious tolerance, democracy and what Hefner calls 'civic pluralism' (2000). We had a long conversation about my origins and research interests, when the *kyai* opened a photo album from his pilgrimage to Mecca and showed me the picture of a *syekh* (an Islamic scholar who claims descent from the Prophet) he had met there. 'You look like him', he said. Despite the photo portraying a much older and bearded man, *kyai* Saiffudin was struck by the similarity of the long nose and skin complexion (at that point I was quite tanned), adding 'Are you sure you do not have Arabic blood in your veins?'. Somewhat embarrassed due to my Greek upbringing, I replied negatively.

Kyai Saiffudin's comment was an invitation to bridging the gap that separated us. The comment was intended neither as a covert attempt at proselytisation nor as a mere compliment. 'Forced' conversion to Islam is not expounded as an option because, as the *kyai* explained, only conversion that comes from the *hati* (the inner most centre), that is, through the wilful realisation of Truth, counts as sincere and authentic. What this gesture intended to effect was the opening of the possibility of finding some common ground, of establishing some sort of similarity between us on the basis of which our interaction could proceed further. This possibility was extended when he proposed that I take up residence in the boarding school in exchange for teaching the students English and paying a substantial amount of money each month as rent, a practice that did not apply to the other students there who were mostly children of poor farmers from the vicinity and beyond. The invitation was presented in the very distinctive terms of the care and affection a good Javanese has to show towards people who live far from their relatives, coupled with the Islamic value of the hospitality one has to display towards travellers.

To say that his invitation to become a *santri*, that is, a student in an Islamic boarding school, was about establishing rapport and reducing social distance does not mean that it was devoid of other considerations of a more strategic kind. *Kyai* are informal political leaders who are supposed to offer protection for the 'little people' (*wong cilik*, Javanese) from all kinds of dangers, both supernatural and secular, political and economic. Seen in this vein, his invitation to join the boarding school was an attempt at encompassment and eventual domestication of the potential danger I represented with regard to my foreign origins and undetermined intentions. The local community was safe from potentially disruptive influences, cocooned by the *kyai*'s protective umbrella. Moreover, the invitation placed me in an ideal position in which both my everyday routine and research agenda could be under constant surveillance, control and evaluation. I was destined to become the object of observation as much as the subject of participation.

Taking up residence in the *pesantren* was an opportunity that I found myself unable to refuse. I had chosen Indonesia as my fieldsite for it was a Muslim country, sharing some strong similarities to Greece's neighbour and long time rival, Turkey. Though classic ethnographic accounts of the Javanese society and culture construed Islam to be only a 'thin veneer' or a 'container' enclosing the essence of 'Java', in this case, a unique mixture of animism and Hindu-Buddhist traditions, a debate was raging over the subject after the publication of a series of studies in the 1980s that provided fertile ground for contestations and further explorations. Compounded with these personal and academic issues was my uncertainty and insecurity in the field. By accepting the offer, I put myself in the position of a client. The *kyai*'s family was to be my hosts, fieldwork family and patrons. I was to live in the same compound with the rest of the students and the *kyai*'s extended family. I was thus to be classified as an *oreng dalem* (Madurese), meaning a person of elevated status because of his/her proximity to the *kyai*. Later on, I often overheard people in the village market commending on the possibility that I would get married to one of the *kyai*'s sisters-in-law, a pretty girl in her late teens. Moreover, I was to be invulnerable to theft, scorn or any other activity that could be seen as offensive towards the *kyai*'s honour. Living in the *pesantren* and showing in practical terms respect towards Islam and an inclination towards learning about my interlocutor's faith provided a solid basis for introducing my self to the village.

Domesticating Alterity, Transforming the Self

The *kyai*'s offer of a place to stay, sleep, eat and socialise, however, is not so easily construed in terms of strategic considerations only. I believe that it was a gesture that makes full sense only if considered in terms of the history of the locality and of the wider area in which it belongs. In other words, the invitation to become a *santri* was informed by particular local histories and cultural themes; in principle, it rested on indigenous modes of reflexivity and self-understanding.

The inhabitants of Alas Niser and Probolinggo frequently assert to foreign anthropologists, unfamiliar civil servants and visiting tourists, both overseas and fellow Indonesians, that they and, more generally, the people who live in a region covering most of the east coast of Java, facing the arid south of the island of Madura, are *orang pedalungan* (Indonesian) – 'mixed persons' (also *oreng camporan*, Madurese). In so doing, they place themselves in between the two major categories of kinds of people that demographically dominate the area outside the *pedalungan* region, namely the 'Javanese' and the 'Madurese'. Alas Niser locals' self-identification as 'mixed people' indicates a sense of identity founded both on an intimacy with their significant Others and a substantial degree of separation. In other words, they identify themselves as neither 'Javanese' nor 'Madurese' but rather as a kind of people produced by the very conjunction and the blending of 'Javanese' and 'Madurese' kindedness.

As in other places of the world, the idiom of 'mixed personhood' is evoked as a convenient category at the contact point of migration. It refers to a 'third person' and a 'third space' (Bhabha 1994) shaped by ambivalent and incomplete combinations of opposing elements culminating in the domestication and partial displacement of difference (see Retsikas 2007a). In my case, the contact point of migration owes its emergence to colonial times – from the early nineteenth century onwards – when a series of demographic movements, vividly remembered today, brought together in the same place a divergent set of migrants from both Madura and western East Java, with the Javanese that were concentrated mainly on what is today downtown Probolinggo. These migrants also went to re-populate the city's periphery that was demographically devastated by the colonial wars, pushing the frontier further to the south, away from the coast. Madurese migrants arrived en masse in Probolinggo in response to the excessive demands of the local aristocracy and Madura's largely arid landscape, in search of jobs in the lower sectors of the burgeoning economy of Java (see also Husson 1995). They were also looking for large tracts of superior, unclaimed land in the shape of thickly forested areas they proceeded to clear and put to cultivation. In contrast, the majority of the Javanese migrants who arrived a bit later were primarily young and better educated, attracted primarily by the needs of the colonial and post-colonial administration for professionals and civil servants. They too were seeking to set themselves relatively free from the combining effects of poverty, under-productivity and population growth that have engulfed Javanese society for more than two centuries. The opening up of the frontier in the nineteenth century saw, in addition, an increase in the number of Chinese and Arab traders and entrepreneurs who were present in the area from earlier times, and who nevertheless have remained outside the moral space that mixing designates, for reasons I will briefly explore later.

The agentive capacities and processuality on which the creation of 'mixed personhood' is predicated is readily acknowledged by those partaking in it today. One of the most potent images of mixing that the locals of Alas Niser offer as a narrative account, a mythology of the self, if you like, is that of a newly arrived migrant who marries a local, settles permanently in the area to raise his/her children, builds a house in the village and is eager to create and maintain the state of harmony people in Java call *rukun*. *Rukun* is established and maintained through participation in the networks of reciprocity and exchange, both ritually marked and informal, that bring forth the neighbourhood (*kampung*) as an important category of thought and action. The agency involved in these exchanges rests with both parties; the incomer's willingness to settle, commitment to marry locally, and striving for the realisation of that particular state of affairs encapsulated in the term *rukun*, which, according to my informants, is also a way of feeling (see Beatty 2005), implying emotions of tranquillity and contentment. Such agency is met with what Carsten (1995), writing about another South-east Asian migrant society, calls 'forced incorporation', that is, the power the community, however recent and unstable might be, exercises on the new arrivals and the demands it makes for conformity through incorporation, exemplified by marriage with a fellow Muslim and the co-production of children.

In Alas Niser, sociality is seen as emerging out of a refashioning of migrant identities and the domestication of certain kinds of alterity. Such understandings of society are embedded in spatial arrangements and practices. The latter construe Alas Niser as a hybrid, third space. Such a space is experienced as both recent in achievement and unfinished as a project, and thus unstable and in danger of disintegration. Collective memories make the case that throughout the colonial era and until the first decades of national independence, specific residential quarters within the municipality of Probolinggo were almost the exclusive domain of either Javanese or Madurese, Dutch, Chinese or Arabs. The advent of the Indonesian state and the instigation of more flexible patterns of social mobility, which allow for greater geographic mobility on a national level, have contributed towards bringing about important changes in this respect so that spatial cum ethnic exclusivity is no longer the case. Especially with reference to people of Javanese and Madurese ancestry, the aforementioned factors have combined with local demographic pressures on converting fields into residential areas and the participation of increasing amounts of residential land to markets as commodities, so as to create a situation in which what was before readily distinguishable has been turned into a terrain of intermingled living. Such intermingled living, though, still carries the effects of history since 'mixed personhood' is thought of as unequally distributed in space. The town centre, is talked about as 'more Javanese' due to older settlement there and the Javanese language is predominant in casual conversations. In contrast, the soundscape of the town's periphery is animated by the everyday use of Madurese and considered as populated by 'mixed persons' who are closer to 'pure' Madurese persons (*orang Madura asli*).

Agency is necessary for the production and reproduction of mixing, least its formula of intermingled living, ritual exchanges and affinal transactions in the present falters, stabling upon the predicates of a history of divergent places, different languages and varied ancestors. Overall, hybridity, and the agency it presupposes, is celebrated for being both disruptive and productive. It is productive in the sense that it highlights a conception of the self as fluid, contextual and relational. Persons are thought of as capable of transformation since human life and human growth is predicated on a spatialised mode of sociality that revolves around reciprocity. The discontinuities that demographic movement introduces in human growth are compensated with the avenues for new sources of expansion that engagement in new locales provides for. In this regard, proximate transformation is made to appear as depended upon the instantiation of new sets of relationships – the acquisition of new neighbours, new relatives, new friends. These acquisitions or additions work their way to conceptions of the self and mark a point of departure. However, for transformable personhood to exist as a possibility, an assertion akin to essentialism is involved by necessity. 'The positing of an anterior "pure" that precedes mixture' (Hutnyk 2005: 81), offers images of the intimate Others. 'Mixed persons' are composed of as stable in space and fixed in essence. This fixity, however, does not contradict the logic of transformable personhood. It merely highlights it by providing a counter-example that is also a caricature of the Other.

My presence in Probolinggo as a student in search for knowledge was made sense of by my interlocutors in terms of the demographic movement either their ancestors or they themselves had to undergo in their own trajectories of a 'search for living' (*cari nafkah*). Though I was not conceived to suffer from the economic deprivations that force one to leave his/her village, the pursuit of knowledge is readily recognised as a valid reason: students of Islamic boarding schools often leave their natal villages to take up residence in schools far away, sometimes in the Middle East if they come from wealthy families, where famous and revered scholars teach. In more recent years, the expansion of higher education has also made it possible for relatively few young men from Alas Niser to pursue studies in secular subjects in localities often as far as Surabaya and Jakarta. In addition, several comments made in my presence about the personal qualities ancestral migration was said to require, such as bravery and lack of fear, put me in a recognisable place in reference to local history. As it is to be expected, my fate was sealed by historical precedent. The deployment of transformative agency was extended in my case to encompass and draw in a stranger who did not, however, belong to those intimate Others of 'mixed persons' consist. What is more is that such a deployment was congruent with a mode of attention to my body, its habits and embodied ethical dispositions that were bound to be remade.

Attending the Body

Several days after I accepted the *kyai*'s invitation of entering the *pesantren*, I received a visit at downtown Probolinggo where I was staying at the time, by the *kyai*'s elder brother-in-law who was also involved in the running of the school, in charge of finances and administration. He asked to talk in private in the seclusion of my bedroom, saying that it had to do with my move to the school. He started off with the usual polite language, explaining that the purpose of his visit had to do with preparations about my arrival, to check what kinds of furniture I would need in order to arrange their purchase. He proceeded to give me a rather extensive account of the establishment of the school, with a long list of the *kyais* that had run it over a period of eighty years, then switched to the topic of ancient Greece and the philosophers Greece was 'famous throughout the world' for producing. This turn of subject was followed with the observation that Greeks were also known to be *homo* (Indonesian), engaging in sex with (young) men. 'Are you *homo*?' he asked rather uncharacteristically, to which I replied in my rudimentary Indonesian, that the practice was common some 2,500 years ago and that today among Greek men there is a norm for heterosexuality, though homosexuals do constitute a minority. At that point, I offered him photos of my girlfriend, now hastily 'upgraded' to the status of fiancée, as a proof of my sexual orientation. He commented that his brother-in-law who had seen the photos in a previous occasion, had informed him about it all but he wanted to check himself. There was something else too though, that he wanted to discuss with me, he continued, and without providing for any kind of introduction this time around, he asked to inspect my genitals for proof that I was a Christian and not an *orang Yahudi*, a Jew, and thus, circumcised. Being overly shocked, offended and embarrassed, I replied rather angrily that this was not possible, that my genitals were 'private' (*pribadi*). A short silence followed and the conversation abruptly, awkwardly switched back to preparations for my entry to the boarding school in two weeks' time, right after the end of Ramadan.

Not all kinds of difference are held to succumb to mediation and domestication. As with Chinese (*orang Cina/Tionghoa*) and Arabs (*orang Arab*) who fall outside the moral space of mixing for reasons of being too different – the first in terms of religion (being predominately Christians), and wealth, the second in terms of occupying a superior position due to claims of direct descent from the Prophet – so too, in the case of homosexuality and Jewish identity, the divide is deemed as too big to bridge. The body, its features and its dispositions occupy a particular place in these negations of mediation. Chinese bodies, for example, which are marked as distinct due to the particular shape of the eyes and skin complexion, are also deemed as incapable of experiencing *rasa kasihan*, the feelings of pity and mercy that ideally motivate every good Muslim to be generous and pay *zakat fitrah*, the tithe in rice or money paid on the last day of the fasting month, and *zakat maal*, the tithe paid by the rich only. Similarly, Arab-Indonesians, whose bodies are demarcated by long noses and almond shaped eyes, are also marked by a high degree of purity and inner perfection, being descendants of the Prophet (*sayid*). While this elevates them, it also furnishes 'mixed persons' with a certain ambiguity towards them since Arab-Indonesians are often accused of displaying arrogance and excessive superiority to the extent that they prefer not to opt for inter-marriage. These latter characteristics Arabs are said to share with Westerners (*orang Barat*), familiar to the inhabitants of Probolinggo since the town is often a resting point for those travelling to Mount Bromo, the major tourist destination in East Java. Whenever tourists appeared in town, they were construed also as loud, extremely serious, for they rarely smiled, were rather rude and without the capacity of displaying reserve and modesty in their interactions. The assumption that some of my interlocutors shared that tourists and I were kin, was very telling of the way I too was conceived.

Attention to my bodily presence, comportment and behaviour was coupled with the desire to teach me local modes of appropriateness early on. In this regard, teaching did not primarily take the form of linguistic instructions and propositionally articulated advice, though these were by no means absent. More importantly, the education I received was aimed at my body's surfaces and was explicitly directed towards their reconstitution. The surfaces in question corresponded to a re-training of my senses through a myriad of techniques that aimed at refashioning the way I comprehended and engaged with the world, in this instance, Muslim Java.

Upon hearing that I was to enter an Islamic school, a family I had come to know very well in downtown Probolinggo, invited me to spend *Idul Fitri* (the holiday that marks the end of Ramadan) in their company. This particular family's extended kindred consists of descendants of migrants from South Kalimantan, intermarried with peoples of Javanese and Madurese ancestry in Probolinggo, who are all very active in entrepreneurial circles. Much to my surprise, I was invited to join them not only in their annual rounds of feasting, but also to accompany its male members to the mosque for the performance of the prayer. Commonly, *Idul Fitri* celebrations, along with the festive consumption of food and the customary exchanges of forgiveness, involve the wearing of new sets of clothes, especially by the young ones. New sets of clothes are taken to signal the state of purity one has achieved through fasting, a state that is renewed every year. It was in this set of circumstances that, after having lunch at the family's paternal house, I was presented with the gift of an Islamic attire by the eldest male relative. The attire itself consisted of a *sarung pelékat,* the block patterned sarong worn by Muslims in the archipelago, a fine *dakwah* shirt made of silk with Arabic inscriptions on it in the button and flat collar area, and a white *kopiah*, the rimless cap normally worn by those who have performed the pilgrimage to Mecca. What was more was that I had to try them on immediately. Accompanied by four men of my age, I retired to one of the bedrooms and under their instructions, I learned how to put on a *sarung*; first, envelop myself in its cylinder-shaped cotton cloth after stepping in it with my right foot first; then, tighten the *sarung* against my right side ribs, fold it horizontally across the chest first to the right, then to the left, and then, fold it gently again, though vertically this time, towards my waist line, and tight enough so it can hold itself there. With the *sarung* wrapped around my waist, my continuous body was made into a bifurcated, divided entity, endowed with an upper and lower part, the latter marked as dirty and inferior. Putting on the shirt was the next step. The *dakwah* shirt with its soft, silky feeling, having an immediate cooling effect on the body, brings into being and adorns the chest. There lies the heart/liver (*hati*), the seat of emotions and knowledge, and the seat of *roh*, the invisible essence of life human beings receive from Allah when still in their mother's womb. The adorning of such important faculties and essences is coupled with a stress on the care one has to show to regulate one's emotions so that one is always tranquil and peaceful. Finally, the rimless cap was fitted, covering my head, the seat of intellect and reason (*akal*, also *fikroh* from *fikr*, Arabic), which one must guard and attend to with concentration and purposefulness. Apart from highlighting such desired qualities, this particular type of *kopiah* has a 'whitening' effect on the face, mirroring and enhancing one's inner purity and sincerity of intentions and motives. To all these, a borrowed set of flip-flops were added and with the laudation *amin*, we exited the room to face the anxious crowd.

To my surprise, my admittedly odd appearance, for this is how the whole affair felt to me, was met with sober approbation and favoured consent by older men, while the women present cheered and praised how handsome I looked. Feelings of embarrassment soon gave way to ethical questions. Was I going too far? By accepting to live in an Islamic boarding school and to be dressed as a Muslim, was I unwittingly giving the false impression that I was willing to convert? If such was the case, should I backtrack and explore different avenues to do my research? And if I was to do so, would this not be offensive, most of all to the *kyai*? The affirmation my new bodily presence was met with in that fateful afternoon in downtown Probolinggo, was solidified with *kyai* Saiffudin's commendation, who, wishing to inspect my dress code in my first day at the *pesantren*, applauded my by now rather skilful use of the *sarung* and the *kopiah*. Under his instructions, I was not allowed to wear any kind of short trousers at all. While in the environs of the school and the neighbourhood, I was expected to wear the *sarung*, though I was allowed to opt for trousers when visiting acquaintances beyond its boundaries. That same night, my first in the *pesantren*, I was formally introduced in the neighbourhood. A marriage was being celebrated and the *kyai* presented me in his speech as a student from Greece, a Christian single man, who wishes to know about *adat Probolinggoan* (the customs of Probolinggo).

For the duration of my fieldwork, I was a hybrid: a white Christian pupil of a Koranic boarding school. My anthropological training laid emphasis on experiencing Otherness through the intimacy of the senses. Anthropological knowledge, I was taught, was not to be achieved through abstract reflection and library research only, but it was to be grounded on a personal experience, an event unlike any other facilitated and brought into being through the employment of the physical, sensing and moving body *qua* self. This epistemological position was seized upon by the people of Alas Niser within the precedents set by historical efforts of domesticating certain kinds of difference. Ethical questions can now find relief in the historical positionalities of my research subjects that determined my own research trajectory. In other words, their hybridity was replicated in my own hybrid positionings and, despite being a Christian, I was often honourably addressed as *ustadz*, meaning young Islamic teacher, not withstanding my inability to utter but a few words in Arabic. The partial transformation corresponded to a rite de passage that did not, however, involve changing roles, statutes or anything remotely sociological. The transformation was existential for my body was taken over.

Wearing the *sarung* entailed an apprenticeship in new capacities for ethical ways of movement. Walking was now dictated by the span of the cloth, which, though wide, was constrained by its double sideways folding and waist tightening. Such limitations made movement possible only in shorter steps, unlike the ones trousers allow for with one being able to capitalise more fully on the legs' spread. As a result, movement was slower and more graceful. Slowness is understood in Java, amongst other things, to indicate modesty and humility, virtues that any good Muslim should display in his/her behaviour. Slow movements are also commonly taken as indexical signs of *halus*-ness, that mode of temperament that bespeaks internal control of socially undesirable emotions, and effects a sociality of respect towards superiors and exquisite politeness. Wearing thus the *sarung*, was not about a masquerade, a new-age rendition of 'going native'. Rather, the *kyai* and the family from South Kalimantan employed it as a 'body technique' in Mauss's (1979) famous words, with the intention of honing and cultivating a particular set of sensibilities and embodied values in the young fieldworker. The covering of my legs down to the angles also gave rise to a sensing of them as a part of my body that women in the neighbourhood, especially young ones, should not gaze at. Lifting the *sarung* when moving through the mud or walking up the couple of steps towards the front porch of neighbouring houses, became an exercise in modesty as I became aware of my legs' sexual meanings. At the same time, the *sarung* allowed for the uninhibited movement of the air in my lower body, counteracting the excessive heat of tropical afternoons, and provided me with the practicality of being able to sleep in neighbouring houses and the small prayer house without the need for a cover since, unfolded, it is also used as a blanket.

Using a *kopiah*, though only occasionally for it gave me acute headaches, also involved the acquisition and deployment of new habits and volitional-affective capacities. Resting on top of my head, it changed the balance of my bodily movements through affecting the centre of gravity, and brought attention to the care I should exercise regarding the deployment of the senses located at my face the *kopiah* was now crowning. The facial orifices, that is, the nose, the ears, the eyes and the mouth are sometimes referred to as *tretan se pa-empa* (Madurese), literally translating as the four siblings, with the corresponding sensory organs held as animated by these invisible entities after one's birth. In this regard, the fifth sense, that of *rasa* (taste/touch/ feeling), goes unmentioned here as a separate faculty, for its place is taken over by the body, that is, the fifth element, as a whole. My informants relate the *tretan se pa-empa* to perception and action in a complex manner. *Fikroh*, the faculty of thought, located at the head, is conceptualised as receiving and processing all information one gets through the senses and sending them to *sirri*, the upper part of the heart/liver. *Sirri*'s function is to reflect upon the information by way of the emotions which arise. Finally, *kolbih*, the lower part of the heart/liver, after measuring and evaluating these emotions, decides about the appropriate response and course of action. Then, this decision is transmitted to *fikroh*, which, in turn, orders the body to respond accordingly. What the *kopiah* underscored was the caution and circumspection I should display with regard to external stimuli that penetrated me by the mere fact of living and interacting with the environing world, and the attention I should bring to bear in relation to acting appropriately and purposefully, that is, in accordance with the emotions generated, the feelings contained in the interaction itself. Attention, care, caution and circumspection are modes of being, ways of engaging with the world and others, attitudes and dispositions of relating. What such a mode of being emphasises is that control of oneself and by implications of one's environment is paramount in matters of sociality. In Java, the uncertainties and dangers of engaging with others are thought to stem from an inability to foresee events and evaluate appropriately, both amounting to a substantial loss of agency. Achieving control is generally sought through multiple ways, the most extreme of which is asceticism and meditation (see Anderson 1972; Keller 1987). More commonly, wearing the *kopiah* as a protective helmet and a reminder of the circuits of perception was a training device aimed at the cultivation of a particular set of appropriate emotional-kinesthetic experiences of the body for understanding and enacting sociality 'from the native's point of view'.

To feel (*rasa*, Indonesian, also to taste and to touch) is equated in Java with understanding, the latter informing action. To enable feeling, village children of primary school age attend Koranic classes in the *pesantren* and the mosque led by senior students and those learned in religion. To them and to their parents, religious education is of the utmost importance in leading a good life, and the pursuit of Islamic knowledge is seen as a religious obligation, the performance of which is said to bring about future well-being and prosperity. Islamic education involves instruction in the rudiments of Islamic theology and the practice of the five pillars of the faith, with the emphasis put on the recitation of the Koran. Reciting the text is a practice that stresses not linguistics and contemplative, interpretative knowledge as these can be acquired later on when one has mastered more fully the oral and auditory perception of sacred words and has attuned one's speech and auditory habits to correct modes of apprehension (see also Hirschkind 2001). The proper vocalisation and audition of the Koran recruits the sensing and experiencing body, and, ideally, hones particular emotions in the believer's body, such as tranquillity (*ketenangan*) when the passage recited evokes the gardens of Paradise, fear (*rasa takut*) in corresponding sections portraying the torments sinners will face in Hell, humility (*kerendahan hati*, literally lowering the heart) when Allah and the Prophet are mentioned.

Though I consciously decided not to embark upon learning to recite the Koran for such could have been construed as in preparation to conversion and, thus, misleading of my intentions, my daily routine and its alternating rhythms, was very much shaped by the five daily prayers, anticipated by the hard beating of the large drum (*gendang*) located just outside my room, and the melodious call to prayer (*azan*) broadcasted by two loudspeakers, one of which was fixed in a bamboo pole at the roof of the building in which I was staying. *Azan* spreads in waves and infuses the air with the aura of sacredness, while demanding concentration, remembrance and stillness by all listeners, Muslim and non-Muslim alike. The words of a friend and a senior *santri* of the *pesantren* that 'the heart of every good Muslim weeps when listening to *azan*' have stayed with me to this day with an immense force that is re-activated every time my ears happen to hear it, taking me back to Java, albeit momentarily. Learning to respond emotionally, affectively to the *azan*, is fundamental. When a baby is born, and a corpse is undergoing the funeral rites, the recital of the call to prayer marks these points of transition; the first opening up one's senses to the Prophet's Message, the second, completing the closing of the corpse's orifices with memories of devotion.

The same goes for all the other senses. The capacity to speak, the faculty of taste and smell, the habits of seeing received a re-training. Generating unfamiliar sounds like the sound *–ng* involved the acquisition of a new skill of using the larynx and the tongue in such a combination so that the sound produced is sharp, clear and short in duration, or the sound *–r* through bringing the tongue behind the upper central teeth and reverberating it; learning to appreciate the taste of *nasi goreng* and *sate kambing*, or, in most cases, simply endure the spiciness of raw chillies consumed in hot afternoons with rice, itself often mixed with corn; the heavy smell of rain and moisture during the wet season and the sweet smell of mangoes of which Probolinggo is generously endowed, conditioned my sense of self *qua* body in the field and gave rise to an appreciation of the second life, an unexpected addition, a surplus, I was given.

If my knowledge of my co-villagers' lives is partial, it is not only because of the particular position I occupied in the field and the assumptions, or rather, embodiments I was (still am) consisting of and thus, carried in the field. From the perspective of the people I lived with, such knowledge is partial because the transformation I underwent was incomplete, disrupted by a future that is un-shared. This was made aptly clear to me a month or so before I was to leave the village. I had spread the word that I will be returning to Europe after the *Idul Adha* festivities were over, a total of fourteen months since I first entered the Koranic school, and since I had no wife and thus no relatives in the village so as to help me give a *slametan* (ritual feast), I decided to sacrifice instead a young bull whose meat was to be distributed locally. The limits imposed by my bachelor status – by then my fiancé was an ex – were highlighted when that same period, a long month of goodbyes and promises of a quick return to Java, I found myself at the receiving end of two marriage proposals; the first one was by the village headman who was also distantly related to the *kyai*'s family, and the second one, by a rich trader from another village who employed a neighbour of mine as a go-between as is common in these situations. I declined both as politely as I could, indicating that I could not support a family due to being a student.

The marriage proposals which were made on the basis that I would convert first to Islam and that I would stay in the village as a permanent member, rather than taking the young bride to Europe, were primarily a test of my commitments – to my studies, parents, place of origin, the Javanese village and its inhabitants, my friends and neighbours there – and an attempt to re-constitute my personhood through shaping its future contours by regulating its sexuality and channelling its productive and reproductive capacities. These contours were predicated on becoming a *bapak*, a father, the next stage to which male *santri* who leave the *pesantren* progress, usually having found a sweetheart from amongst the female students – I know they will resent me for publishing this – who they meet at the *pesantren*'s backyard early in the evenings. Being a *bapak* is about assuming the responsibilities of adult life, acquiring property most commonly through the wife who is given a house, and land if there is enough of it and generating a new set of relatives, the relationships to whom are physically embodied in the figure of the children the union has procured. *Bapak*-ship is then followed by the acquisition of grandchildren and finally, the achievement of ancestorship after death and burial in the family cemetery, often visited by descendants in ritually marked and unmarked occasions dedicated to remembrance. Property, children, fields and gravesites, the activities that go in their making, maintenance and multiplication, are the stuff that local life revolves around, and the loci through which 'mixed personhood' amongst a diverse set of migrants has been achieved. By declining the offers, I was putting myself outside the frame of an ongoing process of growth and maturation, stepping outside a trajectory consisting of the means of mixing and geared towards homogeneity. Such options and acts come to define the self by means of their very products and consequences. The refusal to disperse further my personhood in the physical and bodily landscape of the locality through labour and procreation, amongst other things, has left the project of my transformation unfinished. Partial knowledge, my co-villagers indicate, stems from partial embodiment. I only hope that such embodiment is however deemed adequate enough for offering a vivid account.

Conclusion

I began this paper by arguing that the postmodernist focus on reflexivity as a disembodied intellectual exercise taking place in an after-the-fact mode mis-apprehends the realities of fieldwork, itself based on the deployment of the fieldworker's body as a living, physical, sensing and experiencing agent enmeshed in practical and intimate encounters. The privileging of the dialogic as a commanding metaphor of the negotiations over identity and representation taking place during fieldwork is grossly inadequate for capturing the complex terrain in which culture, selves and fieldwork are constituted. Despite acknowledging that identities are not natural and fixed, but contextual and historically shifting, postmodernism has retained, nevertheless, a degree of fixity in relation to its understanding of the role of the fieldworker in the image of a transcendental analytical consciousness. This article has instead, argued for fluid, alterable embodiment being a more productive way for thematising the production of knowledge. In this regard, I have argued that the anthropological knowledge arises from the transformable body, in particular the ways the body is re-fashioned and reconstituted by its active taking up of new cultural themes and practices in situations of initial alienation and subsequent immersion. True, the process of fieldwork is a process of familiarisation. Familiarity is, though, a sensation of confidence and comfortability that bespeaks a certain degree of control over cultural conventions permeating sociality. Such control is the effect of the saturation of the body and the sedimentation of cultural themes by means of training, incorporation and everyday use. What this implies is that changes in the everyday habits that have historically created and sustained particular kinds of bodies as an assortment of dispositions, tastes, skills and capacities, will inevitably lead to changes of the experience of the self. This is culture rising to awareness through, with and in the body. As Hastrup writes, 'sedimentation implies a degree of solidification of the world as incorporated, which will gradually make the fieldworker experience a reshaping of the body's actual ability … In this sense, too, culture, becomes 'naturalised' in socialisation and experience' (1994: 231).

The practice of embodiment takes place within an arena of interaction between self-conscious subjects, including the fieldworker and his/her significant others. Such interaction is defined by the parameters set by history and power: that is, the biography and agency of the fieldworker and those of his/her informants, both individually and collectively. In such encounters, Jackson contends, 'each person is at once a subject for himself or herself – a *who* – and an object for others – a *what*' (1988: 8). To be more precise, however, the ethnographic project is also grounded on the processual conversion of the fieldworker from a what to a who as the distinction between object and subject becomes blurred by means of intimacy and shared experiences. Turning into somebody was, in my case, predicated on moving from the category of a being of foreign origins, indeterminate intentions and ambivalent powers to a *santri*, a neighbour, a friend and a potential affine. This is not to say that such a process is by necessity always linear and that I was all these things to every single person I interacted with during fieldwork. Rather, this conversion was more apparent in my relationships with a limited number of persons I came to know well and it was far more complex that a lineal model can render. What is of particular importance, however, is that this movement rested very much on the agentive capacities on behalf of my 'informants' to inscribe culture onto my body and make it proximate to theirs. In other words, fieldwork revolved around the exercise of a power I found myself relatively unable to resist had I wanted to, though this should not be taken to mean that I was totally devoid of agency since I did make choices amongst a limited set of options.

The ethnographer-informant relationship has during the last couple of decades, been intensely scrutinised by post-modernists and post-structuralists alike who, working in the immediate aftermath of the process of decolonisation, made us aware of the power matrix inherent in the creation of knowledge, anthropological ones included. The remedy for the objectification of the other as embedded within colonial anthropology has been sought in the textual humanisation of that other, that is, his/her rendition in the ethnographic writing as a negotiating, skilful and competent social actor with a distinctive voice. However, power has always been assumed to be on the side of the ethnographer-writer as the epistemological pairing of the concepts of author and authority denote in the Anglo-American context. My suggestion here is that this power imbalance can no longer been taken for granted and that we need more nuanced accounts of the knowledge/power equation as enacted in the field, and not only in its aftermath, as writing by and large surely is.

References

Anderson, B. 1972. 'The Idea of Power in Javanese Culture', in C. Holt, B. Anderson and J. Siegel (eds), *Culture and Politics in Indonesia*. Ithaca, NY: Cornell University Press, pp. 1–69.

Beatty, A. 2005. 'Feeling Your Way in Java: An Essay on Society and Emotion', *Ethnos* 70(1): 53–78.

Bhabha, H. 1994. *The Location of Culture*. London: Routledge.

Bloch, M. 1991. 'Language, Anthropology, and Cognitive Science', *Man (N.S.)* 26(2): 183–98.

Bourdieu, P. 1977. *Outline of a Theory of Practice*. Cambridge: Cambridge University Press.

Carsten, J. 1995. 'The Politics of Forgetting: Migration, Kinship and Memory on the Periphery of the Southeast Asian State', *Journal of the Royal Anthropological Institute (N.S.)* 1(2): 317–35.

Clifford, J. and G.E. Marcus (eds). 1986. *Writing Culture: The Poetics and Politics of Ethnography*. Berkeley: University of California Press.

Csordas, T.J. 1990. 'Embodiment as a Paradigm for Anthropology', *Ethos* 18: 5–47.

Geertz, C. 1993. 'Deep Play: Notes on the Balinese Cockfight', in *The Interpretation of Cultures*. London: Fontana Press, pp. 412–53.

Haraway, D.J. 1991. *Simians, Syborgs and Women: The Reinvention of Nature*. London: Free Association Books.

Hastrup, K. 1994. 'Anthropological Knowledge Incorporated: Discussion', in K. Hastrup and P. Hervik (eds), *Social Experience and Anthropological Knowledge*. London: Routledge, pp. 224–40.

Hastrup, K. and P. Hervik. 1994. 'Introduction', in K. Hastrup and P. Hervik (eds), *Social Experience and Anthropological Knowledge*. London: Routledge, pp. 1–12.

Hefner, R. 2000. *Civil Islam: Muslims and Democratization in Indonesia*. Princeton: Princeton University Press.

Hirschkind, C. 2001. 'The Ethics of Listening: Cassette-sermon Audition in Contemporary Egypt', *American Ethnologist* 28(3): 623–49.

Husson, L. 1995. *La Migration Madurese vers l' Est de Java*. Paris: L'Harmattan.

Hutnyk, J. 2005. 'Hybridity', *Ethnic and Racial Studies* 28(1): 79–102.

Jackson, M. 1983. 'Knowledge of the Body', *Man (N.S.)* 18(2): 327–45.

———. 1988. *Minima Ethnography: Intersubjectivity and the Anthropological Project*. Chicago: University of Chicago Press.

Keeler, W. 1987. *Javanese Shadow Plays, Javanese Selves*. Princeton, NJ: Princeton University Press.

Mauss, M. 1979. 'Body Techniques' in *Sociology and Psychology: Essays*. London: Routledge and Kegan Paul, pp. 95–123.

Merleau-Ponty, M. 1962. *The Phenomenology of Perception*. London: Routledge and Kegan Paul.

Okely, J. and H. Callaway (eds). 1992. *Anthropology and Autobiography* (ASA Monographs 29). London: Routledge.

Retsikas, K. 2003. '"People of Mixed Blood": Ethnicity, Personhood and Sociality in East Java, Indonesia', Ph.D. thesis. Edinburgh: University of Edinburgh.

———. 2006. 'The Semiotics of Violence: Ninja, Sorcerers, and State Terror in Post-Soeharto Indonesia', *Bijdragen tot de Taal-, Land- en Volkekunde* 162(1): 56–94.

———. 2007. a 'The Power of the Senses: Ethnicity, History, and Embodiment in East Java, Indonesia', *Indonesia and the Malay World* 35(102): 187–214.

Retsikas, K. 2007b. 'Being and Place: Movement Ancestors and Personhood in East Java, Indonesia'. *Journal of the Royal Anthropolgical Institute* 13(4): 969–85.

Spencer, J. 1989. 'Anthropology as a Kind of Writing', *Man (N.S.)* 24(1): 145–64.

Turner, A. 2000. 'Embodied Ethnography. Doing Culture', *Social Anthropology* 8(1): 51–60.

Watson, C.W. 1999. 'Introduction: The Quality of Being There', *Being There: Fieldwork in Anthropology*. London: Pluto Press, pp. 1–24.

Chapter 7

What is Sacred about that Pile of Stones at Mt Tendong?

Serendipity, Complicity and Circumstantial Activism in the Production of Anthropological Knowledge of Sikkim, India

Vibha Arora

The *rite de passage* of fieldwork that transformed me into a competent fieldworker and an anthropologist was undertaken by me in Sikkim, situated in the Eastern Himalayas of India. The former Buddhist kingdom of Sikkim was incorporated into India in 1975 as its twenty-second state.[1] I conducted multi-sited fieldwork in Sikkim and the Darjeeling Hills of West Bengal between August 2001 and September 2002, primarily among the Lepchas and the Bhutias, but also the Nepali groups and the Tibetan refugees.[2] This paper discusses my fieldwork experiences to highlight the role of serendipity, complicity, circumstantial activism and archival research for the production of ethnographic knowledge of Sikkim. As Marcus explains in his book *Ethnography through Thick and Thin* (1998), these ideas inform multi-sited ethnographies.

The Sikkim of my fieldwork experience neither resembled the picturesque mountainous Himalayan landscape of any current tourist brochures nor any ethnographic description of a Himalayan sacred landscape that other anthropologists wrote about. There were no recent ethnographic voices that could caution me about this ethnically fissured land.[3] I did not conduct fieldwork under fire, but the field was politicised with the Lepcha and Bhutia groups ceremonialising their identity to assert their indigeneity and rights to

Sikkim's landscape, while expecting this ethnographer to document them for the wider world.[4] The initial weeks upturned all fieldwork plans and I had to mould the direction of my research inquiry to an ethnically unpredictable eruptible crucible.[5] Documenting those ethnic encounters, the ethnic fissions and fusions among the Lepchas and Bhutias, created conditions to encounter serendipity and I seized the chance when it occurred.[6] Serendipity accounts for my making two ethnographic discoveries. These are discussed later in this paper.[7]

I begin by introducing the ethnographic context, mapping my multi-sited fieldwork in it, explaining my positioning in this field, and discussing the fieldwork encounter(s) that shaped my multi-sited ethnography, in order to emphasise the role of complicity and serendipity. I found myself witnessing ethnic encounters, documenting discourses around the Rathongchu hydroelectric project controversies, and participating in rituals that could not have been anticipated by any scientifically prepared research design.[8] The second section emphasises the role of serendipity by briefly mentioning an ethnic skirmish among the Lepchas and the Bhutias at Kabi village, which facilitated my entry into and participation in the world of Lepcha revival. My presence as a witness during that ethnic skirmish explained my inclusion into their annual pilgrimage to worship Mt Tendong, although there were differences between these situations. These two field experiences resulted in ethnographic discoveries that I suggest will influence any understanding of ethnic groups and sacred landscapes in Sikkim. The concluding section underscores circumstantial activism in multi-sited ethnography and expectations of an ethnographer by their informants. It emphasises the necessity of regaining a critical perspective in the post-fieldwork phase by relating the fieldwork experiences to secondary and archival data. I also discuss the ethical issues involved in any ethnographic representation of Mt Tendong and the dissemination and validation of its sacredness to the wider society by me.

Multi-sited Ethnography, Serendipity and Complicity

My ethnography of Sikkim is a product of multi-sited fieldwork, archival research in India and England and a result of serendipity and, to some extent, complicity during fieldwork. Understanding the dynamics of ethnopolitics of Sikkim required a thorough knowledge of the history and culture of the Lepchas and the Bhutias of Sikkim, and some familiarity with regional economic development, Buddhism and the culture of other Himalayan groups residing in Sikkim. The key to my 'knowing how to know' lay in a dynamic interaction between the archive and the field, relating significant events to social developments, understanding myths, participating in rituals and people's practices, understanding encounters that disrupt everyday life, and serendipity.

As an ethnographic context, Sikkim represents a picturesque Himalayan watershed composed of twenty-two Indo-Tibetan and Indo-Aryan ethnic groups.[9] Broadly, this ethnic diversity is categorised into three groups: the

Lepchas, the Bhutias and the Nepali groups. Currently Sikkim's population is predominantly Hindu (68%). The Buddhists comprise a large community (27%). Christians comprise a small minority (about 3%). Muslims are present in insignificant numbers (Lama 2001: 7). The main ethnic boundary is between the Lepchas and the Bhutias, who comprise an indigenous minority and, since 1978, were accorded Scheduled Tribe status by the Indian Constitution. The numerically dominant category of Nepali persons that comprises several ethnic groups is internally differentiated by differences of religion, caste and class among groups that have varying migration histories into Sikkim (Arora 2006b). In Arora (2004) I emphasise that the ethnic relations between these diverse groups follow segmentary principles of situational selectivity and complementary opposition. There are tensions within the Lepcha-Bhutia ethnic alliance although they are united in their opposition towards the Nepali groups.[10]

Multi-sited Ethnography of Sikkim

My fieldwork was a combination of localised dwelling in a village and a series of ethnographic encounters in different sites to which I travelled to attend rituals. As places, locales sustain meanings in communicative acts (Giddens 1984: xxv).[11] Yet, I felt a single-sited study would neither adequately represent the contested discourses around Sikkim's landscape nor document the differences in perceptions within an ethnic group and between different ethnic groups. A multi-sited study is designed around 'paths, conjunctions, or juxtapositions of locations' in which the ethnographer establishes some form of literal, physical presence, with a posited logic of association between them shaping the argument of the ethnography (Marcus 1998: 90). This multi-sited fieldwork was guided by the logic of association that was given by some Lepcha-Bhutia ideologues and by reading two texts, namely the *History of Sikkim* (Dolma and Namgyal 1908) and the pilgrimage guide to Sikkim.[12]

The Lepcha and Bhutia-dominated Kabi village of North Sikkim constituted the primary site for this localised dwelling and I was based here between September 2001 and February 2002.[13] Thereafter I used Gangtok, Sikkim's capital, as my base. I undertook short-term fieldwork in Kalimpong in the Darjeeling area of neighbouring West Bengal, the Lepcha reserve area of Dzongu (see Arora 2006b), Chungthang, Guru Dongmar Lake, Lachen and Lhonak valleys of North Sikkim; Gangtok in East Sikkim; Mt Tendong in South Sikkim; and Yoksum, Lake Kacheopalri, and Tashiding and Pemagayantse monasteries of West Sikkim (Arora n.d.).[14] After completing fieldwork, I consulted the archives at Kolkatta in India (September 2002), Oxford, Cambridge and London (June 2003 to August 2003), and Delhi in India (December 2003 to January 2004) to give historical depth to my ethnography. Archival research was essential since my fieldwork was conducted in historically significant sites, as is explicit in the worship of Mt Tendong and discussed later by this paper.

Ethnographic Positioning in the Field
at the Macro and Micro-level

The perceived identity of the ethnographer influences the interaction in the micro-setting and access to macro-level to produce 'ethnography through thick and thin'. I was neither exploring another land nor did I ever feel that I was conducting fieldwork in my own society and culture. Sikkim's sensitive geo-political location situates it in an extremely restricted access area of North-east India. Despite being an Indian national, I had to renew my entry permit for fieldwork in the restricted-access areas of North Sikkim every ninety days.[15] During multi-sited fieldwork, the anthropologist needs to assume diverse identities, negotiate cross-cutting affiliations and reconcile contradictory personal commitments (Marcus 1998). I was perceived differently at the micro-level (Kabi village) and the macro-context of ethno-politics, which afforded differential access to knowledge and enabled a range of fieldwork experiences. The field was generally hostile towards anthropologists in general.

The thesis contains *in-situ* discussion of how my ethnic identity and research questions became occasions for the Lepcha-Bhutia elites to reflect on ethnicity and the anthropological (mis)representation of the Lepchas and the Bhutias in earlier ethnographies (Arora 2004: 121–24, 131–34). Initially all of them distrusted this Indian anthropologist who was studying in England, and some members of the Sikkimese nobility were hostile towards my Indian identity.[16] Inevitably, all political discussions on Sikkim focused on the events of 1975 that culminated in Sikkim's loss of independence. The upper caste Hindu denigration of these beef-eating Mongoloid Lepcha-Bhutia tribals and their kinship customs (such as bride-price, polyandry and polygyny) directed much criticism in my direction as an upper-caste Punjabi Hindu woman. I ignored these undercurrents effectively since there were many other unforeseen issues. For instance, some Nepali bureaucrats at Gangtok were hostile to me as they could not comprehend the expectations of a research-design or why I selected the Lepcha-Bhutia groups rather than a Nepali group as my subjects. While the Lepcha-Bhutia bureaucrats decided that they had to support my study, ethnic fissures of Sikkim are reflected in its bureaucracy.

Kabi as Microcosm of North Sikkim

Kabi village of North Sikkim is located about sixteen kilometres from Gangtok and lies on the border between East Sikkim and North Sikkim.[17] It is a multi-ethnic settlement, with Bhutias comprising the majority in the consolidated figure of 778 Bhutias and Lepchas, while the remaining persons are categorised as being Nepali (about 213 persons).[18] Kabi is the historic site of the blood-brotherhood treaty that was enacted between the representatives of the Lepcha and the Bhutia tribes in the fourteenth century by keeping the sacred mountain Kanchenjunga as the divine witness. The treaty legitimised the migration and settlement of Bhutias to Sikkim and is symbolised by a shrine of stones in a sacred grove that is the locus of an annual ritual commemorating the historic Lepcha-Bhutia alliance during the worship of Mt Kanchenjunga.

These sacred stones materially represent the sacred mountain Kanchenjunga, which makes the grove sacred and inviolate from human interference. I chose Kabi as a fieldwork site because of its politico-symbolic role in sustaining the Lepcha-Bhutia alliance while reinforcing the migrant status of the Nepali groups in Sikkim. This had been mentioned in passing by some studies of Sikkim. Kabi is also close to Tumlong, which used to be the third capital of the kingdom of Sikkim and the residence of a powerful Lepcha lineage of the Karwang which gave Sikkim many military commanders and a Prime Minister during the nineteenth century.

Please Give Me a Room to Stay at Kabi

Concerned about the fragile ecology of Sikkim, the Supreme Court issued a directive in 2001 to prevent the illegal felling of timber in Sikkim's forests. Hence, the Central Bureau of Investigation initiated several investigations into the illegal felling and sale of timber. During one such investigation, the Central Bureau of India (CBI) cross-examined a resident of Kabi, who later committed suicide a few weeks prior to my first visit to Kabi in August 2001. The villagers were mourning his death when I entered this village with a research project to study Lepcha-Bhutia attitudes to the environment by studying Sikkim's sacred groves and Kabi sacred grove in particular. In this atmosphere, it became quite impossible to focus on sacred groves and I modified the project into a study of sacred landscapes of the Lepcha and Bhutia tribes of Sikkim. I decided not to abandon Kabi as it is a sacred site. However, unfortunately someone spread the rumour that I was a forest official investigating timber theft. There were other issues such as that Sikkim was neither exposed to the idea of a single Indian woman travelling alone nor were there any precedents to legitimise my status as an anthropologist. The field repulsed all my attempts to find a place to stay at Kabi, despite officials at Gangtok trying to persuade the villager's that I was a *bonafide* researcher.

I was exploring possibilities of shifting to other sites when by chance I interacted with a local journalist while attending some rituals at Pemagayantse monastery of West Sikkim. The journalist (mis)quoted me in his article that was published by a Sikkimese weekly newspaper in English. Nevertheless, this article presenced me in Sikkim's landscape and its urban elite. This article and my chance meeting with a Bhutia bureaucrat who had studied at Delhi and was visiting his family at Kabi ultimately led to my being given a place to stay at Kabi and near its sacred grove. To assuage villagers's suspicions that I was not an informant and explain how I knew about the historic importance of Kabi, a sympathetic villager floated a rumour that perhaps I was originally a Sikkimese resident of Kabi who had been reborn at Delhi. I compromised with this reincarnated (re)definition of myself.[19] My repeated reference to historical texts or a research design to justify my selection of Kabi and the interventions of my Gangtok friends were floundering when this rumour succeeded in naturalising my presence.

'She is Like an Inept Child'

I became an object of villagers' curiosity with my host initially restricting my interaction to select Lepcha-Bhutia households. I was further immobilised in those initial fieldwork weeks, as I was unused to footholds that passed as village-tracks, to the blood-sucking leeches, the practicalities of collecting water and vegetables, getting hot-water and the privacy of a bath, cooking on an open hearth, and dealing with nuisances such as drunks.[20] Two (un)lucky falls into village ditches yielded a twisted ankle and many blues, which, combined with my screaming at the blood-sucking leeches on my body during the monsoon, convinced all villagers that I could not be a forest official.

These villagers began to regard me as an inept child asking stupid questions, such as uses of some kitchen equipment (that were not familiar to me). They accepted me into their fold after I befriended some schoolchildren who became my friends, teachers, human-newspapers, chaperones and companions in discovering Kabi in its houses, fields, cardamom forests, the sacred grove, the village shops, the dispensary, the school, and the Buddhist temple. Some children started calling me *ani* (meaning father's sister or a Buddhist nun in the Bhutia language) and this sealed my kinship with Kabi. My interaction with the Nepali residents of Kabi was curtailed by the Lepcha-Bhutia villagers. However, these compromises were unavoidable in the early phase of my fieldwork.[21]

'She Knows Doctors in Gangtok. She Writes Constantly and Can Use the Camera'

The inept child was transformed into a resourceful figure and an ethnographer when someone fell sick in my host household and my medical box proved handy. My friends in Gangtok were doctors and I consulted them on the phone (there were four phones at Kabi village) before giving out these medicines.[22] Another village child injured his head in a fall and luckily my friends at the Gangtok hospital were on duty when the villagers took him to the hospital.

My positioning was altered when I started introducing the notebook in noting down names of things and opening the Tibetan and the Nepali dictionary. My hosts allowed me to take photographs of a ritual they sponsored in the Kabi temple. The children were always ready to pose for me and their parents were delighted with their pictures. The pen and the camera became twin instruments to document Kabi's public and private spaces. I was allowed to take pictures of a private moment of shamanic healing when a neighbour's repeatedly became sick and a Bhutia marriage in December 2001. People related to me as a photographer.

'She is Lepcha-Bhutia Sympathiser'

The micro-level of Kabi village was not impervious to the ethnic-politicisation at the macro-level, as is evident in my subsequent discussion of a local dispute among the Lepcha-Bhutia tribes at Kabi. As mentioned earlier, my mobility was restricted and I could not interact at length with the Nepali section of this ethnically divided village. The Nepali residents labelled me as a Lepcha-Bhutia sympathiser despite my repeated attempts to incorporate their perspective. A breakthrough came when a 45–year-old Sherpa man died. Death united all villagers in their grief and I participated in his mortuary rituals that presenced me among the Nepali residents. This is how I discovered that the Nepali Buddhists at Kabi (Sherpa and Tamang) had a separate cremation ground and were constructing another temple. The Lepcha-Bhutia villagers were angry with them as their temple constituted a symbol of Nepali mobility. The President of the local government at Kabi was a Sherpa youth who facilitated my interviews with Nepali elders about their migration to Kabi. I was tracing the historic migration of Nepali groups to Kabi with the Lepcha-Bhutia elders as part of my efforts to understand the history of Kabi. Hence, these interviews did not raise any eyebrows. These Nepali narratives were supplemented by those collected in other parts of Sikkim.

Undoubtedly, Kabi legitimised my participation in various rituals in other parts of Sikkim by claiming me as their historian, while I used their kinship and friendship links at other sites. I will restrict myself to a brief comment about my experience of staying in urban Sikkim. Urban Sikkim is used to foreign tourists visiting Sikkim but a single Indian woman anthropologist was a novelty. I was not a bureaucrat or a teacher who was associated with any institution that justified my presence. I was based at Sikkim's capital Gangtok for the latter phase of my research, where I lived in a multi-ethnic neighbourhood with Nepali and other Indian tenants and near the Sikkim Government College and the army cantonment. My Bhutia landlord treated me like a family member. My frequent travels did not elicit any suspicions as the neighbourhood was an 'urban fish-bowl'. I had limited privacy as I used the nearby public telephone booth's to make all travel bookings and to contact people.[23] My parents regularly called me up at a local call centre or at my landlord's house and my mother visited me for a fortnight in April 2002. The entire neighbourhood accepted my 'traveller's-dwelling' presence, as my research took me into other parts of Sikkim. There were many bureaucrats living in the same neighbourhood and they also helped me in my research with contacts and information. Fieldwork was not an easy experience, yet in the last leg of my fieldwork, many of my Sikkimese informants commented: 'you have experienced and travelled to more places during this period of your fieldwork in Sikkim than we have in our entire lifetime'.

Circumstantial Activism and Complicity in Multi-sited Ethnography

My fieldwork was a tangled web of negotiations and complicities with diverse sections, including the villager's (Lepcha, Bhutia and Nepali persons), the ethnic associations of the Lepcha and the Bhutia tribes, the Buddhist monastic association, the Lepcha ideologues, including their shamans, the bureaucracy of Sikkim, the Indian judiciary (Gangtok and Delhi), the army, and other Indians residing in Sikkim. Personal conflicts and contradictions were 'resolved not by refuge in being a detached anthropological scholar but in being an ethnographer-activist renegotiating identities in different sites' (Marcus 1998: 98). My constant movement between sites and different levels of Sikkim's society inevitably gave it an activist character.

The ideologues and the leadership of the cultural associations of some ethnic groups, more specifically the Lepchas and the Bhutias, perceived me to be a useful instrument who would disseminate information about them to the wider world. Hence, the Lepcha-Bhutia ideologue consciously directed me into documenting specific aspects of their culture and transformed my research into a collaborative project to document Lepcha and Bhutia cultural revival in contemporary Sikkim.[24] I was encouraged to interview members of these associations, attend rituals that they organised at various sites, and document their efforts to develop their communities. My fieldwork progressed accordingly although this transformed me into a circumstantial activist (an ethnographer-accomplice) of the indigenous Lepcha-Bhutia tribals while placing me at the receiving end of hostile comments from the Nepali category. Issues of knowledge and its construction were brought to the forefront specifically after my participation in the Lepcha pilgrimage to worship Mt Tendong. The collaboration between the ethnographer and the participant-hosts produced knowledge of Sikkim for a third, the wider world.[25] Tropes of exit and entry do function to construct the field in my narrative and authorise the material (Gupta and Ferguson 1997:17), but my thesis does not privilege the authorial voice of its ethnographer.[26] Without subverting ethnographic knowing, I tried to document the polyphony of voices constituting Sikkim into a multi-ethnic society.[27]

Serendipity and the Anthropological Journey: Kabi to Mt Tendong

Many anthropologists are recognising the methodological value of serendipity as a strategy of ethnographic discovery, as 'epistemologically it will help us understand how we and others make sense of, and simultaneously create, the reality we live in' (Pieke 2000: 149). Some anthropological journeys are simply the unanticipated, unintended consequence of being in a place at a particular moment. If I had not witnessed a local dispute at Kabi then I would not have become the official ethnographer of the Lepcha pilgrimage to worship Mt Tendong in August 2002. This journey was definitely a result of serendipity, which radically altered my perspective on sacred landscapes in Sikkim while raising ethical issues around ethnographic representation and the anthropologists' role in emphasising the sacredness of sacred sites by undermining the instrumental act of their social construction. I begin by discussing the dispute that culminated in some ethnographic discoveries.

On 16 October 2001, I witnessed a dispute at Kabi that not only influenced my research agenda but furthered collaboration with the Lepchas. While passing the sacred grove, I noticed several jeeps parked near its entrance and some visitors in traditional Lepcha attire. These visitors appeared to be embroiled in an argument with the local villagers.[28] The visitors explained that the day was marked in the Lepcha calendar for making first fruit offerings to the protective deities of Sikkim and to commemorate the blood-brotherhood treaty at Kabi. They complained that the local villagers were not letting them enter the grove. The villagers (mostly Bhutia youth) had locked the gates of this sacred grove. On their part, the villagers of Kabi were uncompromising in their demand that the Lepchas should participate in the annual celebrations scheduled after a fortnight. There appeared to be no possibility of compromise, hence the Lepchas decided to go back after placing their offerings outside the sacred grove.

The Lepchas departed with a sense of humiliation and powerlessness while the Bhutias of Kabi arrogantly celebrated their victory by scattering their offerings.[29] As one Lepcha leader stated, 'this incident aptly summarised Bhutia domination over us [the Lepchas], and the inequalities within the alliance'. The desire to perform the ritual separately symbolised their alienation while the inability of the Lepchas increased their anger. It was this act of witnessing that later facilitated complicity with the Lepcha ideologues.

A fortnight after this dispute the annual ritual was performed at Kabi. It was attended by the officials of the district administration, including the District Collector himself, the representative of Kabi in the Sikkim legislative assembly, officials from the Culture Department in Gangtok, members of the press and electronic media, and the schoolchildren of Kabi. Not surprisingly, the Lepchas boycotted these celebrations in 2001, although the chief celebrant of the ritual was a Lepcha shaman based at Kabi.

If Kabi is sacred then for whom is it sacred and why? What kind of blood-brotherhood treaty was being commemorated if the Lepchas were denied the right to worship here? What is the nature of this historic Lepcha-Bhutia ethnic alliance? The local dispute raised more questions for research and resulted in the ethnographic discovery of the Bhutianisation of the Lepchas. I was thoroughly intrigued that none of the Lepchas of Kabi had voiced any criticism of the way the other villagers had handled the Lepcha delegation. As Kabi is the site of the blood-brotherhood treaty, the Lepchas should comprise the majority of its residents. Today, approximately ten to fifteen households in Kabi identify themselves as Lepchas. So where have the Lepchas of Kabi disappeared? Solving the mystery of the missing Lepchas became critical for my research on Sikkim. A Lepcha of Lhabi (Kabi's neighbouring Lepcha village) once seriously stated to me that the Lepchas were Bhutianised after assuming Bhutia identities and lifestyles. It was while recording the genealogy of a Lepcha lineage and locating them at Kabi that I discovered approximately 200 Bhutianised Lepchas at Kabi itself. Even the Lepcha shaman is listed as a Bhutia in Kabi's voters' list and the land revenue records.

No other ethnography on Sikkim and the Lepchas discusses the 'Bhutianisation of the Lepchas', which explains the degradation of Lepcha cultural identity and their loss of social and political power in Sikkim after the Lepcha rebellion of 1826. Bhutianisation refers to the social mobility of Lepchas but not the entire Lepcha group, as these individuals assume Bhutia identities. The boundary between the Lepchas and the Bhutias is not too rigid due to kinship alliances between the two communities. Both the Lepcha and the Bhutia tribes enact distinct lineage rituals that underscore their ethnic differences. The process of Bhutianisation assimilates the Lepcha elites at the lower end of the Bhutia group, although they enjoy higher status than the Lepchas. On their part, many Bhutias complained that the Bhutianisation of the Lepchas had diluted their identity and allowed for incorporation of some elements of Lepcha culture into Bhutia culture: this explains the interpenetration of Lepcha-Bhutia culture and the subordinate position of the Lepchas in the Lepcha-Bhutia ethnic alliance. Nevertheless, unlike other cases of social mobility such as Sanskritisation (Srinivas 1989), Bhutianisation is restricted to families and is not a group strategy for social mobility.

The following indicators signal the process of Bhutianisation of the Lepchas that effectively involve abandoning of Lepcha culture: those Lepchas who do not use the Lepcha language and cannot read the Lepcha script, those who do not perform the rituals prescribed by the Lepcha calendar, those who do not participate in shamanic rituals and follow only Buddhist practices, and those who do not wear Lepcha but Bhutia costumes are discarding Lepcha symbols of identity and becoming Bhutianised. In law, the Lepcha and Bhutia tribes enjoy equal status and entitlements. One Lepcha leader stated that many Lepchas have Buddhist names and are intermarried with the Bhutias. Hence, with politico-economic mobility the Lepchas instrumentally assume Bhutia identities to improve their standing in the social hierarchy.

In contemporary Sikkim, the Lepcha association is trying to reverse the historic Bhutianisation of Lepchas by rediscovering Shamanism, which valorises Lepcha identity and their indigenous knowledge. Paradoxically, individual shamans are disappearing yet the ideology of Shamanism as indigenous knowledge is emerging as a political tool for negotiating ethno-politics and pressurising the state for privileges as Scheduled Tribes. Over time Lepcha identity had become ethnically inferior to Bhutia identity. The rise of Shamanism in contemporary Sikkim and the Darjeeling Hills of West Bengal is a rediscovery of Lepcha cultural roots guided by an instrumentalist-pragmatic need of the Lepchas to assert prior claims over the region's resources and to bargain for power. The rise of Shamanism expresses both their self-consciousness and agency to other groups and the state (Arora 2005a). This explains the paradox of the vanishing Lepcha shamans and the simultaneous rise of Shamanism as epitomised by the worship of Mt Tendong as a sacred mountain.

The Lepcha association instituted the ritual of worshipping Mt Tendong in the early 1990s as part of the process of retribalisation.[30] A major achievement of this cultural revival has been to reinvent Lepcha identity as that of nature-worshippers and the vanguards of environmental wisdom and prevent further Bhutianisation of the Lepchas. The rituals for the worship of Mt Tendong were instituted in 1991 with the Lepcha shaman Sonam Tshering composing its prayers and performing the ritual in Darjeeling and Sikkim. The Lepcha leadership surmised the need to initiate such cultural festivals in order to express their distinctive Lepcha identity, since Mt Kanchenjunga is jointly worshipped by the Lepcha and the Bhutia tribes in another ritual (*dpang lha gsol* in the Tibetan language). Mt Kanchenjunga is a sacred mountain of the Lepchas and was incorporated into the Buddhist pantheon as a defender of the Buddhist faith. Hence, Mt Kanchenjunga has predominantly Buddhist connotations today as its pre-Buddhist identity as a Lepcha mountain god is receding in social memory.

The incorporation of Mt Kanchenjunga in the Buddhist pantheon was central to the consolidation of the power of the Bhutias and the Namgyal dynasty in Sikkim. I concur with Humphrey (1995) observations on Chiefly and Shamanic landscapes in Mongolia, and trace similarities in the Sikkim case. In the past, Shamanism expressed decentralised power and countervailing tendencies in Sikkim's landscape while Buddhism consolidated the power of the Namgyal dynasty, although kingship patronised Lepcha shamanism to legitimise their rule. The present state government is secular and democratic and is neither dependent on Shamanism nor on Buddhism to legitimise its rule, yet in practice it actively seeks legitimacy by sponsoring many rituals instituted by the Namgyal dynasty. The rise of Mt Tendong in contemporary Sikkim symbolises the subversion of the Bhutia hegemony through the empowerment of the Lepchas, and it is not merely about reviving a disappearing Lepcha culture. Shamanism does not express any separatist or secessionist aspirations of the Lepchas. It expresses Lepcha political consciousness within the Lepcha-Bhutia alliance and the wider society. State patronage of Lepcha culture was a prerequisite for the rise of shamanism in contemporary Sikkim and the Darjeeling Hills. This is explicit in the sponsorship of the worship and recognition of Mt Tendong as a sacred mountain.

The Lepcha ideologues explained to me that the ritual for the worship of Mt Tendong has its genesis in an ancient Lepcha myth of deluge. According to their myth, the river Teesta flooded Sikkim and almost caused the extinction of all forms of life.[31] During this deluge the peak of Mt Tendong gave sanctuary to human, animal and other forms of life and saved them from being drowned. The rest of Sikkim was flooded and all life perished in the great deluge (L. Tamsang 1997). Mt Tendong is annually worshipped on 8 August, and in 1997 the government of Sikkim declared it to be a state holiday (L. Tamsang 1997: 23). The ritual has two components and the government of Sikkim sponsors the entire celebration. Firstly, prayers are offered by a small group at the summit of Mt Tendong. Secondly, the entire Lepcha community worships it on 8 August in Gangtok in Sikkim.

On 6 August 2002, a group comprising twelve Lepcha men and myself travelled to South Sikkim to perform the ritual to worship Mt Tendong (South Sikkim). The journey represented a pilgrimage for the Lepchas, and a Lepcha revival to the others. The ages of this delegation ranged between eighteen and seventy-four years, while five members (excluding Sonam Tshering) were participating in the ritual for the fifth time. This was the first time that a woman, a non-Lepcha and an anthropologist, was participating in and documenting the rituals at the summit of Mt Tendong.[32] Women do not normally attend lineage rituals among the Lepchas and the Tamsang clan worships Mt Tendong to ensure the continuity of their lineage. The importance of documenting the worship of Mt Tendong became explicit later although there had been no indication of this responsibility prior to commencing this journey.[33]

Our vehicle was flying the Lepcha flag, the stereo was playing melodious Lepcha songs, the entire delegation excepting me was in traditional Lepcha costumes and the passengers were periodically shouting *Aachuley*.[34] The vehicle was carrying offerings sent by Lepchas from various parts of Sikkim and the Darjeeling Hills. These included silk scarves, incense, fruits, flowers, rice, cash offerings and fermented millet beer. Additionally, the jeep was carrying cement, sand, iron rods, a metal trunk of ritual artefacts and Lepcha manuscripts belonging to the shaman Sonam Tshering. The metal trunk containing Lepcha texts symbolised their indigenous knowledge. The sand, cement and iron rods were for constructing a permanent shrine for the midnight-to-dawn celebrations at the summit that would monumentalise the decennial anniversary of the worship of Mt Tendong.

By afternoon our group reached Damthang village at the base of Mt Tendong. The entire group changed into trekking clothes and, carrying assorted backpacks, commenced the trek. From here Mt Tendong's summit is a five kilometre, steep, uphill trek on a slippery clayey floor through dense sub-tropical forests, bamboo thickets, and bushes infested with thick blood-sucking leeches. The pilgrimage began with Sonam Tshering offering fermented millet beer to the spirits of the mountain and seeking their permission before climbing the mountain. But the material they carried made their political objective explicit to me. During this journey, the Lepchas continuously joked with each other, sang songs, narrated myths and generally indicated their interest in Lepcha indigenous knowledge that had been degraded as being inferior with the Bhutanisation of the Lepchas.

On reaching the summit, Sonam Tshering offered millet beer to the spirits, stated the intention of this group, explained my presence and requested their cooperation in constructing the shrine. We set up our base camp in the lighthouse for the duration of our visit, as the only other building is a Buddhist hermitage.[35] The men gathered firewood and then built a fire. Sonam Tshering unpacked the Lepcha material artefacts and his books. I was the official ethnographer but also assigned the job of supervising two Lepcha youths who were cooking our dinner. Sonam Tshering divined and selected the site for constructing the shrine. Some members of the group mixed the sand, cement and the soil while other members selected long stones to symbolise the iconic representations of Mt Tendong. The participants believed that they were making history on 6 August 2002 when the Lepcha youth under the supervision of Sonam Tshering constructed the sacred shrine. The shrine consists of upright stones fixed in the ground.

One Lepcha youth aggressively stated, 'in case the shrine is desecrated and destroyed, we will rebuild it next year'. The Lepchas had informal permission to construct the shrine on this land belonging to the Forest department. However, they admitted the possibility of its vandalisation by other ethnic groups objecting to the shamanic conversion of Mt Tendong. The Buddhists have a hermitage, and the Hindus of the area celebrate the birthday of Lord Ram at the summit. Members of the Lepcha delegation admitted to me that if the shrine was undisturbed then they could plan the construction of a shed in the subsequent years. Their argument explicitly acknowledged that the construction and retention of that shrine at Mt Tendong involved careful political negotiations with other ethnic groups. The Lepchas cannot ignore the claims of other ethnic communities over Mt Tendong.

Around 7 PM Sonam Tshering started reciting the verses from the Lepcha book of predictions. He had already narrated the myth and explained the significance of this ceremony during our journey from Gangtok. However, while reciting the verses he would pause to explain the meaning of his song to the participants. His songs are composed in a metaphorical language that is comprehensible only to other Lepcha shamans. After these prayers there was a break, during which the group had dinner and rested before commencing the prayers at midnight at the shrine.

At midnight, Sonam Tshering performed the rituals under a plastic sheet protecting us from a heavy downpour with leeches crawling over us. Candles and torches illuminated this shrine. Sonam Tshering recited his songs and prayers by reading them from a Lepcha manuscript, *Chyu Ten Malong*, which he had complied himself. The text collated Lepcha myths such as the myth of creation, the myth of deluge, the myth of the origin of different Lepcha clans, the description of the Lepcha sacred sites, and prayers to various spirits and gods. During these prayers, Sonam Tshering would pause to explain to us the meaning of his songs, the significance of these offerings and the myths that he was narrating. He explained that the prayers propitiated the gods and requested their protection from any future deluge. He requested their cooperation in ensuring the fertility of the land, in maintaining the environmental balance and in ensuring peace and harmony in Sikkim and the world. At dawn Sonam Tshering proudly outlined the entire spread of Sikkim from the top of the lighthouse and narrated the glory of the former Lepchaland to us. Then he thanked the spirits for the successful completion of the rituals and the construction of the shrine. He then requested their permission to descend from Mt Tendong, and sought their blessings for our safe return journey to Gangtok. The tired group trekked back to Damthang village in a euphoric mood having accomplished their mission.

What explains the construction of this shrine in August 2002 and my inclusion in the delegation? The construction of this new shrine at Mt Tendong in 2002, is a response to their not being able to worship at the Kabi shrine in October 2001. This Kabi incident was an ethnic skirmish that was cited to be the cause of tensions between the Bhutias and the Lepchas during the period of my fieldwork. Some members of the Lepcha community decided they needed an exclusive shrine of their own. I had witnessed their humiliation while conducting fieldwork in Kabi. Partially, this explains why they responded with enthusiasm when I expressed my desire to join the Lepcha delegation. The leadership wanted me to document the act of constructing a separate shrine as I had witnessed their humiliation and powerlessness at Kabi. It was a different kind of witnessing as the Lepchas wanted me to record and disseminate the rise of Mt Tendong as a sacred mountain into the wider society. Both these events highlight the tensions and the continuing negotiations in the Lepcha and Bhutia alliance. This participation in the pilgrimage to Mt Tendong marked the completion of my ritual of ethnographic documentation. The segmentary character of inter-ethnic relations is clearly explicit, as in 2002 the Lepcha-Bhutia jointly performed the annual ritual at Kabi after the Sikkim government announced that elections for the local government were to be held in early 2003. The Lepcha-Bhutia ideologues quickly cemented their fractured alliance to pose a united front against the Nepali groups.

What is Sacred about that Pile of Stones?

The rediscovery of the shamans' song at Mt Tendong metaphorically expresses the emergence of Lepcha self-consciousness and as a countervailing trend against the centralising tendencies of Buddhism. The shaman's song at Mt Tendong was not just a song praising the gods or a song reviving Lepcha culture, because its melody belies its political purpose. Recent developments in Sikkim suggest that myths and rituals are critical arenas for observing the development of political consciousness and understanding transformations in the symbols of power. Rituals can reverse hierarchies and 'the symbol of the ritual leads us to the discovery of structural conflict, contradiction and stress in the wider social and cultural world' (Ortner 1978: 4). Scholars also emphasise that collective memory works over time in forgetting the active construction of social processes by mythologising its origins (Vansina 1985

Connerton 1989). Here I need to direct attention to another discovery that I made during fieldwork and participation in the annual ritual at Kabi. The elders of Kabi confessed to me that the sacred shrine identified as the site of the blood-brotherhood treaty at Kabi is a reconstruction of the original shrine worshipping Mt Kanchenjunga. The knowledge of the existence of the original and the constructed shrine is not widely known but restricted to the Lepcha shamans and Kabi's elders.

The desecrated original shrine is now a weathered pile of stones that is located near the entrance of the sacred grove that was destroyed during the construction of the national highway in the 1940s. The original shrine is distinguished from the surrounding stones by the white silk scarves tied around one of its big stones. The currency of the Kabi myth and the continued performance of the annual commemorative ritual testify to the symbolic power of these sacred stones. This also expresses the dynamic relation between shamanism and Buddhism over time in legitimating political authority in Sikkim. The ascendancy of Mt Tendong and the declining importance of Mt Kanchenjunga in Lepcha culture express the negotiations within the Lepcha-Bhutia alliance and changes in the valuation of Lepcha culture with recognition of their environmental knowledge.

Sikkim's landscape is constructed by the cultural performances that are enacted in it and the meanings the diverse ethnic groups residing in it give during their engagement and dwelling in it. The landscape constantly oscillates between a foreground of everyday emplacement and a background of social potential (Hirsch and O'Hanlon 1995: 3, 22–23). Scholars argue that the landscape mediates between the cultural and the political processes by becoming their material expression and the locus of social actions (Duncan 1990; Duncan and Ley 1993; Hirsch and O'Hanlon 1995; Strang 1997; Lovell 1998; Stewart and Strathern 2003). My research documented the politicisation of sacred landscapes (such as Kabi, Mt Tendong and Mt Kanchenjunga) that are regarded as being repositories of Lepcha and Bhutia indigenous knowledge. The sacred site is a space to which people give material form, content and boundaries in order to reimagine themselves while responding to changes in the wider society (Parkin 1991). The fieldwork experience of Mt Tendong gave me a processual perspective on sacred sites. It simultaneously provided evidence of their construction as acts of monument construction to represent social transition materially. The idea of a monument explains the rise and the symbolic power of the constructed shrine at Kabi and the receding social memory of the original shrine for worshipping Mt Kanchenjunga. The act of creation of a sacred landscape such as Mt Tendong may be forgotten as the site is mythologised, ceremonialised, monumentalised and sometimes dissipated into insignificance.

Although the worship of Mt Tendong was part of the general worship of sacred mountains, it did not have any specific rituals prior to the 1990s. My familiarity with other ethnographies and the honest admissions by two Lepcha ideologues guided this ethnographic discovery. In the pre-1975 period ethnographic descriptions of the Lepchas were given by some Europeans (de

Beauvior Stocks 1927 [reprinted 1975]; Gorer 1938; Morris 1938; Siiger 1967; Siiger and Rischel 1967). Since the merger of Sikkim into India in 1975, the Lepchas themselves have conducted research and published books such as studies by K.P. Tamsang (1983), A.R. Foning (1987), and Gowloog (1995).[36] There have been some studies by other (non-Lepcha) scholars (such as Thakur 1988; Bhasin 1989; Chattopadhyay 1990; Ghosal 1992); nonetheless, I could not find any description of the rituals to the worship of Mt Tendong in them although they do mention the Lepcha myth of deluge.

I was in a big dilemma about representing Mt Tendong and its worship in my writing. Do I privilege the Lepcha performance? Or write the performance expected of me of naturalising Mt Tendong as a sacred mountain? Or do I write what is my own understanding? Mt Tendong can be defined as a sacred mountain according to Lepcha mythology. It does not represent historical expression of collective representations among the Lepchas. It is partially an ethnic assertion and expression of fractures in the negotiated alliance among the Lepchas and the Bhutias. It is also partially an expression of Lepcha culture and knowledge as primordial nature worshippers. It is partially an expression of the contribution by Sonam Tshering towards Lepcha culture based on his knowledge and dedicated work during his lifetime. The banner on the stage of the celebrations at Gangtok in August 2002 proclaimed that the Lepchas were conscious that they were celebrating the tenth anniversary of this ritual. The average person in Sikkim does remember the inception of this ritual. Consequently, in my thesis I wrote: 'the worship of Mt Tendong is a recently invented ritual, although I admit that its importance has increased to such a level that it is now at the heart of Lepcha cosmology' (Arora 2004: 282). Visual evidence such as the picture of that banner and the new shrine are part of my thesis.

The historian and ethnographer is an active constituent in the process of naturalising and mythologising sacred sites, and my participation in these diverse rituals was perceived to be essential to gain further recognition and disseminate the knowledge of Mt Tendong to the wider society. Ethics of ethnographic writing demanded that I distance myself from that circumstantial-activist of the field to accept my responsibility as an ethnographer by adopting a critical stance.[37] I am conscious that some sections of my data will elicit critical reactions from different sections of Sikkimese society that will influence my future field visits and collaboration. Further, I am a sociologist at an Indian University with students from Sikkim.

Postscript

Some of the methodological, representational and ethical issues around fieldwork discussed in this paper were raised by me during two ASA workshops on 'Professional Practice in Anthropology' organised by Andrew Garner at the School of Oriental and African Studies at London in May 2003 (where I was a student-participant) and at the University College London in

March 2004 (where I was transformed into a resource person). They were briefly raised by me in September 2003 at the BSA-ESRC Summer School at the University of Bath. Discussing them at these professional fora was an essential pre-condition to writing about them.

Notes

1. My fieldwork was conducted in what existed as the undivided kingdom of Sikkim, as the Darjeeling Hills were annexed by British India and incorporated into Bengal in 1835. I am grateful to the Commonwealth Scholarship Commission (UK) for funding my doctoral research, and the Beit fund for Commonwealth History and Linacre College at the University of Oxford for giving me grants for fieldwork and archival research in India and England. I was awarded my doctorate in November 2004 by the University of Oxford. I am indebted to my supervisors Marcus Banks and David Parkin for believing in me, and my thesis examiners Caroline Humphrey, Wendy James and Robert Parkin for their critical insights, as well as Narmala Halstead and Eric Hirsch for their constructive comments that improved this paper. Some sections of this paper were presented at the ASA Decennial Conference at Manchester in 2003 in P. Sillitoe's panel on Indigenous Knowledge, and at an anthropology seminar at the London School of Economics in October 2004.
2. A forthcoming publication discusses the ethnic identities of the Bhutias and the Tibetans in detail (Arora 2006a).
3. Prior to my fieldwork, no recent in-depth studies were available for any consultation. Sikkim studies were dominated by Tibetologists or anthropologists using a Tibetologist perspective. Between 2002 and 2004 three anthropologists (including myself) received our doctorates in this field, while some others have entered the field. There are hardly any media reports about Sikkim. The incorporation of the former kingdom of Sikkim into India was a front-page story in 1975 and in the 1980s it re-entered news with the death of the Karmapa and the Sikkim's last king, *Chos-rgyal* Palden Thondup Namgyal. In the 1990s and until recently, Sikkim's presence in the Indian and International mass media was limited to news-items about its three famous son's (Bhaichung Bhutia's football exploits and Danny Denzongpa and Ugen Chopel's films), frequent landslides, orchids, masked dances and occasional reports about the Karmapa controversy and the Indian army guarding this borderland. Sikkim is in the process of opening itself to the world by promoting itself as an alternate Buddhist Shangri-la. The Maoist insurgency in Nepal and the current ethnic cleansing in Bhutan are not appealing to tourists any longer.
4. The ethnic encounters I documented among the Lepcha-Bhutia of Sikkim neither challenged the authority of the state nor showed that these groups have any secessionist agendas, unlike other parts of North-east India as in Nagaland. I will admit the presence of 'retrospective' nationalist sentiments about Sikkim as a nation among some elite families and some sections of the Sikkimese nobility.
5. Many collections of fieldwork by anthropologists and sociologists emphasise that fieldwork experiences produce ethnographic knowledge although theory informs the writing of these fieldwork experiences (Clifford and Marcus 1986; Marcus and Fischer 1986; Okely and Callaway 1992; Marcus 1998; Dresch, James and Parkin 2000; Gellner and Hirsch 2001).
6. A point Pieke (2000: 142–45) reiterates about his fieldwork in China.
7. The pre-fieldwork period at Oxford (October 2000 to June 2001) was spent by me in language training (Nepali and some literary Tibetan) and reviewing the relevant theoretical and ethnographic literature on the Himalayan region, specifically relating to Sikkim. Parkin (2000: 270) reiterates that intensive linguistic, ethnographic and regional preparation and around-the-clock participant observation and patient listening, are in fact the conditions for serendipitous discovery.

8. In the last leg of my fieldwork even the Indian army and the government of Sikkim complemented me by giving the rare permission to conduct short-term fieldwork among a small Tibetan yak-herders community living in a sacred site that lies in the land-mined areas of the Indo-Tibetan border.

9. The area is considered one of the wettest regions of the Himalayas.

10. These broad categorisations underplay the competing definitions, the internal variations and the transnational connections between ethnic groups residing in Sikkim and the neighbouring countries of Nepal, Bhutan and the Tibetan Autonomous region (for details refer to Arora 2005b).

11. Giddens defines them as 'a physical region involved as part of the setting of interaction, having definite boundaries, which help to concentrate interaction in one way or another' (1984: 375).

12. The pilgrimage guide (*gnas yig* in Tibetan) is a religious text written in the Tibetan language that was compiled in the thirteenth century and was later translated for me by the learned Tibetologist Chewang Acharya of a monastic college at Gangtok.

13. During this period, I visited the Lepcha reserve area to attend their New Year celebrations and a ritual at the Tholung monastery and also the Gaebo Achuk celebrations in the Darjeeling Hills of West Bengal.

14. These sites of West Sikkim constituted the area of the Rathongchu hydroelectric project controversies (Arora 2006c). My fieldwork on the Rathongchu project was supplemented by an analysis of the Rathongchu project case file. To cite relevant sections of the case file in the thesis, I obtained formal permission from the Chief Justice of India at the Supreme Court of India, Delhi, in January 2004.

15. Getting it was not easy and I had to obtain clearances from the office of Chief Secretary of Sikkim, the Home Department of the government of Sikkim, the Sub-divisional Magistrate (North Sikkim) and sometimes even the Commander of the Indian army at Gangtok. After China's recognition of Sikkim as being an integral part of India, access to many of these areas became easier.

16. There is a large corpus of literature on this issue of incorporation (annexation or peaceful merger by referendum) that is beyond the scope of this paper. For instance, see *Enchanted Frontiers* by N. Rustomji, *Smash and Grab* by Sunanda Datta-Ray, *China's Shadow over Sikkim* by Bajpai, *Sikkim: A Story of its Integration* by Raghunanda Rao, *Sikkim: A Short Political History* by L.B. Basnet, *Against the Tide* by Jigme N. Kazi, and last but not the least is Sikkim's former Queen Hope Cooke's autobiography *Time Change*.

17. North Sikkim is a restricted access area that is predominantly inhabited by the Lepchas and the Bhutias.

18. The Nepali category includes the Tamang, the Limbu and the Rai groups who settled at Kabi in the early twentieth century (Arora 2005b).

19. The villagers interpreted my vegetarianism as conforming to the austere diet of a Buddhist nun.

20. Thanks to a friend I acquired a gas-stove later. Alcoholism is a major social evil leading to the death of many persons.

21. I even had to ignore the exploitative relationship between the Bhutia landlords and their Nepali tenants and servants.

22. My visits to Gangtok became essential for restocking my medical kit.

23. It was not possible for me to install a land-line in Sikkim and mobiles entered Sikkim just before I quit the field.

24. Some members came forward to educate me as they did not want me to make mistakes in my documentation and representation. I am extremely grateful to many of them.

25. Marcus' notion of complicity establishes equivalence between the ethnographer and the informants, as both situate themselves in constructing a larger picture for the wider world (1998: 28). The hostile reactions of the Nepali groups constituted an essential background to this study.

26. Social anthropologists such as Okely and Callaway (1992) argue that anthropology cannot be reduced to the autobiographical experiences of the ethnographer in the field, but 'incorporating them in the text indicates how others related to the anthropologist while conveying the ethnographic moment' (Okely and Callaway 1992: 27).
27. I had to anonymise many such voices.
28. The Lepcha delegation comprised approximately fifty to sixty Lepcha men and women and three shamans (two male shamans and a female shaman).
29. During the entire period of my stay at Kabi, this incident was the only occasion when the gates of the sacred grove had been locked.
30. Retribalisation is a term used to refer to the ways in which the community recovers lost traditions and introduces processes for ensuring the continuation of the group traditions (Cohen 1969).
31. I will admit the influence of the Biblical myth of deluge here in the Lepcha case.
32. The worship of Mt Tendong is also a ritual for the continuity of the Tamsang clan.
33. On that day there was some initial disappointment as there was to be no video recording of the construction of the shrine. The group had wanted me to record the event although they had not communicated this desire prior to the journey. This explained why my gender was overlooked and I was included in the delegation. However, they had to be content with my stills camera and continuous note taking. I even ran out of photographic film while documenting the ritual on the mountain.
34. A Lepcha invocation that praises the Himalayas.
35. The government constructed it to promote the scenic vantage point of Mt Tendong among the tourists and it functions as an observatory.
36. I am excluding recent short descriptions in various articles published in *Aachuley* and other Lepcha magazines.
37. The ASA and BSA guidelines mention this point.

References

Arora, V. 2004. 'Just a Pile of Stones!: The Politicization of Identity, Indigenous Knowledge, and Sacred Landscapes among the Lepcha and the Bhutia tribes of contemporary Sikkim, India', Unpublished D.Phil. thesis. Oxford: University of Oxford.

_____. 2005a. 'The Shamans' Song at Mt. Tendong: Lepcha Environmental Wisdom' in the compilation of documents relating to the *3rd South Asian Solidarity for Rivers and People Forum*, June 13–16, Nirjuli, Arunachal Pradesh. CORE Guwahiti: Assam, India and WAFED Kathmandu: Nepal.

_____. 2005b. 'Being Nepali in Sikkim', *Contemporary India*. 4 (1/2) 127–48.

_____. 2006a. 'Changes in the Perception of Tibetan Identities in Contemporary Sikkim, India', in C. Klieger (ed.), *Identity Along the Margins*. 10/2. Proceedings of the 10th International Association of Tibetan Studies Conference. Leiden: Brill, pp. 31–52.

_____. 2006b. 'The Forest of Symbols Embodied by the Tholung Sacred Landscape of North Sikkim, India', *Conservation and Society* 4(1): 55–83.

_____. 2006c. 'Texts and Contexts in Sikkim, India', in E. Arweck and P. Collins (eds), *Reading Religion in Texts and Contexts*. Aldershot: Ashgate, pp. 83–102.

_____. n.d. 'Text, Ritual and Context in the Sacred Landscape of Sikkim, India: The Bumchu Ritual at the Tashiding Monastery', Unpublished paper presented at the *Second International Conference of Religions and Cultures in the Indic*

Civilization, Delhi, India, 17–20 December [2004].

Bajpai, G.S. 1999. *China's Shadow over Sikkim: The Politics of Intimidation*. New York: Lancer Publishers.

Basnet, L.B. 1974. *Sikkim: A Short Political History*. New Delhi. S.Chand.

de Beauvior Stocks, C. 1975 [1927]. *Sikkim: Customs and Folklore*. Delhi: Cosmo Publications.

Bhasin, V. 1989. *Ecology, Culture and Change: Tribals of Sikkim Himlayas*. New Delhi: Inter-India Publications.

Chattopadhyay, T. 1990. *Lepchas and their Heritage*. Delhi: B.R. Publishing.

Clifford, J. and G.E. Marcus (eds). 1986. *Writing Culture: The Poetics and the Politics of Ethnography*. Berkeley: University of California Press.

Cohen, A. 1969. *Custom and Politics in Urban Africa*. London: Routledge.

Connerton, P. 1989. *How Societies Remember*. Cambridge: Cambridge University Press.

Cooke, H. 1980. *Time Change: An Autobiography*. New York: Simon and Schuster.

Datta-Ray, S.K. 1984. *Smash and Grab: Annexation of Sikkim*. New Delhi: Vikas Publications.

Dolma, Y.M. and T.M. Namgyal. 1908. *History of Sikkim*. Gangtok: Namgyal Institute of Tibetology.

Dresch, P., W. James and D.J. Parkin (eds). 2000. *Anthropologists in a Wider World*. Oxford: Berghahn Books.

Duncan, J.S. 1990. *The City as Text: The Politics of Landscape Interpretation in the Kandy Kingdom*. Cambridge: Cambridge University Press.

Duncan, J.S. and D. Ley. 1993. *Place/Culture/Representation*. London: Routledge.

Foning, A.R. 1987. *Lepcha: My Vanishing Tribe*. Delhi: Sterling Publishers.

Gellner, D.N. and E. Hirsch (eds). 2001. *Inside Organizations: Anthropologists at Work*. Oxford: Berg.

Ghosal, S. 1992. *The Lepchas of Darjeeling and Sikkim: A study in Cultural Ecology and Social Change*. Unpublished Ph.D. Thesis: University of North Bengal.

Giddens, A. 1984. *The Constitution of Society*. Cambridge: Polity Press.

Gorer, G. 1938. *Himalayan Village: An Account of the Lepchas of Sikkim*. London: Michael Joseph.

Gowloog, R.R. 1995. *Lingthem Revisited: Social Changes in a Lepcha Village of North Sikkim*. New Delhi: Har-Anand Publications.

Gupta, A. and J. Ferguson (eds). 1997. *Anthropological Locations: Boundaries and Grounds of a Field Science*. Berkeley: University of California Press.

Hirsch, E. and M. O'Hanlon (eds). 1995. *The Anthropology of Landscape: Perspectives and Places*. Oxford: Clarendon Press.

Humphrey, Caroline. 1995. 'Chiefly and Shamanist Landscapes in Mongolia', in E. Hirsch and M. O'Hanlon (eds), *The Anthropology of Landscape: Perspectives and Places*. Oxford: Clarendon Press, pp. 135–62.

Kazi, J.N. 1993. *Inside Sikkim, Against the Tide*. Gangtok: Hill Media Publications.

Lama, M.P. 2001. *Sikkim: Human Development Report 2001*. Delhi: Government of Sikkim, Social Science Press.

Lovell, N. 1998. *Locality and Belonging*. London: Routledge.

Marcus, G.E. 1998. *Ethnography through Thick and Thin*. Princeton: Princeton University Press.

Marcus, G.E. and M.M.J. Fischer. 1986. *Anthropology as a Cultural Critique: An Experimental Moment in the Human Sciences*. Chicago: University of Chicago Press.

Morris, J. 1938. *Living with Lepchas: A Book about the Sikkim Himalayas*. London: Heinemann.

Okely, J. and H. Callaway (eds). 1992. *Anthropology and Autobiography*. London: Routledge.

Ortner, S. 1978. *Sherpas through their Rituals*. Cambridge: Cambridge University Press.

Parkin, D.J. 1991. *Sacred Void: Spatial Images of Work and Ritual among the Giriama of Kenya*. Cambridge: Cambridge University Press.

_____. 2000. 'Templates, Evocations and Long-term Fieldworker' in P. Dresch, W. James and D.J. Parkin (eds), *Anthropologists in a Wider World*. Oxford: Berghahn Books, pp. 91–108.

Pieke, F. 2000. 'Serendipity: Reflections on Fieldwork in China', in P. Dresch, W. James and D.J. Parkin (eds), *Anthropologists in a Wider World*. Oxford: Berghahn Books, pp. 129–50.

Rao, R. 1978. *Sikkim, The Story of its Integration within India*. New Delhi: Cosmo.

Rustomji, N. 1987. *Sikkim, A Himalayan Tragedy*. Ahmedabad: Allied Publishers.

Siiger, H. 1967. *The Lepchas: Culture and Religion of a Himalayan People, Part 1*. Copenhagen: National Museum of Denmark.

Siiger, H. and J. Rischel. 1967. *The Lepchas: Culture and Religion of a Himalayan People, Part 2*. Copenhagen: National Museum of Denmark.

Srinivas, M.N. 1989. *The Cohesive Role of Sanskritization and Other Essays*. Delhi: Oxford University Press.

Stewart, P.J. and A. Strathern (eds). 2003. *Landscape, Memory and History*. London: Pluto Press.

Strang, V. 1997. *Uncommon Ground: Cultural Landscapes and Environmental Values*. Oxford: Berg.

Tamsang, K.P. 1983. *The Unknown and Untold Reality about the Lepchas*. Kalimpong: Lyangsong Tamsang and Mani Printing Press.

Tamsang, L. 1997. 'Offering to Mt. Tendong and its Significance', *Aachuley* 1: 22–23.

Thakur, R. 1988. *Himalayan Lepchas*. New Delhi: Archives Publishers Distributors.

Vansina, J. 1985. *Oral Tradition as History*. Oxford: James Currey.

Chapter 8

Learning to See: World-views, Skilled Visions, Skilled Practice

Cristina Grasseni

Those who cannot explain the irruption of objects in human collectives, with all the manipulations and practices that they request, are not anthropologists, because they are missing what constitutes the fundamental aspect of our culture since Boyle: we live in a society that is bound to objects built in laboratories. Practice substitutes ideas, controlled doxa takes the place of apodictic reasoning and specialists' teams that of universal consensus (Latour, We have never been modern, 1991: 35)

Most of the ethnographer's anxiety when first confronted with the field comes from the sense of not knowing what to look for. This article addresses the process by which the ethnographer may become involved in processes of apprenticeship and 'enskilment' (Ingold 1993c: 221), which may allow her to 'learn to see anew'. The theoretical tenet of the essay in fact is the idea that *skill* may be a way of embedding relations between human beings and the environment they inhabit. I draw different examples from my fieldwork conducted in the valleys north of Bergamo, in the alpine region of northern Italy, which began in 1997 and continues to this day. This mountainous area, traditionally characterised by a pastoral economy of dairy farming and by seasonal migration, is now being repositioned in the 'global hierarchy of value' (Herzfeld 2004) as either a 'marginal rural area', in need of development and support, or as a potential tourist resort.

Here I recount how I came to reposition myself in the field several times through different uses of camerawork (both for observational and for analytic purposes) during fieldwork. This repositioning was also the result of my participation in different 'communities of practice' (Lave and Wenger 1991).

The phenomenological tenet of the primacy of emplacement guided my participant observation of the practices of dairy farming, orienting me to an analysis of what I have elsewhere called 'skilled visions' (Grasseni, 2007), that is, the diverse processes of developing 'an eye for' something. The main example I shall draw from is my apprenticeship into looking at cattle. In the field, I derived great frustration from not being able to absorb certain capacities for looking that my host's grandchildren leisurely exercised (such as cow-spotting, i.e. making out their herd's cows on the pasture, recognising them and calling them each by name). This failure, combined with my philosophical keenness for understanding world-views in relation to perceptual experience, prompted an 'epistemological crisis' that led me to rethink several times over the meaning I ascribed to vision and observation. I shall anticipate here that by world-views I mean not only the peculiar perspective that an educated capacity for perception affords, but also the whole cluster of cognitive, aesthetic and moral stances that accompany such perspective.

Learning How to Know as 'Legitimate Peripheral Participation'

The enskilment of vision goes along with the enskilment of the other senses, and, in particular, of bodily movement and dexterity, as part of a progressive process of joining a particular 'community of practice' – a process which Jean Lave calls 'legitimate peripheral participation' (Lave and Wenger 1991). In many ways, to be able to *see* means, in local discourses, more than just using one's eyesight. For instance, in my fieldwork setting, it means to be able to move through the pastures by noting the relevant features of the mountainous landscape, to have a particular sensory relationship with one's cattle and to be able to carry out certain processes (such as milking and cheese making) with dexterity. Often, for my hosts, to be able to 'see' becomes shorthand for being well-integrated into the environment of one's practice, and especially to have certain socially accepted skills – including that of knowing how to learn by paying attention to the right people and to the right features.

'Legitimate peripheral participation' can also work as an apt description of the way field encounters can be shaped, especially when the anthropological methodology of participant observation focuses on the phenomenology of lived experience. 'Situated learning' plays a vital role in imbuing everyday practical contexts with skills: practical, cognitive and social. Hence, investigating the process of the enskilment of vision allows us to reflect on the heuristic value of participant *observation*, meant itself as a controlled practice of ethnographic *presence* that involves entering relations of apprenticeship that grant understanding. 'Legitimate peripheral participation' may thus stand also for a process of enskilment of the ethnographer's senses in fieldwork encounters. The ethnographer is effectively trying to share the same lived experience from an 'adjacent' position.[1]

Ways of knowing are embedded in social practice. Drawing on my previous analyses of 'breeding aesthetics' and 'skilled vision', I have elaborated elsewhere on how specific 'skilled visions' grow and are constituted around aesthetic and practical standards (Grasseni 2004a, 2007). Since identity and cultures are rooted and reproduce themselves in the naturally and culturally constructed environments we thus inhabit, practices literally shape the way we look at the world, through technical mediation. Indeed, as a growing literature on cultural psychology and distributed cognition demonstrates, specific technological or cognitive artefacts may be instrumental in mediating skill. This raises issues of commensurability and understanding between different ecologies of practice: the outlook of a modern breeder that selects his cattle according to the US-imported 'linear module for the morphofunctional evaluation' of dairy cattle differs from that of a transhumant herder who conceives of his cattle as a long-standing part of a seasonal routine tied to the terrain. 'Sharing a world-view', for an ethnographer, may thus mean learning to inhabit local ecologies of vision that structure 'the public organisation of visual practice within the worklife of a profession' (Goodwin 2000: 164). She may then find that acquiring specific skills may serve to access such world-views and to document how ways of knowing are embedded in social practice.

A sense of propriety, of aesthetic accomplishment and of moral order is developed and transmitted in communities of practice. In fact, local ecologies of practice orient not only strategies for developing ethnographic participation and field relations, but also a theoretical search for the ways and tools through which everyday activities are organised (spatially, socially, cognitively). I refer here to the identity-making processes through which, by encountering, perceiving and investing the objects and spaces of everyday activity with meaning, people form attachments and a sense of themselves. For instance, a modern and a traditional breeder will hold opposing 'breeding aesthetics', each being attuned to an intimate appreciation of what is deemed as 'a beautiful cow' – whether a squat and sturdy heifer, adapted to the mountain climate and terrain, or a lean milk-making machine with bulging udders. These aesthetics derive from the complex histories of animal husbandry and biotechnology, the latter facing the economic imperatives of competitive production. In this scenario, one or the other 'skilled vision', once acquired, is not so much a code, a tool for actively manipulating messages, but rather the background that makes those messages meaningful.

The use of visual media is a legitimate part of an 'anthropology of the senses', which studies the cultural uses of the senses to observe, empathise with and record reality, while revealing the functional and symbolic predominance of different senses in different contexts of practice. Here, I would like first to elaborate on the use of visual media as both a synthetic and analytical tool. Visual anthropological methods for research and representation are being widely used outside a strictly 'ethnographic' concern, to investigate ecologies of practice, especially in the areas of education and psychological research (e.g. studying children's interaction in clinical settings or in natural, on-camera interactions), linguistic analysis (socio-linguistics, applied and comparative linguistics, ethnography of communication), ethno-methodology, as well as management and organisation studies. The analytical precision of audio-taped material is methodologically presumed, and even privileged, in a number of 'cognitive ethnographies' of the working environments (see, for instance, the series of studies sponsored by the Xerox Research Institute in Palo Alto, which produced high-quality data on human interaction and theories of mind, practice and cognition by academics such as Lucy Suchman, Charles Goodwin, Michael Cole and Yrjo Engestroem). These works highlight how the emergence of 'intelligence' and 'responsiveness', as the collective property of a human-technological system, are the result of a fine-grained interaction between human observation, speech acts and cognitive artefacts.

This style of ethnographic research studies the ways in which the social and material environment is organised, and how this has implications for the ways in which we understand and act in the world. Their main tenet is the idea that human cognition is *embodied*, situated, relational and interactive, hence social.[2] Some of these scholars have now almost abandoned the 'textual' mode of scientific communication – if not for the sake of the high status that journal publication still enjoys – and are now producing 'hybrid' texts[3] which comprise multimedia or audio clips, disseminating their work on their websites or through CD-ROMs. Such hybrid texts make full use of the spectrum available to enhanced analysis of data, using fine-grained formalisation in the analysis and punctuation of transcripts and diagrams, and introducing grids and filters to orient the reader amongst text, image and voice (for instance they use arrows, magnification or repeat functions in their clips or photographs).

For a visual anthropologist who watched Tim Ash's *The Ax Fight* this may come as no news at all. But what is interesting about this is the fact that the objects of analysis here are mainly everyday and mundane linguistic or voice-eye-body interactions, in typical Western (mainly professional and educational) settings. If we think about what visual techniques positively afford in analytical terms, one must list the possibility of in-depth, repeat analysis of taped materials; the constructive and creative use of video-diary as field notes and even research reports; the camera as a catalyst of the ethnographer's attention and tool for self-distancing from a familiar situation; the 'transparent' definition of roles deriving from holding a camera in ethnographic settings; the possibility to give footage or edits as gifts in exchange for time, access, etc.; and the use of feedback elicitation through footage or edits. Nevertheless, one wonders how much of the anthropological interrogation on the status of visual evidence and on the role and positionality of the observer has actually seeped through in these studies. In fact, the ethical and epistemological problem about this kind of application of visual media to ethnographic analysis is the fact that they are largely used to record 'typical' or 'standard' situations which, especially in work settings, result from the privileging of a distant, wide-focussed, third-person type of perspective, while not leaving any representational space to acts of resistance, situations of discrimination or non-collaborative practices. In other words, power relations are simply not part of the analytical framework and as such they are not allowed to emerge from the flow of data.

The skill of the ethnographer, therefore, is different from the simple application of analytical grids to settings of activity, but rather is itself similar to the ability of learning, resulting in the capacity to recreate particular conditions which allow her to engage in a 'community of practice' (Lave and Wenger 1991), with all its internal articulations and positionalities of meaning. How can one acquire such skill? Unless we rely on the conviction that one is born a sensitive and good ethnographer, or consider the ability to improvise in complex situations as the only possibility, we can draw a comparison between learning to do fieldwork and the general issue of how one learns how to learn. One way of answering the question is to 'go neural' – following models that explain the emergence of recursive patterns of interaction as the result of the reinforcement of spontaneous neural connections. Successful connections would be reinforced more than others and would sediment into patterns of satisfying recursive interaction (Edelman 1992; see Whitehouse 2001). Or we can adopt the system-theory notion of 'emergence' of complex abilities as the result of 'structural coupling' of complex systems (Varela 1991).

If we prefer to stay safely on the shores of social science, one epistemological notion that allows us to analyse practice at the macro level, without entering the depth of individual minds, is Wittgenstein's notion of *agreement in practice* (Wittgenstein 1953). According to this philosopher, engaging in a common performance in congruent ways would basically be the result of sharing a common *practice*: 'if both learning and the subject learned are embedded in participation frameworks, then the portability of learned skills must rely on the commensurability of certain forms of participation' (Lave and Wenger 1991: 20). In other words, understanding human practice requires sharing a cultural, social and linguistic framework. Eventually this leads to a notion of anthropological understanding (Dilthey's and Weber's *Verstehen*) that is meant more as a practical and relational wisdom than as knowledge of the contents of someone else's mind. The notion of *Verstehen* means that the understanding we have of human activities is gained from within that activity, and not by the observation and inference of 'rules' for social action. This requires 're-living' a situation through a process of empathy, from the point of view of other people. Anthropological knowledge is therefore the capacity to comprehend facts at once synoptically and also according to their proper sense, namely, in their character of being intrinsic in a form of life. This does not mean somehow accessing a domain of private consciousness, but socially sharing a way of being in the world, a *Lebenswelt*. Irreconcilable world-views are not impossible to 'understand' in the sense outlined above. On the contrary, to some extent anthropology is exactly about seeing someone else's point of view. In other words, 'understanding' provides a useful theoretical angle for anthropologists to interpret the methodology of participant observation. Appreciating this belief requires a brief definition of both 'form of life' and of 'incommensurability'.

Traces of World-views

'World-views'[4] and 'understanding' are philosophical keywords connected to the concept of 'forms of life'. By the latter, I refer to the different world-views expressed by a community, as a result of their practices. A 'form of life' is what constitutes the boundaries of sense of a certain group of individuals. Ludwig Wittgenstein, who used this phrase, imbuing it with philosophical content, maintained that the bounds of sense that define forms of life cannot be expressed from a point of view that is external to those boundaries. In his own philosophical jargon, he distinguishes between 'what can be said' and 'what can only be shown'. For instance, subjectivity pertains to experience – there is no experience without a subject – but the subject is not itself an object of experience and observation; similarly, the eye is relevant to a visual field but is not an object of its own scrutiny. In other words, there are limits to what can be legitimately expressed in our language, or, to put it in Wittgenstein's words, 'the limits of my language are the limits of my world' (1922: 5.6). For example, Wittgenstein maintains that ethical values cannot be conveyed in words. He suggests instead that the cogency of ethical convictions 'displays itself', by some sort of personal illuminating experience, similar to that of wondering at the existence of the world.

Since Winch's sociological reading of Wittgenstein, suggesting that culture is a set of meanings that are only shared internally, the debate has focussed on the issues of incommensurability and relativism.[5] Kuhn explored the notion of incommensurability in his *The Structure of Scientific Revolutions* (1962) to account for competing scientific theories. Ian Hacking's wider notion of 'style of reasoning' (1982) takes into account not only scientific theories but also issues of communication and understanding between communities in a broader sense. Both Hacking's notion of 'style' and Wittgenstein's 'form of life' stress that sense is internal to a certain system of belief – even though there may be several of these 'styles' or 'forms of life', with competent agents shifting between them. For instance, scientific truth is always internal to a style.[6]

The reason these theories are attractive for anthropology is the fact that they shift the problem of incommensurability away from the debate on 'the other minds', which reaches a stalemate when dealt with solely by using the tools of analytical philosophy. In Hacking's view, incommensurability does not prevent understanding: what makes a style of reasoning *alien* to us does not necessarily prevent us from *understanding* it. Understanding means picking up 'chains of reasoning' and not strictly *translating* from one code to another (Hacking 1982: 60–61). To take Hacking's example, we may 'learn hermetic lore' in order to understand Paracelsus, but this does not amount to its translatability into our scientific frame of mind; similarly, a bilingual person is not automatically a competent translator. On the other hand, the fact that we practice understanding does not refute incommensurability, either. Incommensurability could then be considered – to use Kant's language – a regulative principle, something to remind us that sense is grounded in specific forms of life. Paradoxically, if we reduced world-views to the private sensations and thoughts of each individual, there would only be one way of having someone's world-view, that is, having lived her own life.

The fact about world-views being binding is not that people cannot get out of their world-view for another: a cow-breeder can take to painting or film-making, and by doing so she joins the relevant community of practice, with its sociality, its shared standards of beauty and accomplishment, a series of sensibilities and moral order that accompanies her perception of the world. A botanist can take up running and 'see' the mountain landscape with new eyes, as a marathon runner. But the point is, a world-view shapes the way I look at the world and it does so through relevant practice. Another world-view cannot be accounted for in terms of a different practice than the one that shapes it. One shares a world-view through handling brushes, or cameras, rather than cows.

Participant observation may then be seen as a technique that solves phenomenologically, on the ground, so to speak, the issue of incommensurability, since by coupling participation (i.e. the proximity of bodily knowledge) with observation (i.e. the detachment of vision and of representation) it can make sense of others, experiences and world-views. It was the issue of incommensurability between forms of life that led me to ethnographic film-making. I believed that one way to provide insight into one form of life would be literally to 'take on' a world-view through film. Making a film and learning to look at cows were my own ways of accessing world-views by sharing practices of skilled vision.

On my first and second visit to the field in 1997 and 1998, my wish was to edit a visual monograph from the perspective of the field, an ethnography that could capture a 'form of life' using film as a holistic expressive tool, conveying the ineffable substance of identity. To an extent, ethnographic film was for me about getting hold of a world-view 'intuitively', by stressing its moral, existential and aesthetic dimension. It did not mean bringing a 'visionary', a-logic sensibility to the field, but rather an attempt to reveal a particular 'way of seeing' by sticking to the practices of the ethnographic 'subjects'. The aim of my film was not only to document skilled processes, such as cheese-making or cow-tending, but also to give an insight into the 'form of life' of the characters in relation to their practices. I was trained in the techniques of observational cinema at the Granada Centre for Visual Anthropology, and absorbed the observational style that characterises in different ways the film-making of Judith and David MacDougall, David Hancock and Herb di Gioia, Nick

Broomfield and Toni de Bromhead.[7] The code of practice of observational film-making as it was taught to us hinged on self-censoring all attempts at directing, according to the instructions that we were given as apprentice film-makers. I was influenced particularly by those films which, though focusing on working practices, transcend the mere process of handling materials and tools to render the world-view of the protagonists. For instance, Herb di Gioia's film *Peter Murray* is not just about the skill involved in chair making, but about Peter Murray, focussing closely on the chair-maker's body, on the tactile experience of wood-carving, respecting the time-scale of the process, making the audience re-enact the experience of looking at the design of the chair in its making. It aims beyond the surface, to the agent's world-view behind the process, and yet conveys a sense of immediate participation in a whole sensory experience.

Coming from a philosophical background, I was stunned by the resemblance of the observational film-maker's code of practice to a Wittgensteinian philosophy of silence, whereby the recourse to figurative means seems to testify a crisis in classical anthropological representation. By producing a complex audio-visual text that speaks for itself, one would bypass the interdiction against speaking of that which cannot be talked about (Wittgenstein 1922: §7). When I produced a visual monograph, an ethnographic documentary called *Those Who Don't Work Don't Make Love* (1998), I nurtured the ideal of representing the lived experience of my hosts, and their bounds of sense, as a wholesome whole, without attempting to analyse or fragment it. In a sense, I envisaged film as a tool for understanding rather than explaining, for synthetic representation rather than for analytic dissection. In Anna Grimshaw's words, the ethnographic approach associated with observational film-making privileges the visionary quality of Malinowskian fieldwork (Grimshaw 1997: 45). And, in fact, the paradox of naturalism lies at the core of visual anthropology: romantic vision denies its constructed nature. An 'innocent eye' requires sensibility, embodied knowledge and personal experience, but rejects acknowledging technical mediation.[8]

Conveying world-views on film reproduces a dichotomy between film as a holistic revelation and film as a scientific endeavour, as the product of a surveying eye. In this sense, the vision entailed in observational film-making is not the same as that in ethnographic observation, as the latter allows for a wide-ranging spectrum of viewpoints including that of analytical detachment, while the former aims at conveying a sense of immediate participation in a whole sensory experience. This is not because film is any less mediated than a rich description accomplished in an ethnographic text, but because, precisely through the many contrivances of technological mediation and especially of montage, the observational style wishes to maintain the highest possible degree of fidelity to the film-maker's perception of what unfolds around her. My position nowadays is that an attunement to world-views also allows one to contemplate a modernist fragmentation of viewpoints. In other words, one should not confuse the *process* of getting attuned to particular skilled visions. In fact, skilled visions can also be objects of analytical study as well as of holistic representation.

Different ways of seeing reveal different ways of knowing: the lived experience of the landscape is different for planners, tourists, herders, housewives, apprentices, children and fieldworkers, with different political, economic, aesthetic and ethic views. My participation in a project to draw a map of Valtaleggio – my fieldwork site – with the village Mayor and other locals marked a pivotal point in my switching attitudes to the visual 'traces' that I myself had produced. This was a local initiative that I shadowed during my fieldwork in a village of the Italian Alps. Local villagers got together to draw a tourist map of their valley. From their meetings, some interesting connections emerged between practices of locality, ways of seeing and the phenomenology of the landscape. The mayor of the village chaired a group of volunteers to design and publish a tourist map of the valley. A tourist guide and map had just been issued by the province administration, but they felt that only locals could be the sources of local knowledge of the territory. The group included, amongst others, expert mountain-goers, a university student, a cheese retailer, a marathon runner, a botanist and a hunter. Alpine guides, amateur photographers and habitual hikers engaged in an exercise of 'embodied imagination', re-living the experience of walking along the paths. But each saw the landscape differently. Their description of the hiking routes matched their experience of the landscape in ways that are closely related to their visual and bodily experience of the land. There were in fact different timescapes and different landscapes: those walked by the hiker and those studied by the botanist, those run by the marathon man and those seen through the eyes of nostalgic memory. In each case, a different experience of locality would amount to a different perception of duration and different time projections, so that the fittest would tend to underestimate hiking times, whilst the botanist insisted on allowing time to look around. The map became the sediment of a complex negotiation between different ways of envisioning and perceiving the landscape. The point about this is not simply that every person is different, and that different people hold different perspectives of the landscape. The point is that their practices make a difference to such perspectives, which are not private but shared within a community of practitioners, and practice-oriented.

Stephen Daniels has stressed 'the implications of the aesthetics of space in the culture of modernity', which is mediated through a variety of 'imaginative geographies': 'maps, regional surveys, topographical verse, travel books' (Daniels 1993: 243). Participating in the map-making exercise alerted me to the fact that, just as I was entertaining an exercise in accessing world-views through film-making, so others had devised different ways to share their respective repertoires of competent knowledge of the valley. During further fieldwork, in 1999, I used the camera differently, as a catalyst for my attention for a skilled practice and as a tool of self-distancing from a familiar situation. I used various technical approaches, including an analysis of local visual production, a personal apprenticeship to a breed inspector and the production of short edits on specific topics (such as cheese-making or contact with cattle on the pasture). I also used footage or edits from my film for feedback elicitation, asking the protagonists to monitor/evaluate/disagree with my work. Rather than as the entry point into a world-view, I now tended to see my ethnographic film-making more as a map-making activity, as a trace of my own outlook on fieldwork.[9] My own experience of ethnographic film-making amounted to mapping, that is, to a visual mediation into a specific 'form of life'. Drawing a parallel between mappings and filming, the film became a sketch, or trail, that testifies to the success of creating commensurability between the film-maker's viewpoint and that of the interlocutors, in the form of a visual trace. Just as a map needs a legend, namely a key to interpreting it, so would ethnography provide a legend to ethnographic film.[10]

For Merleau Ponty, 'the body is our general medium for having a world' (1962: 146). On the score of his lesson, phenomenological anthropology recommends to 'advance *a grounded view* which begins with interactions and movements of people in an organised environment, and considers in detail the patterns of body praxis which arise therein' (Jackson 1983: 340). Nevertheless, it is advisable to describe such movements and such richly textured organised environment by studying and recording them *analytically*. So, if we take world-views as different abilities to see, namely, as modalities of looking, we can interpret them as the expression of different skilled capacities, closely bound up with the skilled practices in which they unfold. For instance, in the example of the map-making group mentioned above, different *skilled visions* comprise different phenomenological experiences and embodied narratives. These are not necessarily made *visible*, as is the case of the map as the final outcome of the map-making exercise, but they are effective in the way in which they structure the environment towards one mode of skilled perception rather than another. The map thus serves at once a geographical, informative, narrative, socialising, phenomenological and mediating role. Similarly to the linear module for the morphofunctional evaluation of dairy cows, it is a tool that directs and orients perception while simultaneously conveying a skilled world-view – that is, a cognitive, emotional, experiential attitude to managing lifeworlds.

If initially ethnographic film-making played the role of providing a visual mediation into a specific 'form of life', my subsequent ethnographic writing has been an attempt at revisiting my ethnographic film-making as a map. I followed up particular ethnographic 'traces' that seemed worth exploring as attempts to bridge different outlooks on landscape and on life and between literally different ways of seeing, rooted in different practices, memories and aesthetic sensibilities. I tried to trace the production and social re-production of a specific local identity down to practices of engagement with the territory, physically and culturally producing the landscape. This shift had important implications both for my fieldwork practice and for my understanding of anthropological theory, as I wish to explain in the following section

Skilled Visions

By 'skilled vision' I suggest that the ethnographer can devise (and reflexively re-visit) ways to attune her vision to the many and multi-faceted native uses of the eye. This means, literally, developing new sensorial capacities, new aesthetic sensibilities and novel ways of educating attention. The anthropologist can reflect on, and represent these processes, accordingly – either in synthetic or analytical ways. 'Skilled visions' are by definition plural, in that they characterise the life of a community of practice. There are then 'skilled visions' of both native and anthropologist; the latter strives to incorporate an understanding of the former's skilled visions in her own fieldwork practice.

My own ways of reflecting on the locality of indigenous knowledge, in a context that privileges standardisation as a passage to modernity, was shaped by the process of apprenticeship to the 'ways of seeing' (Berger 1972) of dairy breeders (see Grasseni 2004a, 2004b). Breed experts judge the beauty of a cow in functional terms. In order to do so, they learn to schematise the body of the cow into traits that correspond to standard models of 'ideal-looking' cows of the relevant breed. A breed expert's job is to judge how close a cow looks to the ideal model that has been elected as representative of the productive potential of her breed. His agenda is hence tightly functional to that of breed selection, intensive agriculture and the 'improvement' of animal husbandry with the available biotechnologies. The criteria by which such recognition is granted may be external to locality, in fact skill in breeding practice is increasingly dictated by standard criteria for genetic selection, which decide which animals are deemed 'worthy' and 'beautiful' by breed experts.

Richard Wilk's notion of 'common structures of difference' may be useful to spell out how these standards work by 'systematically narrowing our gaze to particular kinds of difference': 'They standardise a vocabulary for describing difference, and provide a syntax for its expression, to produce a common frame of organised distinction ... They essentialise some kind of differences and portray them as measurable and scalable characteristics' (Wilk 1995: 130). The fact that Wilk deduces his analysis from an ethnography of beauty pageants rather than cattle fairs does not detract from the applicability of his observations, and in particular how 'the same processes that destroy autonomy are now creating new sorts of communities, new kinds of locality and identity' (Wilk 1995: 131). In fact, the de-localisation of (some of) the criteria that instruct very local practices may affect dairy breeding in northern Italy like beauty pageants in Belize. In my fieldwork experience, apprenticeship in the skilled activity of 'judgement' taught me to scrutinise the animal body, hence to 'see' in new ways.

This is true of other specialised activities, for instance film-making and ethnography. Both can be taken as experiences during which new 'techniques of the body' (Mauss 1935) are developed, according to whatever practice one happens to 'participate in' – as ethnographer, those of one's 'informants', and as filmmaker, those of handling cameras. In particular, when using a tool for a professional vision such as the camera, this becomes an extension of the eye and arm: it shapes the phenomenal word around us and is instrumental in creating the phenomenal objects subject to our scrutiny. In general, processes of 'coding', 'highlighting' and 'producing and demonstrating material representations' of complex phenomenal events and cognitive tasks is of paramount importance to the construction of a *professional vision* (Goodwin 1994). This shapes events and gives them meaning from a point of view that is internal to a community of specialised practice.

An exemplary study of professional vision is provided by Charles Goodwin's comparative analysis of the practices of archaeologists mapping a dirt patch and of police officers justifying recourse to violence – which had been recorded on video – as a methodical and controlled practice. For both, forms and grids provide 'structures of relevance in the material environment' (Goodwin 1994: 610). These shape perception – not only visual – and are the means of sharing such perception with others, accordingly to a shared code of practice. Goodwin's article is particularly interesting because it shows the powerful strategies of 'professional vision' at work in literally constructing events, even in a case – such as the infamous Rodney King's beating – where one would naïvely assume that a video-recording would constitute an unquestionable piece of 'objective' evidence. An exercise in acquiring a 'professional' vision, instead, involves disciplining, selecting, re-interpreting and distancing from the objects of one's naïve and undistinguished vision.

Another example of skilled vision can be found in the way breeders look at cattle and inscribe their vision into paper or electronic forms for genetic evaluation (Grasseni 2004a, 2005). In fact, the ability to evaluate genetically selected traits in cattle is only part of a broader and pragmatic skilled vision, only one aspect of a breeder's practice. Often, breeding mastery involves veterinary knowledge and practical wisdom, gained through experience and, quite literally, touch. This level of personal engagement with one's animals seems nevertheless to be compatible with conceiving of animals as tools for one's economic success, and with the objectification of the animal body according to predetermined 'traits' (Grasseni 2005). The practice of breeding stands in integral relation with the place where the cattle live, the land or the shed. This relation disappears from the exhibition space, which highlights the aesthetic experience of envisioning the desired form of cattle in terms of bodily 'traits' (udder, height, leanness, etc.) that should guarantee a good productive performance of the animal. The breed expert's skilled vision is informed by international standards that respond to global markets and national and international scientific institutions. The herder's skilled vision may well subsume and encompass the competence of a breed expert (a breed expert is often a farmer himself), but becomes employed in a constant negotiation of situated competence on the pastures and in the stable. In the end, the skill of my hosts' grandchildren, which I could scarcely emulate, turned out to be much more encompassing, and at times at odds with the selective gaze of the breed expert that had apprenticed me. Skilled practitioners maintain their expertise through daily experience and personal history, with frequent dealings and acquaintance with practice.

If skill amounts to the capacity to see, learn and act appropriately, the social recognition of the breeder and the aesthetic appreciation of his cows go hand in hand. Though aesthetics alone does not distil a mountain breeder's 'identity', specialist aesthetic discourse implicitly feeds on reference to skill and the moral dimension of practice. 'Skill' is a core concept through which technology, history, social relations and political economy converge. It is an essential aspect, an element of practice, a taste and a meaning-making attitude that is developed and applied in everyday life, thus amounting to a sense of identification or emplacement. Skill can be understood as an encompassing strategy of embedding practical relations between human beings and their everyday environment. In the light of this, and as a final ethnographic example, I would like to dwell on how a cheese maker manages the world through skill. This will allow us to draw some methodological conclusions about the relevance of phenomenological analysis to the construction of fieldwork knowledge.

Towards a Critical Anthropology of Practice

In cheese-making, one of the most important skills is recognising at which point the curd has reached the right temperature and is ready to be cast into the mould. On the high pastures, during the season of summer grazing (*alpage*), renneting is timed after a number of other simultaneous activities, such as cleaning up after milking, washing the milking tools and having breakfast. I video-recorded the following scene in the summer of 1997 on the upper pastures of Valtaleggio, the site of my fieldwork.

After milking, Guglielmo, born 1931, is training Oscar, age 15, to tend the curd. Sara and Marco, Guglielmo's grandchildren, aged 8 and 12, join in to check the temperature on the wood-mounted thermometer in the faint light of the cellar.

Oscar:	I checked it before, it was 48 degrees.
Guglielmo:	It should be 49.
Oscar:	No, it's still 48.
Guglielmo:	Marco, you read! How much is it?
Marco:	49!
Guglielmo:	You are casting a shade, Away with that head! I can't read.
Oscar:	Sara, be careful! You mustn't take it out of the water!
Sara:	Ehm … It's still 48. It's a bit more, but not quite 49.
	What do we do?

This scene suggests margins for the negotiation of precision in the choral performance of a skilled activity, featuring the master and his apprentice, with the ever-present curious children and apprentices-to-be. Even in artisanal cheese-making, accuracy plays an important role, and – although on a different scale, say, to the physics laboratory – dealing with a simple instrument of measurement, such as the thermometer, allows margins for the negotiation of precision. Learning to deal with such negotiation can be a playful activity – like the game of cow-spotting (recognising cows and calling them each by their name) – which the children indulge in on the pastures. Conversely, there are many ways in which one's 'legitimate peripheral participation' can be a subject of scrutiny, criticism or misdirection (Herzfeld 2004). Paradoxically, only by participating in a skill can one detect it and appreciate it, and only by watching attentively and repeating mimetically can one properly pick it up. Any other non-participatory attitude is likely to be looked down upon by the skilled practitioner as 'blindness'. By acquiring one's master skill, one becomes part of a *'gestural collective'* (Sibum 1995: 77), preserving and reproducing memory and value through the daily performance of a body technique.

In a recent work on the history of science and precision instruments, Otto Sibum argues that a constant dialogue is implicit in the skilled use of precision instruments: skill can be read as a series of 'accepted gestures of precision' tied to the capacity of 'calibrating instruments' (Sibum 1995: 73).[11] This argument imbues the notion of skill with phenomenological meaning, and draws attention to the fact that an element of skill is always present, even in the introduction of modern technology. In other words, there is no zero-sum game of skill and technology, by which an increase of technology means a decrease in skill in absolute terms. Instead, traditional skills may be replaced by other contextual skills that deal with the idiosyncrasy and the local variations of technology. For instance, in the ethnographic scene described above, a similar dynamic seems also to take place in cheese-making, during a process that apparently implies simply reading off the temperature from a thermometer stuck in the milky curd.

Just as practice eschews recasting in rules, so skill would escape formulation in a body of knowledge, an objective system of rational principles – by which we usually think about technology. Moreover, the social dimension of tacit skills does not reside exclusively in the 'traditional' master-apprentice relationship. For instance, classic work on peer-to-peer interactions (Lave 1991: 59–88) has shown how inter-generational processes of apprenticeship rely on replication as much as on memory. During fieldwork on the high pastures, I often observed my host's grandchildren engaging in a spontaneous reproduction of the activities around them. Four-year-old Arianna picked up a rake and her twelve–year-old cousin would help her play to perform the movement of raking. Eight-year-old Marco guided a towering cow in and out of the stable: his confidence and empathy for her movements has been learned playing and climbing on her. As I took part in some basic activities such as guiding the cattle on a path, picking them out of the herd and leading them to milking, I realised that my own body had somehow incorporated my daily contact with their cattle as a kind of phenomenological 'sediment'. Certain levels of physical strength employed in steering, disciplining or making the cows aware of one's presence also shaped the vigour and the quality of touch in other contexts.[12]

Tacit knowledge has been defined as 'the capacity to perform skills without being able to articulate how'.[13] According to this definition, the unspecifiability of tacit skills such as those mentioned above is ultimately due to the fact that the rules for them have lapsed into 'subsidiary awareness' (Polanyi 1958: 62). Similarly, Mauss has defined the 'techniques of the body' as 'actions of a mechanical, physical or physico-chemical order' that are 'effective and traditional'.[14] Conversely, Tim Ingold's work on skill and technology stresses the mimetic and ecological quality of apprenticeship rather than its psychological effects. The fact that the training of the apprentice's eye and body happens in the context of a form of life provides a 'field of resonance', for the apprentice's observation to be 'in tune' with the 'taskscape' around her (Ingold 1993: 170). The 'taskscape' unifies both performative function and aesthetics: acquiring the capacity to perform a skilled gesture means resonating a form of life in one's own body. According to Ingold, skills thus belong to 'developmental systems' as a whole. They are incorporated in the *modus operandi* of the developing human body through a history of training and experience, under the guidance of already skilled practitioners, and in an environment characterised by its own distinctive textures and topography, and littered with the products of previous human activity.[15] Thus 'the acquisition of culturally specific skills is part and parcel of the overall developmental process of the human organism, through which they become embodied in the organism' (Ingold 1993b: 470). 'Sedimentation implies a certain degree of solidification of the world as incorporated, which will gradually make the person experience a reshaping of the body's actual ability' (Leder 1990: 34, quoted in Ingold 1996: 14).

Do these definitions hold in new circumstances, which include the need for the cheese-makers to develop 'new' skill, both in producing and in tasting cheese? A complex physical, economic and legal context of cheese production for a globalised market requires quality certificates, abidance by the EU health and safety regulations and the application of standard protocols of production, etc. (Grasseni 2003b). What's then becoming of my old host's cheese-making skills – for instance, timing the coagulation of the curd or choosing the temperature to which one heats the milk, as I recorded on the high pastures – in the light of recent processes of productive standardisation and sense-disciplining? The cheese-maker's previous experience is a precious element that guarantees rhetorical and genealogical continuity between artisan craftsmanship and scientific standards. Moreover, previous rounded knowledge of the production contexts allow him to respond more quickly to changes, by keeping a constant 'dialogue' in the skilled use of new technology.

As we saw, relevant studies from the history of science stress how standard skills, now ubiquitous in the physics laboratories, originally drew on the very local artisanal practice developed by expert craftsmanship. In nineteenth-century Manchester, the craftsmanship of the brewing community was needed to 'calibrate' rudimentary thermometers in Joule's experiment, to calculate the mechanical value of heat. Analogously, the skill of accurately timing the curdling process is not just about reading a thermometer, but rather about combining standard instructions about humidity and temperature with various indicators of the texture of the curd, such as the size and consistence of the 'grains' into which it is progressively broken. A continuous process of negotiation of difference both favours continuity and highlights the individual capacity to adapt or calibrate standard procedures to local recipes and 'traditional tastes'. Being conscious of the practice that was in place before – not only theoretically, but because this has sedimented in one's body – allows one to gauge what can be acceptably considered as the following step of an – *invented* – 'tradition'.

To conclude, I would like to draw out some implications of ethnographic knowledge for the role of phenomenology in the study of skilled practice. Phenomenological analyses of skill stress perception and interaction as a complex whole, a taskscape. Skill, or body techniques would allow us 'to participate in a world ... and to recognise ourselves as members of a community, of a common body' (Jackson 1983: 340) – not only in ritual contexts but in ordinary everyday practice. That 'indigenous understandings are frequently embedded in practices (doings) rather than spelled out in ideas (sayings)' (Jackson 1983: 340) holds true also in our own globalised, delocalised and hegemonic societies. In fact, the recent focus on the study of taken-for-granted, habitual practices which are typical of Western societies – such as apprenticeship in productive activities – should make us aware of the ineptitude of an implicit dichotomy between Western rational industrialised practice and non-Western, embodied, whole-body sensibility.

This has important implications for the anthropological notion of 'emplacement' too. Edward Casey refers to Merleau-Ponty and to Kant's pre-critical writings to stress the importance of practical experience in the construction of place. According to Casey, the primacy of perception does not mean that human modalities of sensing and moving are pre-cultural or pre-social: 'to be not yet articulated in concept or word is not equivalent to be non-culturally constituted' Casey (1996: 19).[16] In other words, 'to live is to live locally' (Casey 1996: 18). Phenomenological experience is thus at once individual – and so inevitably local, since each and every one of us inhabits a landscape through our body – and universal, because it is unthinkable not to inhabit a landscape through our body. In other words, phenomenological principles must be valid for all human experience, regardless of where that happens: 'place is like a formal universal: a condition of possibility of all human experience' (Casey 1996: 29). As a result, argues Casey, even if bodies may be 'displaced', they shall never be 'placeless' (Casey 1996: 51, note 36). If we accept this, though, it is difficult to agree further with his contention that American Malls – or, *a la* Augé, airports or Disneyland – are mere non-places, 'deficient, or un-aesthetic modes of emplacement' where 'a thin temporality and a sheer spatiality derive from a placial matrix', as 'a matter of surface rather than depth'. This shows how a phenomenological analysis of 'place' as a universal category of perception can be unwittingly overlapped to an organic ideal of 'place' as idyll, following a literary and artistic tradition that selected particular landscapes – such as 'picturesque' alpine landscapes – as icons of harmony and morality. 'Place' must be a dimension common to any experience, not one particular special space where certain aesthetic conditions obtain.

Does a phenomenology of skill suffice to render a complete and critical picture of such processes? We should consider that the practices of emplacement also include the fragmented and kaleidoscopic views of those who think they were in place but no longer are, those who would be in place elsewhere and those who think they can only be in place somewhere specific. In fact, Casey's phenomenological subjects seem to be 'emplaced' in a rather passive, if resonating way.[17] His phenomenology does not seem to take their economic and political strategies into account, that is, the 'bifocal vision' (Peters 1997: 79) induced by self- and media-representation, and the several degrees of construction of what we see and who we are for a specific audience. Phenomenology leaves the unsolved paradox of a sentient body that is universal and yet local, habitual and bound to particular world-views. Instead, places are contested and linked to global processes, and different people have different views of locality, not least because of the different ways they are positioned in power relations. Only through certain modalities of practice and perception is a certain landscape maintained; on the other hand, certain perceptions of the landscape are symbolically charged and constructed even after the landscape has effectively changed. For instance, farming land may be a 'valued landscape' (Lowenthal (1982), a repository of social and aesthetic values. These may well be contested, to the point that landscape-making practices (e.g. constructing conservation parks, hunting reservoirs or tourist resorts) may turn into the focus of political and social divisions and debates.

However, phenomenology contributes the fundamental insight that meaning is rooted in the first-person singular perspective of commitment through practice. Once locality is understood not as an encrusted structure or a symbolic overlay, but as a statement about belonging, the theoretical focus moves away from the fictitious object – locality itself – to start engaging with the subjects making such statements, and with the practices through which they do so. I suggest that we see taskscapes as forms of life, that is, not only as a purely phenomenological series of ecological actions and perspectives, but as anthropologically 'thick' contexts, in which skill is relevant not only as a technical action but also as symbolic meaning, moral judgement, cognitive capacity and aesthetic belonging. This means grasping the background of our everyday practice as a *frame*: namely as a whole whose meaning is also constitutive of its own bounds of sense. Such a frame is not taught like a rule but absorbed mimetically through participation.

In recent analyses of vision and landscape (Okely 2001), stress has been put on the power of a whole-body experience, of 'being there' and of sharing a *life-world*. I prefer to focus on *skill* as it allows a more articulate, historically constructed and socially exposed analysis of meaning. This privileges an analytical study of forms of life rather than a holistic one, while recognising the fact that forms of life are synthetic *loci* of meaning construction. Skill is a privileged site of construction and perpetuation of identity, an ecological complex of metaphysical stances, emotional traits, cognitive and bodily strategies, a way of embedding critical and conflictual relations. Using one's body in the same way as others in the same environment is not only a method to join in esoteric practice or reach speechless understanding of ritual communion, but it is a necessary premise to understanding what is said and thought.

To conclude, I have here sketched an outline of how my 'living with the data' from fieldwork has changed and shifted through time, according to different field and literature encounters. I have tried to show how I came to know the field in different ways through participant observation, shadowing and film-making, focusing particularly on how I used camerawork and film as both analytic and synthetic tools to approach world-views. My main thesis about world-views is that one's practice shapes the way one looks at the world: identity and cultures are rooted and reproduce themselves in the natural and culturally constructed environments of everyday practice. In particular, skill and skilled vision may serve as ways of accessing world-views, as ethnographic work may be experienced as learning to see anew. I take the notion of *skilled vision* as an analytical tool that indicates a process of embodiment and the acquisition of the capacity to see the world with new eyes. This can be the result of involvement in a performance or in a moment of crisis, but also of long-term exposure or direct apprenticeship. The experience of learning to see with new eyes may well be the result of fieldwork, particularly when this involves the attempt to share the ways in which locals understand and construct knowledge in different practices.

Notes

1. I draw this expression from Paul Rabinow's speech, 'Bios Today', given at the 'Anthropology and Science' plenary at the 5th Decennial Conference of the ASA, Manchester, 14 July 2003.

2. These works share a set of main tenets regarding social action. Firstly, they consider *mediated action* as crucial to practice (as in the different traditions of Dewey's pragmatism, G.H. Mead's interactionism, Bateson's ecology of mind, and above all the cultural-historical Russian school of Lev Vygotsky, Alexei Leont'ev and Alexander Luria). Secondly, they focus on environmental systems, including both material and relational structures. As a species capable of mediated action, humankind banks on the socially guided appropriation of environmental resources that are oriented to action by the previous generations (Cole 1997). Thirdly, humans find themselves continuously involved in *performances* and *routines* that allow them to share common fields of action. Culture therefore takes the shape of a set of resources that can be employed creatively in different ways by the social actors: cultural action is the *situated improvisation* that exploits such resources in different circumstances,

rather than an interpretative frame or a fixed repertoire. In turn, contexts are mutually constituted by people's actions rather than fixed scenarios for action.

3. I borrow this expression from Marcus Banks' paper 'Monstrous Outcomes: The Marriage of Ethnographic Film and Anthropological Theory', 5th Decennial Conference of the ASA, Manchester, 16 July 2003, panel: 'Beyond Observational Cinema – Again …'. I have some reservations though about the way he claims a 'Latourian' meaning for the term. By *hybrid*, Latour means a combination of actors and non-human actants in a technological object or inscription. Here instead I simply mean that a 'text' may in fact comprise text, image and voice.

4. I use the term in a different way from Nigel Rapport's 'diverse world-views'. For Rapport (1993: 79–80) these are 'texts' or 'fragments of texts', present in each of our individual minds and thus composing a 'world-view' or 'form of life'. These 'private realities' are then analysable as a form of discourse, by way of linguistic analysis. Rapport does not explain what makes it possible for people with different world-views to communicate with others. In fact, he stresses the failure of communication between our individual and private world-views. More importantly, he does not try to relate lived experience and world-views: there is no sensory or visual pertinence to Rapport's world-views.

5. Winch (1958). There exists a vast bibliography on translation and incommensurability, in history of science, anthropology and cognitive studies. For a comprehensive bibliography on incommensurability and scientific practice, see Pickering (1995).

6. 'The propositions that are objectively found to be true are determined as true by styles of reasoning for which in principle there can be no external justification. A justification would be an independent way of showing that the style gets at the truth, but there is no characterisation of the truth over and above what is reached by the style of reason itself' (Hacking 1982: 65).

7. For a discussion of the meaning of 'observational cinema' and its claim to representing or illuminating the real, see MacDougall (1997), Henley (1998), Grimshaw (2001).

8. Here I am limiting the validity of this statement to what Anna Grimshaw calls 'the romantic vision' in visual anthropology (1997: 43). 'Romantic vision', taken in a wider sense may be difficult to constrict within this argument. For instance, Michael Dettelbach (1996) has shown how Humboldt acknowledged the role of technology as a means of enhancing the capacity of the individual to perceive the world at large.

9. As an alternative to observational cinema, some have turned to performance studies and to the theatre metaphor, differently used by both Turner and Goffman (Ruby 2000). The performative model advocated by Ruby should 'broaden the concept of performance to include the non-dramatic elements of the everyday lives of ordinary people' (2000: 264).

10. This is not a general argument about maps, maintaining that all maps need legends. The argument is rather that the ethnographic observation that accompanied the making of the map can serve as a 'cartographic memoir' that can tell much more about the map than what it can say itself. This is quite beyond and apart from any discussion of cartographic semiotics, for instance of cognitive maps.

11. In particular, Sibum studied Joule's experimental determination of the mechanical value of heat, noticing that 'the act of reading the thermometer requires a certain technique which includes the right timing for taking measurements'. Sibum stresses how skills now implicit in the everyday practices of the physics laboratory originally drew on the artisanal practice developed by the Mancunian brewing craftsmanship.

12. For instance, I came to consider eight year-old Marco's proneness to rather violent attacks on her playmates or on me as a lack of 'calibration' of the physical strength that he was applying on calves and cows all day round.

13. Collins (1985: 56) refers to the earlier work of Polanyi (1958: 49): 'the aim of a skilful performance is achieved by the observance of a set of rules which are not known as such to the person following them'. 'An art which cannot be specified in detail cannot be transmitted by prescription, since no prescription for it exists. It can be passed on only by example from master to apprentice… By watching the master and emulating his efforts in the presence of

his example, the apprentice unconsciously picks up the rules of the art, including those which are not explicitly known to the master himself' (1958: 53).

14. Mauss (1935: 104). Mauss provides a review of historical and geographical variations of techniques, such as walking or swimming, and a first attempt at classifying body techniques by gender, age, efficiency, transmission. For a critique see Ingold (1996: 15).

15. Ingold (1996: 14). The same thesis in different wording appears in a published version: Ingold (1997: 113).

16. Kant stressed the importance of bodily references for indexical emplacement: 'Our geographical knowledge, and even our commonest knowledge of the position of places, would be of no aid to us if we could not, by reference to the sides of our bodies, assign to regions the things so ordered and the whole system of mutually relative positions' (1768: 22–23), quoted in Casey (1996: 21). Notice, nevertheless, that Kant refers to the universal experience of the indexicality of our body in spatial orientation. Hence Casey should not make this equivalent to a culturally and socially constituted body. The Kantian body pre-critical is pre-cultural and pre-social.

17. 'What is kept in place primarily are experiencing bodies regarded as privileged residents rather than orchestrating *force*: my body in place is less the *metteur en scene* than itself *mise en scene* – or rather it is both at once: "passivity in activity"' (Casey 1996: 25).

References

Berger, J. 1972. *Ways of Seeing*. London: BBC.

Casey, E.S. 1996. 'How to Get from Space to Place in a Fairly Short Stretch of Time', in S. Feld and K. Basso (eds), *Senses of Place*. Seattle: School of American Research Press, pp. 13–52.

Chaiklin, S. and J. Lave (eds). 1993. *Understanding Practice: Perspectives on Activity and Context*. Cambridge: Cambridge University Press.

Cole, M. 1997. *Culture and Cognitive Science*. San Diego: Laboratory of Comparative Human Cognition. Online at: http://lchc.ucsd.edu/People/Localz/MCole/santabar.html

Cole, M. and D. Holland. 1995. 'Between Discourse and Schema: Reformulating a Cultural-historical Approach to Culture and Mind', *Anthropology and Education Quarterly* 26(4): 475–90.

Collins, H.M. 1985. *Changing Order: Replication and Induction in Scientific Practice*. London: Sage.

_____. 1997. 'Ways of Going On: An Analysis of Skill Applied to Medical Practice', *Science, Technology and Human Values* 22(3): 267–84.

Daniels, S. 1993. *Fields of Vision: Landscape Imagery and National Identity in England and the United States*. Cambridge: Polity Press.

Dettelbach, M. 1996. 'Global Physics and Aesthetic Empire: Humboldt's Physical Portrait of the Tropics', in D.P. Miller and P.H. Reill (eds), *Visions of Empire: Voyages, Botany, and Representations of Nature*. Cambridge: Cambridge University Press, pp. 258–92.

Edelman, G. 1992. *Bright Air, Brilliant Fire: On the Matter of the Mind*. Cambridge, Mass.: MIT Press.

Engeström, Y. and D. Middleton (eds). 1996. *Cognition and Communication at Work*. Cambridge: Cambridge University Press.

Goodwin, C. 1994. 'Professional Vision', *American Anthropologist* 96(3): 606–33.

_____. 2000. 'Practices of Seeing: Visual Analysis: An Ethnomethodological

Approach', in T. van Leeuwen and C. Jewitt (eds), *Handbook of Visual Analysis*. London: Sage Publications, pp. 157–82.

Goodwin, C. and M.H. Goodwin. 1998. 'Formulating Planes: Seeing as a Situated Activity', in D. Middleton and Y. Engestrom (eds), *Cognition and Communication at Work*. Cambridge: Cambridge University Press, pp. 61–95.

Goodwin, C. and N. Ueno (eds). 2000. 'Vision and Inscription in Practice', Special issue of *Mind, Culture and Activity* 7(1–2): 5.

Grasseni, C. 2003b. 'Packaging Skills: Calibrating Italian Cheese to the Global Market', in S. Strasser (ed.), *Commodifying Everything: Consumption and Capitalist Enterprise*. New York: Taylor and Francis, pp. 259–88.

_____. 2004a. 'Skilled Landscapes: Mapping Practices of Locality', *Environment and Planning D: Society and Space* 22(5): 699–717.

_____. 2004b. 'Skilled Vision: An Apprenticeship in Breeding Aesthetics', *Social Anthropology* 12(1): 1–15.

_____. 2005. 'Designer Cows: The Practice of Cattle Breeding between Skill and Standardization', *Society and Animals* 13(1): 33–49.

_____. (ed.). 2007. *Skilled Visions: Between Apprenticeship and Standards*. Oxford: Berghahn.

Grimshaw, A. 1997. 'The Ethnographer's Eye: Notes from Work in Progress', *Martor* 2: 41–49.

_____. 2001. *The Ethnographer's Eye: Ways of Seeing in Anthropology*. Cambridge: Cambridge University Press.

Hacking, I. 1982. 'Language, Truth and Reason', in S. Hollis and C. Lukes (eds), *Rationality and Relativism*. Oxford: Blackwell, pp. 48–66.

Henley, P. 1998. 'Film-making and Ethnographic Research', in J. Prosser (ed.), *Image-Based Research: A Sourcebook for Qualitative Researchers*. London: Routledge, pp. 42–59.

Herzfeld, M. 2004. *The Body Impolitic: Artisans and Artifice in the Global Hierarchy of Value*. Chicago: Chicago University Press.

Hollis, M. and S. Lukes (eds). 1982. *Rationality and Relativism*. Oxford: Blackwell.

Hutchins, E. 1995. *Cognition in the Wild*. Cambridge, Mass.: MIT Press.

Ingold, T. 1993a. 'The Art of Translation in a Continuous World', in G. Pálsson (ed.), *Beyond Boundaries*. Oxford: Berg, pp. 210–30.

_____. 1993b. 'Technology, Language, Intelligence: A Reconsideration of Basic Concepts', in K. Gibson and T. Ingold (eds), *Tools, Language and Cognition in Human Evolution*. Cambridge: Cambridge University Press, pp. 449–72.

_____. 1993c. 'The Temporality of the Landscape', *World Archaeology* 25 (2)152–74.

_____. 1996. 'Situating Action V: The History and Evolution of Bodily Skills', Unpublished manuscript in possession of the author, now published with modifications as Ingold, T. 1997. 'Eight Themes in the Anthropology of Technology', *Social Analysis* 41(1): 106–38.

_____. 2000. *The Perception of the Environment: Essays in Livelihood, Dwelling and Skill*. London: Routledge.

Jackson, M. 1983. 'Knowledge of the Body', *Man (N.S.)* 18(2): 327–45.

Latour, B. 1991. *Nous n'avons jamais été modernes*. Paris: La Découverte.

Lave, J. and E. Wenger. 1991. *Situated Learning: Legitimate Peripheral Participation*. Cambridge: Cambridge University Press.

MacDougall, D. 1997. 'The Visual in Anthropology', in H. Morphy and M. Banks (eds), *Rethinking Visual Anthropology*. New Haven: Yale University Press, pp. 276–95.

Mauss, M. 1979 [1935]. 'Techniques of the Body', *Sociology and Psychology: Essays*. London: Routledge and Kegan Paul, pp. 95–123.

Merleau-Ponty, M. 1962. *Phenomenology of Perception*. New York: Humanities Press.

Norman, D. 1988. *The Psychology of Everyday Things*. New York: Basic Books.

Okely, J. 2001. 'Visualism and Landscape: Looking and Seeing in Normandy', *Ethnos* 66(1): 99–120.

Peters, J.D. 1997. 'Seeing Bifocally: Media Place Culture', in A. Gupta and J. Ferguson (eds), *Culture, Power, Place: Explorations in Critical Anthropology*. Durham, NC: Duke University Press, pp. 75–92.

Pickering, A. 1995. *The Mangle of Practice: Time, Agency and Science*. Chicago: University of Chicago Press.

Polanyi, M. 1958. *Personal Knowledge: Towards a Post-critical Philosophy*. Chicago: University of Chicago Press.

Rapport, N. 1993. *Diverse World-views in an English Village*. Edinburgh: Edinburgh University Press.

Ruby, J. 2000. *Picturing Culture: Explorations of Film and Anthropology*. Chicago: University of Chicago Press.

Sibum, O. 1995. 'Reworking the Mechanical Value of Heat: Instruments of Precision and Gestures of Accuracy in Early Victorian England', *Studies in the History and Philosophy of Science* 26(1): 73–106.

Suchman, L. 1987. *Plans and Situated Action: The Problem of Human-machine Communication*. Cambridge: Cambridge University Press.

Varela, F., E. Thompson and E. Rosch. 1991. *The Embodied Mind: Cognitive Science and Human Experience*. Cambridge, Mass.: MIT Press.

Wenger, E. 1998. *Communities of Practice: Learning, Meaning and Identity*. Cambridge: Cambridge University Press.

Whitehouse, H. (ed.). 2001. *The Debated Mind: Evolutionary Psychology versus Ethnography*. Oxford: Berg.

Wilk, R. 1995. 'Learning to be Local in Belize: Global Systems of Common Difference', in D. Miller (ed.), *Worlds Apart: Modernity through the Prism of the Local*. London: Routledge, pp. 110–33.

Winch, P. 1958. *The Idea of a Social Science*. London: Routledge and Kegan Paul.

Wittgenstein, L. 1922. *Tractatus Logico-Philosophicus*. London: Kegan Paul.

_____. 1953. *Philosophische Untersuchungen/Philosophical Investigations*. Oxford: Blackwell.

Chapter 9

Rescuing Theory from the Nation

Viranjini Munasinghe

Introduction[1]

I chose to title this chapter 'rescuing theory from the nation' after Prasenjit Duara's title of his inspiring book *Rescuing History from the Nation* (1996) because I believe we are both addressing a similar problematic: attempting to rescue a space for analysis even as we acknowledge and illustrate how the very concept of our object of analysis – the nation – is compromised as an appropriate object of analysis by the conventions of our respective disciplines – history and cultural anthropology. Duara and others such as Chakrabarty (Chakrabarty 2000) have deeply unsettled our notions of history by pointing to the intimate connection between the nation and Enlightenment/Universal History, which they have done by showing the extent to which our assumptions of history are based on (Enlightenment) epistemologies of the nation.[2] Duara's task in his book, therefore, is to 'decouple the deep, tenacious and ... repressive connection between history and the nation' and to explore alternative spaces for history, which he calls 'bifurcated histories', that are not limited to this entangled space (1996: 4–5). In a similar spirit, in this chapter I use the concept of nation as a point of entry to think about another kind of entanglement, which I believe has specific methodological and epistemological implications for our discipline, anthropology, because it undermines our conventional role as translators of cultural difference and thereby questions the legitimacy of anthropological analysis. My aim here is to mine that entanglement critically to explore the possibilities for a privileged space for anthropological analysis.

While anthropologists have for long critiqued the boundary between native informant and anthropologist, more recently there seems to be a shift in emphasis that distills this general critical stance to a particular kind of predicament that faces some, but not all anthropologists – the recognition by anthropologists working in certain arenas that 'our informants are speaking our language'.[3] The dissemination of our theoretical concepts and knowledge to the political and lay discursive levels not only blurs the boundary between subjective informant, who provides the data, and objective scientist, who distills this data to produce comprehensive theory, but it points to what I will term here an epistemological collapse, where theory and evidence (ethnographic data) have become entangled. My attempt here is a preliminary exploration of how we might reconceptualise 'ethnographic' evidence so we can rescue a privileged space for the explanatory power of theory and not surrender to this epistemological collapse as a retreat from theorising.

The chapter will proceed in primarily three parts. The first attempts to illustrate the epistemological collapse between the empirical and the theoretical through the concept of the nation. I analyse this entanglement from the position of ambivalence expressed in the writings of two theorists of the nation – Alfred Cobban and Benedict Anderson – to foreground the truly schizophrenic, irreducible nature of this concept. This first part of the chapter, 'the nation as schizophrenic', then, sets the stage for the anthropological problematic addressed in this chapter: the fact that certain anthropological objects/fields of study, such as nation, ethnicity, race, are not exclusive to academic or theoretical discourse but part of lay and political discourses as well. While I am aware that I pathologise the nation by labelling it as such, I do so to foreground that in identity politics today academic, lay and political convergences in discourse and policy making might not always signal 'racial progress' as we might tempted to thinking – there is no teleology to the direction of a specific nations unfolding. The second part of the chapter briefly engages the works of other anthropologists who have creatively addressed this question of the closing of the gap between ethnographic subjects and anthropologists or data and theory in order to explore what might be at stake for anthropology in such instances. In the final section I turn to my own ethnography in Trinidad to analyse critically a case of epistemological collapse through the concept of creole. I use my ethnographic example of creole to argue that it is imperative that we anthropologists carve out a privileged space for analysis during moments of epistemological collapse rather than retreat from theorising.

Creole is deeply implicated in any discourse of the nation in the Caribbean, and it also metonymises the Caribbean as region (Khan 2001). But creole is also a theoretical frame; it is the dominant analytic of the region for interpreting cultural creation and cultural change (Brathwaite 1971; Munasinghe 2001). Creole, however, is more than just theory, it is national ideology (Bolland 1992) and it connotes an empirical state of being (Segal 1993) – put simply, it functions as a noun for the Afro-Trinidadian. Given the extent of epistemological collapse evidenced in the term creole, I want to propose here that this entanglement had immense symbolic implications for those of Indian ancestry in the Caribbean, specifically Trinidad. It played a crucial role in fostering a particular image of the East Indian in the Caribbean,[4] not only in the lay imagination but, more importantly for the purposes of this chapter, in academic discourse as well – that is, the image of the Indo-Trinidadian as 'culture bearer' in contrast to the Afro-Trinidadian 'culture creator' (Munasinghe 1997). Since the 'theoretical' concept that signified cultural creation was empirically embodied in a group with a different ancestry – Creole as noun to signify Afro-Trinidadians – *there was no theoretical register even to recognise the possibility of Indo-Trinidadians as culture creators.* I use my analysis of creole to argue that moments of epistemological collapse such as this can be understood to constitute a different kind of ethnographic evidence if they are approached from a historical perspective. We need to go beyond the detection of resonances between the discourses of anthropologists and non-anthropologists (lay peoples, experts, knowledge practitioners, politicians, etc.) and critically analyse the larger historicity, and sociological context of this interface – that is, critically probe how this interface is produced and what insights such a collapse elides, precisely because this interface now carries the conceit of theory.

Part 1: Nation as Schizophrenic

I begin with two quotes that register the peculiar ontological status of the concept 'nation': Addressing the vexed nature of the concept, in his introduction to *Imagined Communities* (1991: 5), Anderson makes the following intriguing observation.

> Part of the difficulty is that one tends unconsciously to hypothesize the existence of Nationalism-with-a-big-N (rather as one might age with-a-capital-A) and then to classify 'it' as *an* ideology. (Note that if everyone has an age, Age is merely an analytical expression). It would, I think, make things easier if one treated it as if it belonged with 'kinship' and 'religion' rather than with 'liberalism' or 'fascism'.

In the late 1960s, Alfred Cobban, the well-respected historian of modern France, wrote of the French Revolution's monumental role in drawing the contours of a novel moral and political universe in this way:

> By proclaiming the principle of popular sovereignty, the French revolutionaries fundamentally altered the prevailing conception of the state, and opened a Fresh chapter in the history of the nation state. It was through the combination of the revolutionary idea of democratic sovereignty with the new importance attached to national differences that the nation state ceased to be a simple historical fact and became the subject of a theory. (Cobban 1969: 33)

In their own ways, Anderson and Cobban are referencing the schizophrenic nature of this concept: nationalism as signifying a habitus of sorts – that is, *a way of being in the world – and nationalism also as a theoretical concept*. This duality appears paradoxical only when the concept's historicity is recognised as do Anderson and Cobban. Its origins located in historical contingencies, nationalism constitutes a formal equivalent of other ideologies like liberalism, fascism or even Marxism. In this sense its ontological status is of a different order than that of kinship or religion, despite Anderson's temptation to treat it as such. True, like nationalism, concepts such as 'kinship' and 'religion' also speak to a way of being in the world and constitute abstract analytics. But they, unlike nationalism, index a different kind of relationship between the empirical and the analytic because they *have not been constituted through a certain kind of historicity*. Put simply, the ontologies of 'kinship' and 'religion' as pure analytical expressions are independent of their historicities.[5] By this I mean anthropological theorising, say of cross-cousin marriage in a particular ethnographic setting, is not contingent upon recognising the historicity of the category 'Kinship'. The same cannot be said of the nation and its related cognates. Because historicity is constitutive of its ontological make-up, theorising the nation necessarily foregrounds critical moments of entanglement between the empirical and theoretical realms. Accordingly, nation and its cognates challenge and force us to reconceptualise productively that critical distinction we draw between data and analysis or evidence and theory.

I will use the quotes from Cobban and Anderson to illustrate this peculiar entanglement, even if this was clearly not these authors' intent. The entanglement between theory and raw empiricism of fact – in this instance, ideologies that have arisen through contingencies of history such as nationalism – assume different textures in their respective formulations. True to the spirit of the historian, Cobban identifies a particular event, the French Revolution, as that defining moment when 'nation state' transcends its own raw empiricism 'as historical fact' and attains the status of theory. The historical drama of the first half of the nineteenth century for Cobban is indeed nationalism; of this period he writes:

> The nation state entered on a new stage in its history. Hitherto it had been a historical fact: now it became a theory. It was embodied in the theory of nationalism, which posited as an ideal the identification of cultural and political communities in a universal system of nation states. ... As an agency of destruction the theory of nationalism proved one of the most potent that even modern society has known. Empires or states that were not homogeneous in culture and language were undermined from within, or assaulted from without; nation after nation broke away from its traditional allegiances. (1969: 33–36)

What I want to stress here is the nation state concept's movement between and simultaneous straddling of different ontologies – first as historical fact that organically unfolded in the empirical field independent of a formal ideology, and second in the form of theory, when state and nation become conjoined in the theory of nationalism. Significantly, however, entanglements do not end here. Theory then seeps back into the empirical field in the form of nationalism – one of the most formidable agencies of destruction known to the modern world as Cobban characterises it – to unleash dramatic changes in the real world! Unlike a purely theoretical term like 'habitus' this particular theoretical term, 'nationalism', is capable of 'doing things' in the real world as well as constituting a theory. Thus, the challenge posed by such concepts such as nation and nationalism is that they can be considered simultaneously both theory and ethnographic evidence.

In Anderson's case, as the quote illustrates, a subtle analytical move transfers the concept from the realm of ideology to that of 'kinship' and 'religion', bestowing onto it the ontological status of a universal habitus (because the analogy drawn between nationalism and kinship or religion resonates intuitively with the reader, the epistemological implications of this move – of an intuitive justification extending into an analytical one – are rarely questioned). Yet, throughout his book the theoretical concept of nationalism exists in tension with nationalism as an ideology. On the one hand, one could read Anderson's intellectual labours in *Imagined Communities* as an effort toward understanding how a historically specific and modern way of thinking and being about community trickled into a generalised consciousness that defined in broad strokes a particular way of belonging in the modern world – that is, how modulars of nationalism by way of pirating not only defined the limits of our political and cultural worlds but those of our imaginations as well. I understand Anderson to be saying that it is nationalism considered as a *generalised* consciousness or habitus that constitutes the condition of possibility for Nationalism with-the-big-N – that is, Nationalism as an abstract analytic or theory signifying a quality that everyone has (like Age, Kinship or Religion). The spaces identified as 'theory' are different in Cobban and Anderson and because of this the moments of entanglement that are implicit in their analyses also vary. Anderson's conception of theory is far more abstract, analytical and academic than Cobban's theory of nationalism. But, nevertheless, as Anderson's periodisation of the different modes of nationalism wonderfully illustrate – beginning with creole pioneers and culminating with Third World nationalisms with European vernacular-based popular nationalisms (from the 1820s) and official nationalisms sandwiched in between, – the very conditions of possibility for such a generalised consciousness were the development of historically specific 'modular' nationalist ideologies that possessed the capacity to be pirated. This again reminds us how the ontology of this particular analytic is contingent on the recognition of its own historicity.

It is clear in both Anderson and Cobban that the transcendence of the nation concept to the realm of theory is not a one-way process. Once nation has transcended historical contingency to become theory, the concept seeps back into the level of raw empiricism both as explicit ideas of political ideology (nationalism as theory for Cobban, and modular nationalisms for Anderson) and in the form of a generalised consciousness (Anderson). Irrespective of our specific stances – whether we see nationalism as ideology or more as a generalised consciousness that expresses itself in culturally specific forms that social scientists can decode like kinship and religion – here I want to propose that specific methodological and theoretical challenges face those of us studying processes related to nations precisely because of this epistemological collapse. The schizophrenia of nationalism, with which I began this chapter, is a symptom of this collapse and it threatens a critical convention in our discipline – the epistemological distance we have comfortably assumed between ethnographic data or evidence and our theoretical analysis. The question I want to address here, in a very preliminary way, is how we might reconceptualise alternative spaces for empirical evidence and theory when ethnographic inquiry involves subjects and fields that embody states of such collapse – that is, when they can be simultaneously considered to be both theory and ethnographic evidence. How can we as anthropologists theoretically navigate such an interface? Can we? Should we? What are the stakes?

Part 2: The Stakes for Anthropology

This issue of epistemological distance between data and theory is certainly not new to anthropology and in particular to topics such as ethnicity. Indeed, it was Leach's path-breaking work in highland Burma (1954), later extended by Barth in the now classic *Ethnic Groups and Boundaries* (1969), that foregrounded the significance of subjective claims of cultural markers over so-called objective traits delineated by the outside observer – the anthropologist. Here, I believe they were privileging lay definitions over the anthropologist's[6] in determining the ontology of the theoretical concept of 'the ethnic'. In a later time, among the epistemological issues raised in the period labelled 'the crisis in representation', one could argue that epistemological collapse constituted a defining feature of the anthropology practiced and promoted by those caught up in the 'experimental moment' of the 1980s. Experimental ethnographies deliberately sought to blur the conventional boundaries between that of the scientific observer and the native informant. Their writing strategies of self-reflexivity or dialogical textual production called precisely for a melting of the theoretical and empirical worlds. As Clifford characterised this genre,

> some reflexive accounts have worked to specify the discourse of the informants, as well as that of the ethnographer, by staging dialogues or narrating interpersonal confrontations. These fictions of dialogue have the effect of transforming the 'cultural' text into a speaking subject, who sees as well as is seen, who evades,

argues, probes back. In this view of ethnography the proper referent of any account is not a represented 'world'; now it is specific instances of discourse. ... [dialogical textual production] which locate cultural interpretations in many sorts of reciprocal contexts, and oblige writers to find diverse ways of rendering negotiated realities as multisubjective, power-laden, and incongruent. (Clifford and Marcus 1986: 14–15)

Epistemological collapse expressed through experimental writing styles constituted the methodological and sometimes even the theoretical solution to what these anthropologists then identified as the 'crisis in representation'. The collapse was created by academics as a solution to a primarily academic problem. Seen this way it had very little to do with an organic entanglement between the empirical and theoretical worlds. *It remained largely an entanglement limited to academic discourse. In contrast, the challenge of the present moment seems to be significantly different. The recognition by certain anthropologists working in specific fields, including me, that our informants are using our language and our theories signifies just such an organic entanglement between theory and data in the constitution of our ethnographic evidence.* How do we then methodologically and theoretically navigate this collapse at the levels of evidence and of theory?

In a recent volume, *Global Assemblages*, Ong and Collier (2005: 4) reconceptualise strategies for certain contemporary anthropological problems that have a specific global dimension through the concept of global assemblage (such as technoscience, circuits of licit and illicit exchange, systems of administration or governance, regimes of ethics or values, etc.). While there are many complex aspects to their reconceptualisation of the modern global, what I find significant in relation to the argument I forward here is the reflexive practice they foreground as characteristic of individual and collective life as a consequence of the application of the realm of expertise to non-expert sites. They do this by extending Anthony Giddens' acute observations on modernity, defined as a condition whereby modern institutions understood as both material technologies and social expertise soak into the very sinews of everyday life (Giddens in Ong and Collier 2005: 9). If indeed reflexive practice is a symptom of the application of expert knowledges to non-expert areas due to the penetration of modern institutions into the every day, then the epistemological collapse I refer to can easily be seen as a part of this contemporary modern life as a result of the dissemination of theoretical discourse into political and lay arenas.[7]

Some of the articles in *Global Assemblages* (Ong and Collier 2005) explicitly deal with instances of such epistemological collapse, such as Holmes and Marcus on 'Cultures of Expertise and the Management of Globalization' (2005) and Miyazaki and Riles on 'Failure as an Endpoint' (2005). While Holmes and Marcus are keen on illustrating the parallels between expert knowledge and the anthropologist's through their concept of para-ethnography in their study of central bankers, Miyazaki and Riles propose that we go beyond the recognition of parallels between expert and anthropological knowledge. In their study of Japanese financial markets they suggest that we instead consider formal equivalence between the two forms of knowledge, hence their challenging proposition of epistemological sameness.

The state of epistemological collapse in the field of finance is apparent: 'what defines the "new ethnographic subject" such as finance is a condition in which the subjects of ethnography – the data – are producing "theories"' (Miyazaki and Riles 2005: 327). The Japanese traders are at first voracious consumers of economic knowledge until they come to the realisation of its futility because of their sense of defeat in the market. The change in strategy of the Japanese traders from the use of highly complex trading models to that of very simple models signals to Miyazaki and Riles the failure of economic knowledge and they detect here an intriguing parallel between the *responses* of the Japanese traders and practitioners of the anthropology of the contemporary to the failures of their respective knowledge, which they interpret as a retreat from knowing. Miyazaki and Riles propose that we dwell on the end point, conceived as the limits or failure of knowledge whether it be economic or anthropological. Thus, the traders' acknowledgement of the failure of their knowledge 'allows us to reflect ethnographically in turn on our own moment, and theirs, as a kind of endpoint' (2005: 327), and this reflection is the condition they term epistemological sameness.[8] In recognising epistemological sameness through the failure of knowledge, Miyazaki and Riles refuse to transform this failure into a beginning point or generative moment and the implication for theorising such an interface between data and theory is ambivalent. Indeed, they ask that the 'ethnographer abandon analytical control' (2005: 328).

The stakes of claiming parallelisms between the discourses of subjects and anthropologists, or of formal equivalence between expert knowledge and anthropological knowledge or the reticence to carve out a clear critical space for anthropological analysis, may not be that high when one's ethnographic subjects are central bankers or Japanese financiers. However, Douglas Holme's (Holmes n.d.) provocative analysis of French National Front (FN) Leader Jean-Marie Le Pen, which illustrates the intimacy between the practices of Le Pen and the anthropologist, underscores, at least to me, the importance of rescuing a privileged space for anthropological theory in moments of such epistemological collapse.

Holmes uses his fieldwork conducted in 1990 on European integration to foreground a series of parallels between Le Pen's discourse and practices and those of the anthropologist's. He captures this unsettling complicity between these unlikely partners with terms such as 'intimate artifice' and 'para-ethnography'. Le Pen's deft turning of the tables during the interview process, where Holmes found 'Le Pen was parodying and baiting me' and 'asserting that the distinctive domain of *his* political expertise was culture', prompts Holmes to conclude 'indeed our exchange in some ways sounded like shop-talk among social anthropologists – His narratives were of course hardly disinterested, yet they seem at least superficially to be ethnographic. In other words, what struck me was that Le Pen needed something that approximates an ethnographic purview to pursue his political insurgency' (2003: 6). Thus, Holmes focuses on those practices of knowledge production shared between Le Pen and the anthropologist, but is careful to maintain distinction by labelling Le Pen's as 'illicit discourse'. Here Holmes draws on earlier scholarship which marked Le Pen's discourse as illicit and inscrutable because of his right-wing politics (Holmes, personal communication, March 2005). If for those earlier scholars the disturbing affinity between anthropologist and Le Pen was 'unthinkable' because of politics, then Holmes's concept of para-ethnography and his borrowing of 'illicit' discourse now make this disturbing affinity certainly thinkable. Nevertheless, the extent of this affinity is left ambivalent as with the implications of this affinity for anthropological theory.

Holmes, like Miyazaki and Riles, seems hesitant to claim a privileged explanatory power for an analytical space. Nevertheless, I detect a tension. For example, Holmes identifies the concept of 'society' as paradigmatic of an 'illicit discourse' since both he as anthropologist and Le Pen are heavily invested in this concept for their own specific agendas having to do with the European Union. Thus, he writes:

> Le Pen understands viscerally that *as* society framed by the bourgeois nation-state is eclipsed a space is created for a radical politics that draws on latent *cultural* idioms to align a *new* conceptualization of collectivity. This view of society espoused by Le Pen I described as *Integralist* and I used this concept to frame my analysis of European integration. (2003: 9)

The anthropologist chooses to deploy a 'locally' inflected term to conceptualise the development of new empirical formations – that is, to frame his analysis of European integration. European integration, by eclipsing the role of individual states as the defining frame for society in Europe, forces social scientists to also reconceptualise their conventional units of analysis grounded in Enlightenment Epistemologies like the nation state. In this way, then, Le Pen and the anthropologist are both forced to struggle with the concept of society due to the historical contingencies associated with European integration.

But the similarity ends here. To conclude from this, as Holmes does, that in 'illicit discourse lurks the possibility of a "new" kind of creative process – an "intimate artifice" – whereby the ethnographer and para-ethnographer create either a shared framework of analysis or frame works that operate in some kind of reciprocal relationship'(Holmes 2003: 10) signifies an intimacy between Le Pen and him that is not really evidenced in the material Holmes presents. Instead, Holmes's brief but insightful and compelling discussion of the different stakes distinguishing Le Pen from a social scientist in the way these respective subjects are structurally situated vis-à-vis the waning of the nation state, indicate the significance of analytical privilege because this foregrounds one moment in the paper where parallels, resonances – instances of epistemological collapse – are explained. But, interestingly, explanation goes hand in hand with coding structural difference (by intimating to the *different* stakes attached to different subject positions between the two kinds of experts, Le Pen and anthropologist). Thus, what I want to foreground here is the epistemological space that Holmes elides – that space he occupies when he as anthropologist explains how the waning of the nation state impacts social scientist and Le Pen *differently*, the necessary infrastructure to his explicit argument of 'intimate artifice'. Holmes's objective, however, is not to emphasise difference but intimacy through the evocation of parallels. I, on the other hand, see in this structural difference the necessary epistemological ground to overcome the 'troubling affinities' between someone like Le Pen and the anthropologist.

Holmes's examples of intimacy evidence entanglements that signify epistemological collapse. But, we need to go beyond the acknowledgement of entanglement and conceptualise these moments as constitutive of new types of evidence that urgently call for analysis. Le Pen's discourse needs to be theorised precisely because it carries the conceit of theory,[9] that is, explanatory power that actually masks its truly ideological nature. If we are unwilling to make a distinction between ideology and theory[10] then one has to concede that Le Pen's discourse of 'cultural difference' is no more or less ideological than the anthropologists – it is just different. This I believe is conceding not only unnecessary political but analytical ground as well.

Theorising must include historicity because only such an analytic (as opposed to a purely formalist one) will preserve the entangled ontology of this new type of evidence without risking its reduction to the conventional definition of the unmediated empirical (see Maurer 2002). In short, what I am suggesting is that any theorising of this particular type of evidence must resist reducing its particular ontology to either the purely empirical or the conceptual and instead treat it as a paradoxical combination of both that gives rise to its own peculiar tensions. The most productive way to analyze such evidence and their tensions is to be attentive to their historicity. I will now turn to an ethnographic moment of epistemological collapse to argue for a space for theory when confronted with this "special" type of ethnographic evidence.

Part 3: Theorising Epistemological Collapse: Creole as a New Kind of Evidence

I begin this section with a quote from Earl Lovelace, a prominent West Indian novelist:

> it is the Africans who have laid the groundwork of a Caribbean culture – those Africans who struggled against enslavement and continued their struggle against colonialism – and the reason that they did so is that they had to. They had no

choice but to become Caribbean and address the Caribbean landscape and reality. No other group had to. The Europeans didn't have to … they retained their culture. They couldn't change it because it was through their institutions at home that they were culturally and politically empowered … The Indians also were tied to their culture because in this new land where they were strangers, it gave them a sense of being. They had their pundits and divali and hosay and their weddings and teeluck and had no reason to want to change them. (Lovelace 1988: 340)

This sentiment, that those of African descent were the culture creators par excellence in the New World, and not East Indians, was and to a certain extent continues to be pervasive in the British Caribbean[11] and particularly in Trinidad.[12] In my other work I have illustrated how this image is produced, reproduced and entangled in the three discursive levels of the lay, the political and the academic (Munasinghe 2001, and Munasinghe 2006). For the purposes of this chapter, I will emphasise academic discourses around the East Indian and creolisation as a point of entry to present my argument about why we need to rescue an analytical space to theorise instances of epistemological collapse when they assume an analogous position to theory – that is, when they function as theory.

Until very recently,[13] academic analysis regarding the nature of East Indian culture remained mired around a particular debate – had Indian culture persisted[14] or acculturated into New World forms? Posed this way, the choice for East Indians in the New World was either as *retainers* of traditional 'pure' culture or as *imitators* of 'impure' New World culture. The possibility of East Indians being *creators of novel cultural forms indigenous to the New World* rarely enters the academic discourse of the period prior to the early 1990s. This absence is particularly striking when one considers the fact that the most supreme theoretical symbol defining the region, the creole concept,[15] signifies precisely such creative impulses in cultural dynamics that produce novel cultural forms that are indigenous to the New World. Indeed, scholars outside the region are increasingly 'discovering' in creole an analytic that affords them the tools to conceptualise global cultural dynamics precisely because it embodies attributes with a certain theoretical currency in this post-structuralist moment – attributes that rub against essentialist logic: creativity, change and novelty (Munasinghe 2006).[16] In a region where scholarship has been so obsessed with questions of cultural creation and transformation, the intriguing question for me has been to ask, why this conspicuous silence when such issues involve East Indians? Put simply, why did scholars not ask the same questions of the East Indians in Trinidad?

The answer to this paradox lies partly in the peculiar ontology of the creole concept, which is symbolically positioned as external to the East Indian. This relation of externality resists the application of the creolisation model as a frame to interpret East Indian cultural practices. But the paradox sharpens. In those instances when the creolisation model is applied to interpret East Indian behaviour we are confronted with a fascinating twist in interpretation. At least in theory, creolisation acknowledges the creative capacity of Caribbean peoples to forge new cultural forms that escapes representations of diasporic peoples as mere reproducers of traditional forms or as assimilators of dominant cultures. Ironically, however, when applied to East Indians in Trinidad, creolisation transforms into a principle of acculturation – that is, lay references and even some academic references to the creolisation of East Indians signify assimilation into Afro-Creole patterns. As Mohammed observes of the popular interpretation of the term, '"Creolisation", was viewed as synonymous with the absorption of black culture at the expense of one's own – a process referred to as acculturation' (Mohammed 1988: 381; see also Reddock 1998). The principle of interculturation, so central to creolisation then, becomes conspicuously absent in reference to East Indians.

Here I explore the reasons for this transformation – from interculturation to acculturation – and anchor it in the particular ontology of the creole concept – epistemological collapse. While creolisation carries the conceit of theory (that is, its application as a general theory as distinct from an ideological one), the very historicity of the concept (the limits imposed by its raw empiricism, so to speak) can handle only European and African elements. By uncovering the inextricable link between a theoretical concept, creolisation and a specific empirical field, I argue then that the very theory that speaks so eloquently to cultural creativity and transformation has functioned to occlude recognition of the creative capacity of East Indians as 'culture creators'.

Creole is a familiar term in the Caribbean in all levels of discourse, lay, political and the academic, and it has a long and complex history with a wide array of meanings in the region. It is a concept that epitomises the condition of epistemological collapse in that it functions in the capacity as both supreme theoretical symbol of the region and also an ontological state of being for person or thing of the region, signifying native status. It would be a mistake to interpret the operation of creole in these discursive levels as processes that are independent of one another. In fact they are deeply entangled and mutually constitutive of one another – making separation untenable. Yet, the integrity of the theoretical model of creole, as theory is contingent on the presumption of a state of such disentanglement despite its compromised nature. It is this ambivalence and the costs of not theorising such ambivalence that I hope to foreground here by treating creole as a new kind of evidence.

Due to the early annihilation of the native Carib and Arawak populations, Caribbean cultures have been primarily forged by diasporic peoples – Europeans, Africans and Asians. Creolisation emerged as the key analytical concept to examine the processes of cultural adaptation, change and synthesis within deeply hierarchical relations of power, whereby new cultural forms were developed in the New World by piecing together elements derived from Old World cultural orientations. The concept of creolisation was derived from the word 'creole' (or its Spanish equivalent *criollo*) – a combination of the two Spanish words *criar* (to create, to imagine, to settle) and *colon* (a colonist, a founder, a settler) (E. Brathwaite 1974: 10). While the meaning of creole is subject to much variation depending on the contexts (Allen 1998), in general 'it refers to people who are *culturally distinct* from the Old World populations of their origin' (N. Bolland 1992: 50). In the British Caribbean the term creole 'refers to a local product which is the result of a mixture or blending of various ingredients that originated in the Old World' (ibid.). In Trinidad, Creole as a noun signifies people with primarily African ancestry, while those with European ancestry are signified with an adjectival prefix, as in French Creole or White Creole. East Indians, in contrast, are not considered Creole. Creole, then, signified all those of African and European ancestry who were born in and committed to the New World. As such, Creole Societies were those that emerged out of a colonial arrangement around the plantation/slavery complex – the result 'of a complex situation where a colonial polity reacts, as a whole, to external metropolitan pressures and at the same time to internal adjustments made necessary by the juxtaposition of master and labour, white and non-white, Europe and colony, [and] European and African ... in a culturally heterogeneous relationship' (Brathwaite 1974: 10–11).

This anatomy of definition allows us to see how the semantics of creole, signifying processes of *creation* and *indigenisation*, become annexed not only to a particular historical period – colonialism and slavery in the New World – but also, to specific diasporic populations, namely, those of European and African descent. Accordingly, I argue that efforts to theorise 'creolisation' have been limited by the conflation of a methodological framework – that is, creolisation as process – with an empirically defined field encompassing specific actors located in a particular place and time – that is, African slaves and European masters who were intimately bound to each other by deeply hierarchical relations structuring the plantation/slavery complex. Here is a key defining moment of epistemological collapse.

Elsewhere (Munasinghe 2006) I have illustrated how this epistemological collapse works in various discursive levels – lay, political and academic – to reproduce symbolically the image of East Indians as outsiders by making it impossible for them to be recognised as a people who can authentically embody creoleness.[17] For the purposes of this chapter, I want to focus on the work of Barbadian poet and historian Edward Kamau Brathwaite, the pioneer of the creolisation thesis, in order to illustrate how this epistemological collapse expresses *itself in theory and its implications for analysis when it functions as theory*. I hope to argue for the importance of treating the theory of creolisation as a new kind of evidence.

In the now classic, *The Development of Creole Society in Jamaica: 1770–1820* (1971), Brathwaite argued 'that the people, mainly from Britain and West Africa, who settled, lived, worked and were born in Jamaica, contributed to the formation of a society which developed its own distinctive character or culture which, in so far as it was neither purely British nor West African, [was] creole'(Brathwaite 1971: xiii). This canonic text of creolisation barely mentions

East Indians. Since the East Indian population is less significant in Jamaica one might justify such a position. Yet, the elevation of Brathwaite's theory to canon empowers his particular Jamaica to metonymise the West Indies in general. The dedication of a double issue of the Journal *Caribbean Quarterly* in 1998 to a collection of essays in honour of Kamau Brathwaite entitled 'Konversations in Kreole' attests to the continued significance and vitality of the creole society thesis in the region and, as the guest editors of the volume attest, 'Today, approximately twenty-six years after its public launching, Kamau Brathwaite's creole-society model is generally accepted as the leading interpretation of Caribbean society' (Shepherd and Richards 1998: vii). In this sense the absence of East Indians from the creole society thesis is significant. The very fact that Brathwaite identifies the period between 1770 and 1820 as the formative period of creolisation precludes East Indians, for the systematic entry of East Indians to the Caribbean did not begin until 1845. The 'late' entry of East Indians to the Caribbean has in part contributed to their marginalisation in theories of creolisation. Even Mintz and Price (1976) in their canonic methodological treatise on creolisation, *An Anthropological Approach to the Afro-American Past: A Caribbean Perspective*, barely factor in East Indians. For Mintz and Price, the 'baseline', which informs to this day the cultural practices and institutional forms of Afro-American experience, was first formulated during the initial period of capture, enslavement and transport (the middle passage). As such, one could argue, as many do, that creolisation was well underway by the time East Indians arrived in the Caribbean. Thus, while East Indians are understood as having introduced a novel element to Creole Societies, they are not usually perceived as an integral part of these societies.

Brathwaite, in a later work, *Contradictory Omens: Cultural Diversity and Integration in the Caribbean* (1974), does situate East Indians vis-à-vis creolisation, but significantly the entry of East Indians after emancipation, in his view, changes the trajectory of Creole Society into a Plural one.[18] Plural Societies, by definition, were those that were characterised by an absence of shared norms among the diverse ancestral groups comprising Creole Societies (M.G. Smith 1965) and which were believed to be held together by the power exerted by a privileged minority – Whites. As a critical response to the Plural Society thesis, the creolisation model argued that 'A common colonial and creole experience is shared among the various divisions, even if that experience is variously interpreted' by the groups expressing diverse orientations – European, Euro-creole, Afro-creole (or folk), and creo-creole or West Indian (Brathwaite 1974: 25). That Brathwaite, a staunch proponent of the creolisation model should associate the advent of Plural Society with the arrival of East Indians is revealing. If creolisation was a product of the non-deliberate processes of interculturation that took place between Africans and Europeans within hierarchical structures that put a premium on the conscious adoption of European norms and practices, why should the centre of gravity have shifted from creolisation to fragmentation with the entry of East Indians?

Brathwaite sees acculturation and interculturation as structuring principles for creolisation: 'the former referring, to the process of absorption of one culture by another; the latter to a more reciprocal activity, a process of intermixture and enrichment, each to each' (Brathwaite 1974: 11). Interculturation is also less deliberate, a process that is largely unplanned and unstructured, organic, if you will (Brathwaite 1974: 6), where Black influences White as much as White influences Black. The dual processes of acculturation and interculturation are constitutive of the 'creative ambivalence' characterising the behaviour of Caribbean peoples. Creative ambivalence is also an inescapable fact of creolisation, which involves both imitation/mimicry (acculturation) and native creation (indigenisation). Brathwaite says, 'our real/apparent imitation involves at the same time a significant element of creativity, while our creativity in turn involves a significant element of imitation' (Brathwaite 1974: 160). Thus, acculturation/mimicry and interculturation/indigenisation are not discrete processes but rather each process necessarily calls upon the other. Such dialectics in turn structure the creative genius of Caribbean peoples.

Yet, Brathwaite's astute remarks on creolisation take on a different veneer in his discussion of East Indians. During the colonial period, he argues, both subordinated groups, Afro-Caribbean and East Indian, aspired to 'great traditions' – but the East Indian looked to India while the Afro-Caribbean looked to Europe, thereby becoming an Afro-Saxon. These different orientations in turn shaped subsequent cultural developments of the respective groups. 'The Afro-Saxon "imitates," not modernises, because, unlike the Indian, he has no core culture to adapt from. Yet the Indian's modernisation ... is taking place largely in an endogamous and exclusive manner; *in*- rather than *inter*-culturation, so that despite his apparent disadvantages, it is the Caribbean black who has been most innovative and "radical"' (Brathwaite 1974: 54).

In short, East Indians' orientation toward India only reinscribes their exclusiveness; even when they modernise they *selectively* appropriate modern strains that merely supplement their core culture. The degree of conscious volition imputed to East Indian selections of modern traits militates against the recognition of the 'unstructured', and organic 'flows' earlier associated with interculturation. Indeed, according to Brathwaite, East Indians are not a part of the processes of interculturation. While they may adapt, they adapt *within* their discrete realm and therefore remain exclusive; in contrast, it is the Afro-Saxon who epitomises interculturation and emerges as the cultural innovator *par exellence*. If the dialectic between acculturation and interculturation is what produces the cultural ambivalence that attests to the creative capacity to indigenise, then Brathwaite's refusal to encompass East Indians within the interculturation process not only strips this group of their potential for creative generation of indigenous forms but also positions them outside creolisation proper.

The idea that East Indians possessed a core culture which Africans 'lacked' is rooted in colonial caricatures of the two subordinated ancestral groups. In an essay on the semantics of race categories in colonial Trinidad, Daniel Segal (1993) has argued that East Indian exclusion from Creole or native status was partly premised on the image of East Indians as 'unmixables'. This image, in turn, was a precipitate of the different principles of subordination to which Africans and East Indians were subjected. According to Segal these principles propagated (1) an image of 'Africans' as persons lacking an ancestral 'civilization,' who, through 'mixing' ... acquired 'respectability' [and] could become partially 'white' and inchoately 'West Indian'; and (2) an image of 'Asian Indians' as persons so possessed of an inferior, ancestral 'civilization' that they necessarily remained 'East' (and not West) Indians, regardless of their social entanglements in Trinidad. (Segal 1989: 76)[19]

While plenty of sources attest to East Indians 'mixing' with other ancestral groups, this mixing was denied symbolic recognition either in terms of lexical markers accounting for different portions of East Indian mixture with other groups, or East Indian inclusion in the colour spectrum – privileges that were extended to Africans and Europeans. If mixing defined Creole, and if Creole in turn defined native status in the Caribbean,[20] the denial of symbolic recognition of East Indian mixing effectively defined East Indians not only as outsiders to the New World but also as peripheral to the creolisation process. In fact, Segal argues that the terms East Indian and Creole developed as mutually exclusive categories of identification in Trinidad.

The creolisation model, as articulated by Brathwaite and others, is limited as a general theory of cultural change because its ontology, at least in the Caribbean context, depends ultimately on *who* can be considered creole. The argument therefore is a tautological one where only certain cultures are recognised as privileged enough to be included in an analytic emphasising cultural creation, mixing and transformation. In this way the creolisation model draws sustenance from the semantics structuring colonial race hierarchies that inscribed certain presumptions about cultural change that included some ancestral cultures but not others.

The ideological aspect of the creolisation model also becomes evident when we foreground its productive context. The concepts of creole and nation are intimately linked in the Caribbean region. The works of Brathwaite and other creolisation theorists were efforts by West Indian middle-class intelligentsia to provide models of their societies that dovetailed with the larger political struggle of nation-building.[21] While I cannot go into this aspect at length here, the explicit political agenda of these theorists needs to be acknowledged. To counter the idea that cultural identity was somehow problematic for Caribbean peoples, West Indian scholars, such as Brathwaite, put forward the 'Creole Society thesis'. According to Nigel Bolland this model 'enhanced the emerging Caribbean nationalism of the third quarter of the twentieth century. More specifically, the cultural and populist aspects of the creole society viewpoint, with its emphasis upon the origins of a distinctive *common* culture as a basis for national unity, constitutes the ideology of a particular social segment, namely a middle-class intelligentsia that seeks a leading role in an integrated, newly independent society. The creole society thesis, then, is a significant ideological moment in the decolonization process of the Caribbean'. (1992: 53)

The appropriation of a theoretical model to make a case for independence in the post-1960s period in the British Caribbean meant that the model itself would be substantially influenced by the larger political project. Decolonisation went hand in hand with the positive re-evaluation of formerly despised Afro-Creole lower class cultural forms, such as carnival and steelband. As such, the task for theorists of creolisation was to re-centre formerly marginalised populations, largely the lower class Afro-Creoles, in their critique of colonialism. The politics informing the creolisation model then functioned to highlight the role of those with African ancestry (Lloyd Braithwaite 1954; Safa 1987; Bolland 1992; Munasinghe 2001). The reserved attitude of many East Indians toward independence and their leaders' increasing dependence on India (since the 1940s) for cultural inspiration only served to alienate them from all those forces collaborating toward building an explicitly anti-colonialist nationalist project. The theory of creolisation, which emerged during this highly ideologically charged historical moment, was indelibly marked by the struggles of the period. The empirical context that informed its very formulation remains formidable in that creolisation as theory seems to factor in only those who are not only considered Creole in the New World, but specifically those Creoles who are ascribed the status of 'culture creators' *par excellence* – lower class Afro-Creoles.

The cost of not theorising (and historicising) this instance of epistemological collapse – that is, of not treating the theory of creolisation as a new kind of ethnographic evidence – would be to inherit analytical burdens that are a consequence of blind spots caused by this collapse. If East Indians were for so long represented as culture bearers and not its creators, it was not on the basis of conclusive empirical evidence but because the question of culture creation was never posed in relation to this group in the first place. I have suggested here that the mega-analytic for interpreting cultural change, the concept 'creole', may have partly generated this blind spot because of its ontology of epistemological collapse. Why such a question was so unthinkable in relation to this particular group remains the burdensome historical legacy that needs to be confronted on many fronts, including ours as anthropologists of the region. The general lesson here, I believe, is the call to apply oneself resolutely to the formulation of those unthinkable questions that are invested in the theoretical frames we employ – those blind spots produced by epistemological collapse.

Acknowledgement: We thank the University of California Press for permission to reprint sections of this chapter, which appeared in Munasinghe, V. 2006. 'Theorizing World Culture through the New World: East Indians and Creolization', *American Ethnologist* 33(4): 549–62 and the Rejoinder:

Munasinghe, V. 2006. 'Claims to Purity in Theory and Culture: Pitfalls and Promises', *American Ethnologist* 33(4): 588–92.

Notes

1. This chapter was written for a panel organised by the Wenner-Gren foundation on the theme of Anthropological Evidence for AAA 2003. I am grateful to Dick Fox for having invited me to participate in this panel and Alison Wylie for her astute commentary. I have benefited much from the intellectual exchanges I have had with Doug Holmes, who read my chapter most carefully, and also my colleagues at Cornell, Hiro Miyazaki, Annelise Riles, Steve Sangren, David Holmberg and especially Dominic Boyer, who also read parts of the chapter and provided invaluable suggestions for improvement. I also owe much to Carla Freeman who was always ready to talk through ideas with me. And I am most grateful to the editors, Narmala Halstead and Eric Hirsch for their suggestions for improving the chapter. To all these people I would like to extend my thanks.

2. I am thinking here of the primary lines of argument developed by postcolonial and specifically subaltern theorists.

3. The dissemination of our theoretical concepts to the political and lay arenas was recognised by Brackette Williams in her classic article on ethnicity 'A Class Act' (1989). Since then, however, an exciting literature in anthropology has emerged which explores this dissemination in a variety of analytic forms. See Boyer's (2001) fine analysis of such an instance and many of the articles contained in Aihwa Ong and Stephen J. Collier (2005). See also Munasinghe (2001), where I attempted to explore the implications of such a dissemination (which I now theorise as epistemological collapse in this chapter) for the study of ethnicity.

4. Although East Indians in some Caribbean states, like Guyana, were excluded from the ideological nation on criteria that had little to do with creolisation (Halstead, personal communication, May 2005), the momentum afforded by the convergence of academic, political and lay discourses of creolisation in some islands, like Trinidad and Jamaica, I would argue, projected creolisation as an indelibly Caribbean condition, which implicated all East Indians in the Caribbean, at least semantically.

5. I am not saying that the genealogy of 'kinship' and 'religion' as terms and their application are not embedded in historicity. But as pure analytical expressions, akin to terms like 'Language' or 'Age', these terms signify slices of human belief/behaviour/sentiment that are independent of each term's specific historicity because all peoples through all ages are deemed to possess what these terms signify – Age, Religion, Language and Kinship; hence their status as purely analytical categories. In short, the historical conjuncture affording the creation and theorisation of the terms 'kinship' and 'religion' do not determine their respective ontological make-ups to the same degree as it does for the term nation and its cognates. Historicity weighs in on the category 'nation' in that nationalism, I argue, is a modern sentiment. As such, historical contingencies constitute the very being of the concept – that is, the ontology of – the nation.

6. See for example Barth's objections to Naroll's classic definition of the ethnic unit (Barth 1969: 10–11).

7. This is not to say that people were not capable of reflexive practices prior to this so-called modern moment but to recognise that the nature of this reflexive act is fundamentally different when it involves an articulation or critical engagement between different kinds of knowledge based on different epistemologies, such as say between an anthropologists idea of ethnicity and a particular group's idea of their ethnicity.

8. It is important to differentiate my use of epistemological collapse from Miyazaki and Riles' use of epistemological sameness. First, sameness connotes equivalence, collapse does not; second, and more importantly, our respective terms signify different processes.

Epistemological collapse refers to the simultaneous circulation of similar concepts at different discursive registers, namely, theoretical, political and lay. By epistemological sameness, I believe, Miyazaki and Riles signal a particular anthropological condition where, by reflecting ethnographically on anthropology's subjects' (Japanese financiers) failure of knowledge, anthropology itself comes to grip with its own failure of producing the effects of knowledge it once did, thereby recognising formal epistemological equivalence with ethnographic knowledge.

9. However, I have been told by Holmes that 'Le Pen's para-ethnography provided a far more sophisticated and insightful analysis of European integration and how it would unfold than any scholar I know of' (Holmes, personal communication, March 2005).

10. With the help of my colleague Dominic Boyer I distinguish ideology from theory for the purposes here as the following: ideology as a system of ideas that purposefully cultivates caricature for the explicit function of servicing a political mission whereas theory serves a critical function of deconstructing such caricature through a systematic formulation of underlying relations of connection at a register that offers greater explanatory power.

11. Given the diverse meanings conveyed by the terms 'creole' and 'creolisation' in various parts of the Americas, the discussion in this section of the chapter is strictly limited to the English-speaking Caribbean, given that my purpose here is to ground the concept historically and contextually.

12. The ethnic composition of the two islands comprising the nation state of Trinidad and Tobago is significantly different. People claiming African descent largely populate Tobago. Since this chapter is largely on the dynamics between Afro- and Indo-Trinidadians, my specific spatial unit of analysis is Trinidad. Between 1834 and 1917, 426,623 indentured labourers were brought from India to labour in the sugar plantations of the Caribbean (Look Lai 1993: 19). They were essentially brought to compete with the labour of the newly freed former slave population – this is especially true of colonies such as Trinidad and Guyana. Many of the indentures did not return as was the initial plan and in some countries today, like Trinidad, Guyana and Surinam, their descendents constitute a substantial part of the population. Population of Trinidad according to ethnicity, 1990: African descent 39.6%, Indian descent 40.3%, White 0.6%, Chinese 0.4%, Mixed 18.4%, Other 0.2%, not stated 0.4% (Central Statistical Office 1997).

13. Some of the newly emerging work that speaks to the creative impulse behind East Indian cultural forms by circumventing the persistence/acculturation binary includes Mohammed (1988), Vertovec, (1992), Miller (1994), Reddock (1996, 1998), Gregg (1998), Puri (1999), Manuel (2000), Khan (2001) and Korom (2003). Not all works cited, however, interrogate the creolisation model with respect to its application to East Indians. Reddock (1998) refers to the work of Ravindra Jain (1986), who emphasised processes of interculturation, the core principle driving creolisation proper, with regard to 'Caribbean Indian culture'. I was, however, unable to obtain this source.

14. Morton Klass's book *East Indians in Trinidad: A Study of Cultural Persistence* (1961) is a classic example of the 'persistence' argument.

15. Creolisation denotes the dynamic processual dimension of the theoretical formulation of the creole concept. When 'Creole' is used as a noun to signify a person or ethnic group (namely, those of mixed African and European ancestry and who visibly display African ancestry, as the term is commonly used in Trinidad), I capitalise the C. To denote creole as a theoretical formulation (as opposed to an empirical category) such as the 'creole concept' or 'creolisation', I use the lower case.

16. Some anthropologists of the Caribbean, like Mintz (1994), Kahn (2001) and Sheller (2003), have expressed unease at this global application of this regionally specific term and point to some troubling consequences of this appropriation.

17. Such a view is not limited to non-East Indians. Indeed, Indo-Trinidadians are some of the most ardent proponents of the view that East Indian and Creole are mutually exclusive identities.

18. See also Puri (1999) who makes a similar observation.

19. See Munasinghe (1997), where I anchor the image of the 'culturally saturated' East Indian and the 'culturally naked' African in broader European race and Orientalist discourses of the nineteenth century.
20. See also Allen (1998: 37–42).
21. See Bolland (1992) and Munasinghe (2001) for an extensive analysis of the relationship between the creolisation model and nation-building in the West Indies and, more specifically, in Trinidad.

References

Allen, Carolyn. 1998. 'Creole Then and Now: The Problem of Definition', *Caribbean Quarterly* 44(1–2): 33–49.

Anderson, Benedict. 1991. *Imagined Communities: Reflections on the Origin and Spread of Nationalism*. London: Verso.

Barth, Fredrik. 1969. *Ethnic Groups and Boundaries: The Social Organization of Culture Difference*. Boston: Little, Brown.

Bolland, Nigel. 1992. 'Creolisation and Creole Societies: A Cultural Nationalist View of Caribbean Social History', in Alistair Hennesey (ed.), *Intellectuals in the Twentieth-century Caribbean*. London: Macmillan, pp. 50–79.

Boyer, Dominic. 2001. 'Foucault in the Bush: The Social Life of Post-Structuralist Theory in East Berlin's Prenzlauer Berg', *Ethnos* 66(2): 207–36.

Braithwaite, Lloyd. 1954. 'The Problem of Cultural Integration in Trinidad', *Social and Economic Studies* 3(1): 82–96.

Brathwaite, Edward Kamau. 1971. *Development of Creole Society in Jamaica: 1770–1820*. Oxford: Clarendon Press.

———. 1974. *Contradictory Omens: Cultural Diversity and Integration in the Caribbean*. Mona, Jamaica: Savacou.

Central Statistical Office. 1997. *Statistics at a Glance, 1996*. Trinidad and Tobago.

Chakrabarty, Dipesh. 2000. *Provincializing Europe: Postcolonial Thought and Historical Difference*. Princeton: Princeton University Press.

Clifford, James and George E. Marcus (eds). 1986. *Writing Culture: The Poetics and Politics of Ethnography*. Berkeley: University of California Press.

Cobban, Alfred. 1969. *The Nation-State and National Self-Determination*. New York: Thomas Y. Crowell Company.

Duara, Prasenjit. 1996. *Rescuing History from the Nation*. Chicago: University of Chicago Press.

Gregg, Veronica. 1998. '"Yuh Know bout Coo-coo? Where Yuh Know bout Coo-coo?": Language and Representation, Creolisation and Confusion in Indian Cuisine', *Caribbean Quarterly* 44(1–2): 83–92.

Holmes, Douglas. n.d. 'Intimate Artifice: Two Cases of Para-ethnography', Paper presented at Anthropology Colloquium, Cornell University, Spring 2003.

Holmes, Douglas and George E. Marcus. 2005. 'Cultures of Expertise and the Management of Globalization: Toward the Re-functioning of Ethnography', in A. Ong and Stephen J. Collier (eds), *Global Assemblages: Technology, Politics, and Ethics as Anthropological Problems*. Oxford: Blackwell Publishing, pp. 235–52.

Khan, Aisha. 2001. 'Journey to the Center of the Earth: The Caribbean as Master Symbol', *Cultural Anthropology* 16(3): 271–302.

Klass, Morton. 1961. *East Indians in Trinidad: A Study of Cultural Persistence*. New York: Columbia University Press.

Korom, Frank. 2003. *Hosay Trinidad: Muharram Performances in an Indo-Caribbean Diaspora*. Philadelphia: University of Pennsylvania Press.

Leach, Edmund. 1954. *Political Systems of Highland Burma: A Study of Kachin Social Structure*. Boston: Beacon Press.

Look Lai, Walton. 1993. *Indentured Labor, Caribbean Sugar: Chinese and Indian Migrants to the British West Indies, 1838–1918*. Baltimore: Johns Hopkins University Press.

Lovelace, Earl. 1988. 'The On-going Value of Our Indigenous Traditions', in S. Ryan (ed.), *The Independence Experience, 1962–1987*, pp. 335–44. St. Augustine, Trinidad and Tobago: Institute of Social and Economic Research, University of the West Indies.

Manuel, Peter. 2000. *East Indian Music in the West Indies: Tan-Singing, Chutney, and the Making of Indo-Caribbean Culture*. Philadelphia: Temple University Press.

Maurer, Bill. 2002. 'Fact and Fetish in Creolization Studies: Herskovits and the Problem of Induction, or, Guinea Coast, 1593', *New West Indian Guide* 76 (1–2): 5–22.

Miller, Daniel. 1994. *Modernity, an Ethnographic Approach: Dualism and Mass Consumption in Trinidad*. Oxford: Berg.

Mintz, Sidney. 1977. 'North American Anthropological Contributions to Caribbean Studies', *Boletin de Estudios Latino Americanos y del Caribe* 22: 68–82.

———. 1994. 'Enduring Substances, Trying Theories: The Caribbean Region as *Oikoumene*', *Journal of the Royal Anthropological Institute* (N.S.) 2: 289–311.

Mintz, Sidney and Richard Price. 1976. *An Anthropological Approach to the Afro-American Past: A Caribbean Perspective*. Philadelphia: Institute for the Study of Human Issues.

Miyazaki, Hirokazu and Annelise Riles. 2005. 'Failure as an Endpoint', in A. Ong and Stephen J. Collier (eds), *Global Assemblages: Technology, Politics, and Ethics as Anthropological Problems*. Oxford: Blackwell, pp. 320–32.

Mohammed, Patricia. 1988. 'The "Creolization" of Indian Women in Trinidad', in Selwyn Ryan (ed.), *The Independence Experience 1962–1987*. St. Augustine, Trinidad: Institute of Social and Economic Research, University of the West Indies, pp. 381–98.

Munasinghe, Viranjini. 1997. 'Culture Creators and Culture Bearers: The Interface between Race and Ethnicity in Trinidad', *Transforming Anthropology* 6(1–2): 72–86.

———. 2001. *Callaloo or Tossed Salad: East Indians and the Cultural Politics of Identity in Trinidad*. Ithaca: Cornell University Press.

———. 2002. 'Creating Impurity out of Purity: Nationalism in Hybrid Spaces', *American Ethnologist* 29(3): 663–92.

———. 2006. *Theorizing World Culture through the New World: East Indians and Creolization*. *American Ethnology* 33(4): 549–62.

Ong, Aihwa and Stephen J. Collier (eds). 2005. *Global Assemblages: Technology, Politics, and Ethics as Anthropological Problems*. Oxford:Blackwell.

Price, Richard. 2001. 'The Miracle of Creolization: A Retrospective', *New West Indian Guide* 75(1–2): 35–64.

Puri, Shalini. 1999. 'Canonized Hybridities, Resistant Hybridities: Chutney Soca, Carnival and the Politics of Nationalism', in Belinda J. Edmondson (ed.), *Caribbean Romances: The Politics of Regional Representation.* Charlottesville: University Press of Virginia, pp. 12–38.

Reddock, Rhoda. 1996. 'Intersection of Culture, Class, Identity and Gender in Trinidad and Tobago: The Little Tradition', *Contemporary Issues in Social Science: A Caribbean Perspective* 3: 70–103.

———. 1998. 'Contestations over Culture, Class, Gender and Identity in Trinidad and Tobago: The Little Tradition', *Caribbean Quarterly* 44(1–2): 62–82.

Safa, Helen. 1987. 'Popular Culture, National Identity, and Race in the Caribbean', *New West Indian Guide* 61(3–4): 115–26.

Sampath, Neils. 1993. 'An Evaluation of the "Creolisation" of Trinidad East Indian Adolescent Masculinity', in Kevin Yelvington (ed.), *Trinidad Ethnicity.* Knoxville: University of Tennessee Press, pp. 235–53.

Scott, David. 1991. 'That Event, This Memory: Notes on the Anthropology of African Diasporas in the New World', *Diaspora* 1: 261–84.

Segal, Daniel. 1993. 'Race and "Color" in Pre-Independence Trinidad and Tobago', in Kevin Yelvington (ed.), *Trinidad Ethnicity.* Knoxville: University of Tennessee Press, pp. 81–115.

———. 1994. 'Living Ancestors: Nationalism and the Past in Postcolonial Trinidad and Tobago', in J. Boyarin (ed.), *Remapping Memory.* Minneapolis: University of Minnesota Press, pp. 221–39.

Sheller, Mimi. 2003. *Consuming the Caribbean: From Arawaks to Zombies.* London: Routledge.

Shepherd, Verene and Glen Richards. 1998. 'Introduction: Caribbean Quarterly', 44(1–2): vi–xiv.

Smith, Michael G. 1965. *The Plural Society in the British West Indies.* Berkeley: University of California Press.

Trouillot, Michel-Rolph. 1992. 'The Caribbean Region: An Open Frontier in Anthropological Theory', *Annual Review of Anthropology* 21: 19–42.

———. 1998. 'Culture on the Edges: Creolization in the Plantation Context', *Plantation Society in the Americas* 5(1): 8–28.

Vertovec, Steven. 1992. *Hindu Trinidad: Religion, Ethnicity, and Socio-Economic Change.* London: Macmillan Education.

Williams, Brackette F. 1989. 'A Class Act: Anthroplogy and the Race to Nation across Ethnic Terrain', *Annual Review of Anthropology* 18: 401–44.

Yelvington, Kevin. 2001. 'The Anthropology of Afro-Latin America and the Caribbean: Diasporic Dimensions', *Annual Review of Anthropology* 30: 227–60.

Notes on Contributors

Vibha Arora is Assistant Professor in Sociology at The Indian Institute of Technology, New Delhi. She was a Commonwealth scholar and holds a doctorate from the Institute of Social and Cultural Anthropology, University of Oxford. She has an M.A. and M.Phil. in Sociology from Delhi School of Economics and several years of work experience in the development sector in South Asia. Her research interests include environmental sociology, social movements, Buddhism and shamanism, development, gender, ethnicity, medical and visual anthropology. Vibha is the guest co-editor of the June 2005 special issue of *Contemporary South Asia*.

David P. Crandall, M.Phil. (1989) and D.Phil. (1993) in Social Anthropology at Oxford University, carried out initial fieldwork among the Himba of Namibia in 1990 and 1991. He has continued with research trips to the Himba in 1995, 1996, 1999 and 2003. He took a position at Brigham Young University (BYU) in 1994 and is Professor of Anthropology in the Department of Anthropology at BYU.

Cristina Grasseni is a full-time researcher at the Centre for Research on the Anthropology and Epistemology of Complexity at the University of Bergamo. Her research interests include European ethnography and visual anthropology. She holds a degree in Epistemology (1995) from Pavia University (Italy), an M.Phil. in History and Philosophy of Science from Cambridge University (1995/6), a Master in Visual Anthropology (1997/8) and a Ph.D. in Social Anthropology (2001) from Manchester University.

Narmala Halstead is a Senior Lecturer in anthropology at the University of East London. She was a lecturer at Cardiff University and also taught at Brunel University. She has carried out research in Guyana, the US and the UK. Her research interests include the East Indian Diaspora, conflict and violence, anthropological debates, personhood and fluid bolders. She holds a doctorate in anthropology from Brunel University. She is the editor of the *Journal of Legal Anthropology*.

Eric Hirsch is a Reader in Social Anthropology at Brunel University. He has conducted research in Papua New Guinea and Greater London. His most recent book is co-edited with Marilyn Strathern, *Transactions and Creations: Property Debates and the Stimulus of Melanesia*, Berghahn, 2004.

Viranjini Munasinghe is an Associate Professor of Anthropology and Director of Asian American Studies at Cornell University. She received her Ph.D. from Johns Hopkins University in 1994. She is a historical anthropologist working on the Caribbean East Indian Diaspora. Theoretically, she is interested in epistemological issues to do with the articulation of 'theoretical concepts' with lay and political discursive forms and is working towards an interdisciplinary perspective on the question of historical consciousness.

Judith Okely is Deputy Director of the International Gender Studies Centre, Queen Elizabeth House, Oxford University; Emeritus Professor of Social Anthropology, Hull University and Honorary Research Associate, Brunel University. Her co-edited volume, the ASA monograph, *Anthropology and Autobiography* with Helen Callaway (1992, Routledge) remains a significant text on key issues in anthropological knowledge construction. Other publications include *The Traveller-Gypsies* (1983, Cambridge University Press), *Simone de Beauvoir: A Re-reading* (1986, Virago) and *Own or Other Culture* (1996, Routledge).

Konstantinos Retsikas graduated from Panteion University (Athens) in 1995. He obtained a Masters degree in Social Anthropology at the University of Kent at Canterbury and completed his Ph.D. at the University of Edinburgh in 2003. He was Leach/Royal Anthropological Institute Fellow at the University of Sussex in 2003 and 2004 and is a Lecturer in the anthropology department at the School of Oriental and African Studies.

Helena Wulff is Associate Professor of Social Anthropology at Stockholm University. Among her publications are *Twenty Girls: Growing Up, Ethnicity and Excitement in a South London Microculture* (1988, Almqvist and Wiksell International), *Ballet across Borders: Career and Culture in the World of Dancers* (1998, Berg) and *Youth Cultures: A Cross-Cultural Perspective* (co-edited with Vered Amit-Talai, 1995, Routledge). Her early research was on youth culture and ethnicity, while her current interests centre on the anthropology of dance, the arts, visual culture, transnationality and Ireland. She is a member of the European Association of Social Anthropologists Executive Committee and editor with Dorle Drackle of *Social Anthropology*.

Index

www.ingramcontent.com/pod-product-compliance
Lightning Source LLC
Chambersburg PA
CBHW060038030426
42334CB00019B/2378

* 9 7 8 1 8 4 5 4 5 4 7 7 7 *